AS PUBLIC AS POSSIBLE

Also by David I. Backer

Althusser and Education

AS PUBLIC AS POSSIBLE

RADICAL FINANCE FOR AMERICA'S PUBLIC SCHOOLS

DAVID I. BACKER

NEW YORK
LONDON

Published in the United States by The New Press, New York, 2025
Distributed by Two Rivers Distribution

ISBN 978-1-62097-885-6 (hc)
ISBN 978-1-62097-902-0 (ebook)
CIP data is available

The New Press publishes books that promote and enrich public discussion and understanding of the issues vital to our democracy and to a more equitable world. These books are made possible by the enthusiasm of our readers; the support of a committed group of donors, large and small; the collaboration of our many partners in the independent media and the not-for-profit sector; booksellers, who often hand-sell New Press books; librarians; and above all by our authors.

www.thenewpress.org

Book design and composition by Bookbright Media
This book was set in Bembo and Oswald.

Printed in the United States of America

For Thisbe, who just started kindergarten

Contents

AS PUBLIC AS POSSIBLE

Introduction
Under the Tug-of-War

Call it a culture war, teacher war, or class war—there's a tug-of-war in public education. Over the last few decades, we've seen extravagance for the rich and austerity for everyone else as the ruling class privatized the public. Rightists and centrists from both political parties of America's two-party system slashed public budgets and pushed for the marketization of social democratic structures. Schools were a paradigm case. They imposed high-stakes testing provided by billion-dollar companies and replaced public schools with charter schools in the country's big cities; they also trained educational leaders to think only in terms of market efficiency, weakening unions. Meanwhile, the left—unions' rank-and-file, movements, community organizations—hunkered down, fighting to protect public education from the onslaught.[1]

Despite some victories here and there, the left got dragged along in this tug-of-war and could only ring the alarm as everyone's feet were pulled rightward. The center practically helped the right; while centrists might not have agreed, they had little to offer in terms of resistance or attempts to reclaim ground. They bashed teachers unions, a key source of their past strength, told movements to be quiet, and used nonprofits to knock on doors for their preferred moderate candidates when election time came around, and even today they clutch their pearls and look with helpless horror from the vantage of Democrat-controlled states as the right keeps pulling and pulling.

Meanwhile, teachers in Republican-controlled states go all out to organize wildcat strikes; intrepid public interest lawyers press state governments for more funding, waiting for the courts; students organize walkouts; unions grow and fight. While electrifying and helpful, these efforts have not reverberated enough to prevent that rightward pull on the rope. There's an administration in power at this writing that wants to abolish the Department of Education, and some states that have passed voucher programs are considering dissolving public school districts that don't maintain certain thresholds of attendance.

All the while, school buildings emit the equivalent of 17 million cars' worth of carbon, ruining their students' future world while trying to prepare them for it.[2]

Back and forth the tug-of-war goes, the right side in a Christian capitalist crusade to destroy the public system, the center feckless and aghast, the left scrappy and failing to hold the line, their feet slipping in the dust against a pull whose force has the feeling of gravity, all in the midst of a polycrisis: a climate crisis; a (post-) pandemic crisis; the rise of artificial intelligence; a school shooting crisis; tectonic paradigms like neoliberalism and globalization cracking up; and fascism ascendant.

Yet there's something interesting about the dirt getting kicked up as the tuggers pull. If the left has been losing this game of tug-of-war over education for the last fifty years, perhaps it's time to change the whole game and radically reinvent the terms of the debate.

Do you remember what Ben Stein, the actor who played the teacher droning on in the opening scenes of the 1986 film *Ferris Bueller's Day Off*, was talking about? The subject was so boring that only an affectless man with a voice like a groan could be talking about it. Go back, freeze the frame, and look at the chalkboard behind him. Alongside a bevy of incomprehensible neoclassical phrases, it reads "fiscal policy" and "monetary policy."

More memorable perhaps was how the suburban teen Bueller skipped Stein's class to cruise around Chicago in a leopard-print vest and a borrowed Ferrari, escaping another dull economics lecture. The movie turns on a contrast between this boring economics lesson and the fantasy of life in the 1980s, when one could be free and buy stuff. But that boring lesson was describing the policies that made what we call neoliberalism: (de)regulation by and for the rich, globalization, dismantling social democracy, substantial weakening of unions, and the uncaring political economy that resulted.

To save public education, to change the game in the tug-of-war, we can't afford the intoxication of Bueller's move, which is to both skip economics class and skip class economics. Instead of letting Ben Stein get away with a facade of boring technocracy, we have to reframe finance policy as the blood-stuff of public education's fight for life and death and so much else. It was the economist John Maynard Keynes who said, as he shook his head in disbelief after the atrocities of World War I, that when it comes to government and administration, policy must replace theory. But this theory of no-theory has wrought its own kind of violence. The violence of the esoteric. The violence of the hard to understand. The violence of the technical protocol posturing as visionless while executing its ostensibly nonexistent vision with a ferocious, boring calm.

So let's remember to enliven the polis of policy—that is, to *re*-politicize policy and take it back from the technocrats—and get into the nitty-gritty for the fun of it. This fun isn't the fun of Bueller's ignorant bliss, but rather the joy of engaging in collective struggle, tinkering with and tanking the structures beneath the feet of the pullers in the tug-of-war to change the game.

To do this wonky spelunking, we have to examine what undergirds all the production, distribution, circulation, and consumption through which education itself takes place: the food kids and teachers eat (or can't), the housing they live in (or can't afford), the health care they get when they're sick (if they're lucky), the unions that protect teachers' jobs and retirement (ditto). In conversations critiquing the privatization of public education, we rarely critique private property itself. What this means is that such conversations fail to foreground how the problems we see in education—specifically, unjust distributions and misrecognitions (that is, spiritual as well as material harm)—are grounded in the structural protection and promulgation of private property and its many oppressive articulations. Not only that, but we miss how school finance is a weak link in American racial capitalism. This book describes U.S. regimes of school financing and makes its policy prescriptions from this perspective.

Maybe this is a good moment to say clearly that I'm a democratic socialist, a tradition that demands the democratization of economies: democracy at work, democratic finance, democracy in how we create, distribute, and circulate resources of all kinds.[3] If communities owned and controlled how we make our material lives rather than big corporate firms with yahoo CEOs and dingus underlings, then things could be better.

Now the red-baiters will say, "Oh, he's just a Marxist, communist pinko!" Yet when we slow education policy down and actually look at how school finance works in the United States, we see that racialized private property is at the heart of a lot of the problems that we talk about when we talk about what's wrong with schools. We know education is resource intensive, for example. Translation into democratic socialist terms: Education is best described with a labor theory of value. What makes education valuable derives ultimately from the work that educators and staff do when they educate, and when you pay well for that labor you get a better education.

Despite the neoliberal chicanery in the economics of education over the last forty years—perpetrated by a bevy of deluded souls like Eric Hanushek, who said he'd proved, by god, that schools don't need more money; they just need to be held accountable for the money that they do get (and who concluded recently that he was wrong!)—economists like C. Kirabo Jackson and Bruce Baker and their collaborators have ushered in a new wave of sense, showing that when schools have more money to do what they do, they do what they do better.[4]

Indeed, districts need money to hire teachers and staff, pay livable salaries, offer good benefits, and contribute to pension funds. And those are just some operating expenditures. What about the capital programs school districts need to pay for when their elementary schools fall apart or playgrounds have nails coming out of their slides? Did you know public schools need to sell themselves as financial products on Wall Street to get the money they need for those programs, and also to fill budget gaps between tax grant cycles? They go into debt to pay for items in their budgets like students have to go into odious debt for college, or sick people put medical bills on their credit cards. Public school districts are in more than half a trillion dollars of debt to Wall Street due to the municipal bond market regime. And this isn't a "neoliberal" policy. It's always been more or less like this.

Capitalism generally, and our peculiar version of U.S. racial capitalism specifically, makes it difficult to provide those resources. And guess who doesn't want to provide the resources to fund the public, social democratic structures that public schools need to operate? The rich, their hangers-on, libertarians, privateers of all kinds, enemies of social democracy and unions and the working class generally (the people I call capitalists throughout this book), doing what they do.[5] This happens through vouchers and charter schools, but also through the very fundament of the public school financial policies I examine in this book, like Title I funding, state funding formulas, property taxes, pension policy, and municipal bonding. Of course, we've seen some stop-start progress, and by some measures, education funding has at least stayed steady over the last thirty years thanks to the people fighting on the left side of that rope, but we can do so much fucking better. The capitalist regime of school finance is taken for granted in the education tug-of-war, but no longer!

Here's where it's important to talk about modes of production and state apparatuses and all the stuff of capitalism and socialism, because different ways of organizing material life might treat schools' dire need for more funding differently. Whose responsibility is it to provide and pay for essential public goods and infrastructure? On whom should we rely when it comes to everything from the red bricks of our redbrick schoolhouses to teacher salaries, textbooks, and nourishing school lunches, to name only a few education-related expenditures? Two answers have emerged in modern human social relations: socialize or individualize. Either you can have the group all pitch in and work together, or you can make the individuals, whether people or firms or school districts or schools, fight it out against one another. The United States—shocker—has chosen the second one.

Perhaps you're skeptical about this critique of capitalism and how capital, private property, and the racialized theft of resources that I'll call super-expropriation are fundamental to the battles we fight over education. Maybe you think capitalism is bad but it's the best we can do, that maybe it's a precondition of "freedom," that it has led to incomparable technical advancement, or even that social democracy requires maintenance and engagement with some version of capitalist economy. But a system in which your zip code determines the quality of your supposedly public education, in which property values and commodity prices translate into educational resources—meaning the rich always get more and the working class, less—and in which school districts must enter into creditor-debtor relationships with rapacious firms and markets simply to ensure that their students have safe, clean learning environments is hardly natural, normal, or inevitable.[6]

This book serves as a corrective to those who simply accept, or worse defend, a failing educational status quo, as well as those who attribute that failure to greedy teachers unions or diversity initiatives. By examining policies that have worked in the past, analyzing the present conjuncture, and proposing solutions for leftist campaigns serious about transformation and victory in the short and long term, I hope to shine a light on these school structures as they are and present blueprints for how they could be different, using tools that you can pick up and utilize in your context.

The book is not an "explainer" of school finance policy. Readers can look to Baker's *Educational Inequality and School Finance: Why Money Matters for America's Students* for economics research; find a useful textbook in *Critical Resource Theory: A Conceptual Lens for Identifying, Diagnosing, and Addressing Inequities in School Funding* by Kaplan and Owings; or dive into a more critical explainer in Swensson, Lehman, and Ellis's aptly titled *Thief in the Classroom: How School Funding Is Misdirected, Disconnected, and Ideologically Aligned.*[7] I don't focus exclusively on the terrible wonders of the right wing, like Berkshire and Schneider's crucial *Education Wars* and *A Wolf at the Schoolhouse Door,* or Cowen's *The Privateers,* nor do I tell the story of the privatization of childhood (Erickson's *Class War*) or teachers (Goldstein's *Teacher Wars*) or the energizing wave of teacher strikes in 2018 (Blanc's *Red State Revolt*). This is a book about the guts of public finance and governance in education policy. I will describe and critique the dusty issues at play using stories and snark, to try to make the inscrutable scrutable and even enjoyable.

In part 1 of the book, I draw a portrait of the racial capitalist finance regime that our schools depend on. The first chapter sets up some concepts with which we should understand schools and money, drawing from the theory of racial capitalism. To reimagine school finance from a socialist perspective, I look to Yugoslav political economy and the Illyrian economic model.

Then I look at the local (chapter 2), state (chapter 3), and federal (chapter 4) levels of schools and money. In each case, I survey regimes of financing, stories of injustice and organizing, and provide proposals for policies I think could get things going in a better direction.[8]

Part 2 is all about bonds, or what I call the hidden force behind education injustice. I examine how these bonds work (chapter 5), the toxic political economy growing from and around them (chapter 6), and what to do about them constructively (chapter 7).

Part 3 focuses on teacher pensions, huge pools of capital meant to provide for retired public educators. Understanding teacher pension policy from an ideological perspective, I track different approaches to teacher pensions through the lens of solidarity and how so many popularly available perspectives are anti-solidaristic (chapter 8). Then I look at whether there's a crisis with teacher pensions, like so many of those anti-solidaristic accounts would have us believe. In chapter 9, I take a forensic approach to these claims and show how they're part of the anti-solidarity project. Then I look at some leftist perspectives on pensions and provide my own proposal, drawing from recent historical research to propose a green fiscal mutualism between pensions and school bonds (chapter 10). I conclude by providing what I call a Plan for Public Education under the banner of green fiscal mutualism, gathering together all the alternatives from the book and setting them against the background of the larger political moment today.

Because we live with and in and under capitalism, this is also a book about capitalism and its relationship to education, from a socialist perspective. While the United States (perhaps pathologically) prides itself on its decentralized system of federalism, letting districts, cities, and states make their own policy, there's a notable centricity in all this supposed decentralization: private property. What to say about capitalism, the noble scam of private property propping up the whole edifice of what we call "democracy"? Must we center private property in all that we do for the public? Do we really need private property at all?

The socialist's gamble is that changing whether and how money works—who has it, where it comes from, who gets it, what it even is—goes a long way to changing the whole system, something modern monetary theory has done well recently (and that informs this book).[9] Here we part ways with other accounts of education policy and finance, those that might get lost in the spinning circles of the courts, where the vast majority of the fight for schools and money has historically played out, and the laws and all the policies meant to "protect" the "public." As the founder of critical race theory, Derrick Bell Jr. (a lawyer trying busing cases for the NAACP in the sixties and seventies) said, the courts exist in a world where private property rules, and the rules are meant to protect private property, something even those calling for school finance reparations have to contend with.[10]

Instead, when we're demanding more funding for poor schools, deciding which candidates to support based on their education platforms, and fighting for truly public education, we have to turn to basic structures and nitty-gritty details. What would it mean to democratize school resources? What would it mean to have truly public schools, down to the very means of resource creation and distribution that fuels them and thus the administrations governing them? What will it take to make schools as public as possible?

Ultimately, this book is for the organizers, the campaigners, the teachers, the policymakers, the parents, and the students interested in understanding and transforming the structures on which this whole education mess is predicated. For all those moderates and conservatives wondering what the left might propose—presuming that we are just crybabies with no plans, pragmatically speaking—I also submit this book to you. Here are the policies we might want; the laws we have passed and might pass again; the analysis we have of your precious status quo. Now more than ever, it's socialism or barbarism.

Part I

School Finance WTF: How It Works and the Policies We Deserve

1
Public Schools and Private Property

I got mad reading *Forbes*. Marguerite Roza published an article in 2022 taking school districts to task for lacking "expertise in finance" as budgets crunched in the wake of the pandemic's economic crisis.[1] What infuriated me was that six of the seven cases she examined, in a conveniently cursory manner, focused on pay and benefits for teachers instead of other key aspects of district financing, like debt service or charter school expenditure. I was also frustrated that she didn't focus at all on the context around certain expenditures, the worlds these budget numbers describe and their histories. Her thesis was that teachers unions are greedy and school board members that approve budgets that meet union demands lack a special financial expertise to combat their greed.

Taking recourse in expertise—framed as a simple matter of knowing or not knowing objective truth about naturally occurring facts—can be a powerful maneuver to mask one's ideological, socially situated position. This kind of "you're dumb so listen to me" move is very common in education policy: Many educators (myself included) tend to think of ourselves as bad at math, and the abstract language used in finance and policy makes our eyes glaze over. Inevitably, it's intimidating to confront someone with academic bona fides and fancy-sounding titles when they make these sorts of claims about school and money. But there are always ideological presuppositions behind such claims.

Roza's article is a case in point. She has a material interest in saying school board members need "training" and "expertise" because she directs a privately funded center at Georgetown University that provides this very training through workshops in education finance for educational leaders and policymakers.[2] Tuition for the certificate program is several thousand dollars per participant. And while she has written about equity in school funding, her conceptual and ideological presumptions align with the movement for accountability, which puts the onus on individuals in school districts to make better use of the money they have rather than thinking about where this money comes from.

Roza's *Forbes* piece is in line with the technocratic paradigm common throughout the last forty years in education. This ideology is particularly tricky because it enables technocrats to masquerade as simply "following the data," making "objective," "scientific," "realistic," or "pragmatic" decisions that are "data-driven" rather than being "political," all the while producing knowledge with clear political orientation and impact.

This myopic, overbearing, and semi-invisible approach to education policy speaks to a lot that's wrong with how we analyze and try to change (or not change) the material conditions of schools. A framework that disavows ideology and politics in favor of "objective" technocracy insidiously limits our capacity to analyze and identify both causes and effects in the complex terrain of financial pressures on school districts. This, in turn, limits educational leaders' sense of possibility when it comes to solving budget crises.

Unfortunately, this problem isn't limited to Marguerite Roza. Rather, the explanations, reporting, and terms of debate we receive from academics, education reporters, policy wonks, and school administrators alike instruct us in concepts that direct our gaze toward some issues and solutions, while actively obscuring others. The rub is that the technocratic power brokers of school finance insist that their concepts, always limited and particular in what they show us, represent a full, unadulterated, and objective view of the terrain of struggle.

Technocracy has a politics. In her *Forbes* article, Roza cited West Contra Costa Unified School District in California as an example of a failing district in need of dispassionate "expertise." Without providing relevant context on the district, she argues that, given its budget crisis, West Contra Costa's school board needs to fire teachers. However, it's disingenuous to talk about this diverse working-class district without discussing its long history of struggle.

This struggle began with the passage of California's Proposition 13 in 1978. This law, which is still in effect, placed a cap on property tax increases for homeowners who stay in their houses across the state. Since about half of money for schools comes from local taxes, and increases on these taxes were capped, this meant a loss of revenue for school districts that hit West Contra Costa particularly hard. Compounding this loss, in the late 1980s the district began to suffer budget crises due to declining enrollments and revenues. When people move out of a district, local schools lose money, since funding relies on student numbers. In 1991, the West Contra Costa school district went bankrupt.

The district, which renamed itself Richmond Unified, was one of the first school districts in the country to be put in state receivership, which means having the state assume responsibility for its governance. As part of the receivership, the state of California loaned the district $28.5 million to become solvent. The interest rate was 5.7 percent, which was pretty high considering that the state could have set it at any rate it wanted.

In addition to being saddled with a high-interest loan from the state, the district carried debt from a $5 million loan from IBM.[3]

The company had given the district pallets of outdated computers with the expectation that it would be paid back for them. Given its budget issues, the district asked IBM, a multimillion-dollar company, to forgive this loan in the early 2000s. You'd think that such a big company would help a struggling school district. But no, the company wanted its money—apparently it was the principle of the thing. The district got a few concessions on time, amount, and interest rate, but IBM wouldn't cancel the loan, which pushed the district into even deeper financial trouble.

More than ten years later, in 2004, the district still owed $16.5 million on these loans. In the interim it couldn't afford to maintain its buildings, ended its sports programs, and was forced to shutter many of its buildings. At the same time, Republican governor Arnold Schwarzenegger had cut state funding for schools in half from $4 billion to $2 billion in the budget allocation under Proposition 98, a ballot initiative that set a new, reduced minimum state expenditure for K–12 schools.

Combined with this cut in state aid, the pressure of the loans on the district's budget was the last straw. Parents, teachers, and organizers said enough is enough. They marched more than fifty miles to Sacramento, demanding a meeting with the governor. Schwarzenegger refused. The organizers gathered in a public space and went on a hunger strike that would last twenty-six days.[4]

And they won.[5] Longtime farmworker organizer Dolores Huerta and state legislator Jackie Goldberg worked in solidarity with the movement, getting signatures from elected officials demanding the governor meet with them and act on their demands. Goldberg and others wrote a piece of legislation called the Daucher Bill, which reduced the interest rate for the school district's loans from 5.7 percent to 1.7 percent (even though it really should have been zero). The law also said that any indebted district would not have to make loan payments until changes to Prop. 98 came through. Schwarzenegger met with the fasters when he signed the bill, where the organizers cried tears of joy when they took their first bites of food in nearly a month.

Despite all this, the structures that created the conditions for decades of hardship remained stubbornly in place: relying on private property values frozen in time for public education funding and municipal revenues subject to the forces of racial capitalism, as we'll see later in this chapter; depending on never-quite-enough state aid in the wake of a global financial crisis in 2008 and dominant economic thinking that debases public goods during the recovery; a federal government that provides very little support within the context of a legislative environment where you have to make progress or your schools get turned into charters, which sap money from the public system; and the need to go to Wall Street for expensive private loans for facilities and revenue gaps. That's how school finance works in this country. The district, like so many districts in the United States, simply did not have enough money.

The district couldn't pay off the refinanced loan from the state until 2012, more than twenty years after its initial bankruptcy.[6] Wendy Gonzalez was a first-year elementary school teacher when she marched and fasted with the group in 2004. Interviewed in 2012, when the district paid off the last of its debt, she said it was "kind of a relief." I can imagine it was bittersweet. So much effort for a change in the interest rate on this one loan, when the loan itself, IBM, and the underlying system of property taxation and inadequate state spending that created its necessity remained.

So yes, even now, the district has significant budgetary issues.[7] Prop. 13 is still in place. The district serves 26,000 largely working-class kids, half of whom are Black and Latino. As recently as 2022, the district was facing possible insolvency again. But is that because the people running the district aren't "experts" trained in the right kind of neoliberal thought? Is it because the district isn't run like a business in the private sector? No. If we broaden our scope, use more capacious concepts, and examine the district's political economy through its history of racialized exploitation—viewing it through the lens of struggle, conflict, private property, and repression—a broader, truer picture comes to light. What if it has been the pressures of Prop. 13, low federal expenditure (only 7 percent of the district's funding came from the federal government), interest rate policies, and private property markets and their dynamics in the region that put the district in the situation it's in? What if the school finance regime is actually creating a dog-eat-dog dynamic where other districts get more than they need, leaving West Contra Costa in the dust? What if it's the regional ruling class's treatment of this district over time, like IBM's attitude toward the loan? It's not West Contra Costa's fault that they are not their wealthy neighbors, whose property values are so much higher.

The concepts behind technocratic education policy carry presumptions like Roza's: that financial expertise demands an anti-worker, pro-market rejection of social democratic policies and the provision of public goods, all in the context of an unjust system and history that this perspective conveniently leaves out of the picture. Only that kind of concept could recommend that West Contra Costa be more hostile to unions and fire people.

There are other, nominally more progressive technocratic concepts that accept the legitimacy and inevitability of bourgeois structures made for and by property owners, but which concede that current policies are unjust. These progressive concepts bid us imagine that our policy protocols are like a fundamentally just machine. Well-meaning government officials may need to recalibrate and adjust a few knobs from time to time, but, once they do so, everyone will get what they need: adequate, efficient, and equitable funding. Typically, the progressive recommendation is to increase state spending, which, if you can win it and keep it, leaves root problems unaddressed.

This chapter is all about concepts: how we think about the realities and policies we find when it comes to schools and money. I use two concepts, one critical and the other constructive, and describe each in what follows. The critical concept comes from the theory of racial capitalism—specifically, the notion of super-expropriative kleptocracy—while the constructive concept comes from Illyrian economics, or Yugoslavian-style democratic socialism.

Esoteric distinctions between how different kinds of property are taxed can determine not only how much tax revenue comes into a school district but also how tax revenues are distributed in a region. The historian Esther Cyna's research on North Carolina shows that wealthy elite whites in Halifax County knew this. In her award-winning essay on school finance in rural North Carolina from 1900 to 2018, she tells a story of a debate over Halifax County's school finance policy that helps inform my thinking about funding inequity as racialized theft.[8]

In 1972, there was a disagreement in Halifax over how to allocate the county government's sales tax revenue for schools. There were two positions. The first favored an ad valorem tax, which allocated the countywide sales tax money to districts based on their property wealth. A school district in the county that had high property values would receive more of the revenue than one with less. The second position advocated for a per capita tax, in which districts with more students would receive more of the revenue.

According to Cyna, rich whites holed up in a small district within the county pushed for the ad valorem method of allocating the sales tax revenue because it yielded them a much greater share. Noting this obvious injustice, the Halifax County school superintendent advocated for the per capita position. He argued that the county should use its sales tax to serve everyone in the county, emphasizing the benefits to diverse working-class areas. These districts included both middle-income and poorer whites and middle-income and poorer Blacks.

The rich white district won. With its higher property values, it would receive more sales tax dollars from the ad valorem approach. Cyna is clear: "The *ad valorem* decision was a process of counting lives through property wealth and thus attributing more value to white lives."

Cyna goes further. She makes a move that few others in the motley arena of school finance research do: She rejects the characterization of school finance resource distribution in terms of simple "inequality" or "inequity." This may come as a shock to readers familiar with the literature, since inequality and inequity are the go-to concepts for discussing school resource discrepancies. Instead, Cyna calls the ad valorem policy in Halifax County "kleptocratic." She shows that this policy was *intentional, racialized theft* of the diverse working class's resources, in the form of the county's sales tax revenue, by rich whites. In other words, this wasn't passively "unequal and inequitable distribution," a phrase where even the grammar leaves out the subject of the situation—who distributes what? Instead, Cyna argues that the rich whites who fought for and won the policy debate *stole* from the diverse working class.

While not every disparity will be theft, and Cyna and I have written about a suite of concepts suitable for what we call critical school finance (like dispossession, extraction, and racial capitalism), what's so important about shifting from the language of passive allocation to active kleptocracy is that it presents the whole problem of "school funding inequality" through a different filter.[9] Framing funding discrepancies in terms of unequal or inequitable distribution obscures the political-economic moves that certain groups and individuals make—their choices, their activism, their agency. Instead of understanding school funding as a mechanical, functional, and technical problem abstracted from political economy, Cyna helps us see it through the lens of action, struggle, power, and dominance.

I use this concept in my analysis of school funding. Across the

United States, I find persistent racialized theft of resources by dominant racial and class groups through policy structures so ubiquitous and normalized that the thieves don't even consider their material advantages to be the product of theft at all.

When I think about schools and money, I also rely on the critical framework of racial capitalism, a theory that articulates race and class together dynamically so we can talk about both without analytically subordinating one to the other. Inspired by the anti-apartheid movements in South Africa and most commonly associated with the writing of American political scientist Cedric Robinson (particularly his book *Black Marxism*), but also more recently in interpretations of British-Jamaican cultural theorist Stuart Hall, the framework has won pride of place on the contemporary left because it emphasizes the relative autonomy of race in capitalist society.

In places with histories of colonization and slavery, like South Africa and the United States, for example, you can't just talk about capitalism; you have to talk about racism too. But in doing so—in refusing to abstract racism out of any analysis of capitalism and vice versa—you change each concept.[10] Racial capitalism gets us thinking about how the analytic separation of the concepts of "race" and "class" must be spanned. Researchers Jessica Gerrard, Arathi Sriprakash, and Sophie Rudolph have recently applied the framework to education.[11] The critical theorist of education Zeus Leonardo even says we should talk about them as raceclass, like physicists talk about spacetime.[12]

So what's a racial capitalist concept that goes with Cyna's kleptocracy? Meet Claudia Jones.

The mid-century communist Claudia Jones was a key figure in the American Communist Party in the years before and after World War II. She was one of the few prominent Black female intellectuals whose writing reached a large audience at the time. One of her most famous essays was "An End to the Neglect of the Problems of the Negro Woman!"[13] written in 1949. Generations before the idea of intersectionality emerged as a corrective to siloed race and gender analyses in legal studies, Jones articulated these categories together with class to create a concept through which anti-capitalists could understand the "triple oppression" of working-class Black women in the United States. White working-class men are exploited under capitalism, she noted. White working-class women are too, while that exploitation gets exacerbated by gender-based oppression. But Jones said that Black working-class women face a triple oppression as workers, as women, and as Black people. Rather than capitalist exploitation and gender-based oppression alone, Jones called this triple oppression "super-exploitation" because Black women made exponentially less in wages than white women and even Black men.

Exploitation is capitalism's noble scam. The beating heart of Marx's critique of capitalism was to point out that working people do the labor that produces what we understand as value. Without the labor and value workers produce, capitalists, who own the means of production, wouldn't be able to accumulate by themselves all the wealth they hoard. This is precisely why they pay workers money to do it. And this is, for Marx, the core of capitalist exploitation: When I work, I produce goods or services that are worth a certain amount. But I don't get paid for all the value that I create. Instead, capitalists take the difference—what Marx terms surplus value. That's exploitation. Super-exploitation, then, is a term that Black communists, starting with Jones, used to talk about the way race and gender compound the profit-driven exploitation of workers in the United States.

The contemporary political theorist Charisse Burden-Stelly also uses the concept of super-exploitation because it describes the "conjuncture of white supremacy, racialization, and the 'badge of slavery,' which exacerbates the conditions of exploitation to which the white working classes are subjected." She cites another famous Black communist, Harry Haywood, who wrote that "super-exploitation constitutes a combination of direct exploitation, outright robbery, physical violence, legal coercion, and perpetual indebtedness . . . stifling 'the free economic and cultural development' of the Black masses 'through racist persecution as a basic condition for maintaining' virtual enslavement."[14] Burden-Stelly suggests that we apply the concept of super-exploitation widely to talk about multiple exploitations across social categories like race, gender, ability, ethnicity, and sexuality under capitalism in which everyone—no matter your status in these hierarchies—gets exploited, but, depending on that status, gets exploited differently and multiply.

Where do school and money come into the picture? To talk about racialized accumulation beyond the traditional workplace, the American critical theorist Nancy Fraser proposes we use the term "expropriation," for which she gives the following definition: "Distinct from exploitation, but equally integral to capitalist development, expropriation is accumulation by other means. . . . Commandeered capacities get incorporated into the value-expanding process that defines capital. Simple theft is not enough. Unlike the sort of pillaging that long predated the rise of capitalism, expropriation in the sense I intend here is confiscation-cum-conscription into the process of capital accumulation."[15] In the racial capitalist framework, kleptocratic-dispossessive-extractive school-funding practices fit this description. The white elites in Halifax County successfully accumulated more resources for themselves in the form of better-funded schools, which educated their kids more effectively, thereby increasing their chances of financial success and stability at the direct expense and to the detriment of their diverse working-class neighbors. They confiscated-conscribed those sales tax revenues.

But like exploitation, talking about expropriation alone misses the different and multiple ways this conscription happens across hierarchies. Thus, I will use the term "super-expropriation" to name the school-funding injustice that pervades our so-called public education. In the K–12 systems, property-rich areas wall themselves off like private fortresses, levying taxes at lower rates to get more revenue for their schools, which only the relatively rich can attend. Mostly suburban, the "good" school districts (or, in the case of cities, the rich catchments) get a dividend from their location under the guise of local control, perpetually siphoning off young wealthier and whiter families in search of "better" schools.

Super-expropriation is a concept for critiquing that injustice—the first critical concept I use—which makes space for the second, more constructive concept.

What could a democratic socialist school finance policy look like? In terms of historical examples, I look to Yugoslavia. In its successful fight against fascism in the 1930s through its internationalist and industrial development in the 1970s, the country forged its own complex and successful democratic socialist economy distinct from Soviet communism. It did so as a federation of countries with their own ethnic and regional dynamics. It also placed a high priority on forging solidarity with the international working class, particularly in the third world, helping to build the Non-Aligned Movement. The economist Benjamin Ward called the theory behind this formation "Illyrian economics" after the pre-Roman peoples who occupied the Balkans.[16]

The sociologist Johanna Bockman describes the basic tenets of that model.[17] There's no private property, but rather social property controlled by the state and managed by firms owned by workers cooperating in markets. Instead of shares owned by private shareholders and traded on a stock market, firms produce social dividends that are dispersed to residents through the state. There are managers in each firm, implementing the decisions that the workers make. Further, the firms set their prices equal to the marginal cost of production, charging per unit what it takes to make one extra unit. The firms focus on making as much product as they can for as little cost as possible. What guides their pricing—their bottom line—is not how much they can get for their goods, but rather how well they manage their costs as they sell their goods on the market.

The Illyrian bottom line is therefore not profit but production, foregrounding what the whole point of production should be generally: making sure people get what they need and contribute what they can. Profits are reinvested into the company. They are also distributed into the social dividend, which can then be spent on things like education.

Capitalists critique this model by claiming that workers shouldn't make decisions about how to allocate revenues—surely, they'd just give themselves raises. Of course, it's easy to make the same argument about capitalists, whose entire raison d'être is maximization of profits, getting themselves big bonuses and raises, and amassing as much wealth as possible while so many others struggle. But better than whataboutism is the historical evidence of this critique's worthlessness. The World Bank, according to Bockman, deemed the Illyrian model successful "beyond any doubt," saying economic problems thought to be inherent to the operation of workers' managed firms—including inadequate levels of reinvestment, excessive personal income payments, a bias toward capital-intensive techniques of production, and allocative inefficiency resulting from capital immobility—were either nonexistent or capable of resolution through appropriate compensatory legislation and policy instruments.

The combination of worker self-management, state-owned capital and resources, and production-oriented bottom line makes for what Ward called "the superiority of independent enterprises interacting on a fully competitive global market." (In fact, some economists such as Jaroslav Vanek and Ward claimed that markets in socialism would be freer than in capitalism because there would be fewer monopolies.) Note that this model of market socialism isn't your typical Keynesianism or social democracy in which the state manages a capitalist market economy. In those models, there's private property. Capitalists own and control firms. Workers work for capitalists. Profits go to shareholders. Schools are funded through taxes on various exchanges therein, whether taxes on sales, income, real estate, and so forth. Such an arrangement gives too much power to private property.

The Illyrian model isn't a panacea, and the example of Yugoslavia has issues just like any country, falling prey to the oil shocks and subsequent financial crises of the 1970s, as well as pressure from the U.S. empire's sanctions and intervention.[18]

What the Illyrian model does, at least, is provide a foundation to think about economics and finance in socialist terms. After thinking about schools and money through the critical concept of racial capitalist super-expropriation, the constructive lens of Illyrian economics is like opening a window and getting some much-needed fresh air. What would it mean to think of U.S. school finance policy with the Illyrian model? We can take a guess from the Yugoslav setup.

Yugoslavia was a federation of republics, each of which was composed of communes (which is cool by itself). Within the communes, the federation's education policy became more decentralized over time, focusing on the needs of the commune, eventually forming a network of "self-governing interested communities of education," which observers likened to school districts in the United States except "that they offered a definite and important role for teachers and other school personnel."[19] Imagine the teachers union and the school board merging, for example.

The school finance system itself was complex and there isn't space here to go into detail, but we can judge perhaps on Yugoslavia's approach to capital expenditure, which was based on fiscal capacity of the larger republic, collectivizing cost so that "localities with a per capita income at 20 percent of the average for the republic must fund only 20 percent of capital costs, while those with 91 per cent [of the average] or more must fund at least 80 percent of capital costs." That approach to capital expenditure is much more progressive than the United States', where school districts have to sell themselves as investment commodities to get private credit, paying high interest rates and fees to consultants and investors and private banks, letting anonymous wealthy people make tax-free income, to get money for capital expenditures like new playgrounds (as I examine more in part 2).

The larger policy regime in Yugoslavia made for a more democratic apparatus where shared decision-making was intuitive. In their recent book on Serbian primary school leaders, Jelena Raković, Tom O'Donoghue, and Simon Clarke argue that "the former Yugoslav workers' self-management system required primary school principals to be facilitators of decision-making processes and leading pedagogues who served as role models in their communities," a dynamic they claim ended when Yugoslavia dissolved in the 1990s.[20]

Thus, the twin concepts I'm working with in my analysis are the critical theory of super-expropriation and the constructive theory of Illyrian economics. When I think about schools and money in the contemporary United States—and ask what school funding could look like in a socialist America—these are the ideas that frame my thinking.

I get a common question when I talk about these issues. Stepping back, given how far we are from something like the Illyrian model, how do well-meaning teachers and parents and students and communities change things? How do we exert agency? How effective can this agency be in influencing the government and corporate entities currently responsible for educating our kids? This question pitting big social structures against small, liberties of rhymes with classic controversies in intellectual debates on the left since the 1940s at least.

To handle this question, I look to the sitcom *Abbott Elementary*. The show's protagonist, Janine, is a new teacher of second-grade students in Philadelphia. In the first episode, one of her students has an accident and pees on the classroom's carpet. As all primary school teachers know, carpets are important. They're a collective meeting space and a place of comfort, sharing, and community. So the loss of the rug is a big one. In a poignant vignette, we see one of Janine's students sleeping on the cold floor of the classroom during lunch. He has a difficult situation at home, so he gets the sleep he needs in school, usually on the carpet. Now he has to lay his head on the tiles.

Janine goes on a quest for a new carpet. The problem, as always, is how to pay for it. Earlier in the episode Janine's colleagues also complain about money. It's one of the first things we hear them discussing: how the district can't afford this or that. There's a brief mention of a new football stadium in the works, which, when juxtaposed with the teachers' and students' needs in the school, is absurd—there's enough money for a stadium, but not the city's kids.

Of course, there's not enough money in the budget for a new carpet, nor are there ready replacements available. A veteran teacher tells Janine to be resourceful and figure it out herself. Indeed, she suggests buying a new one with her own money, because, in her experience, leaders in the district rarely deliver things like this. But Janine has too many student loans, along with her rent and car payments, to afford a new carpet for her room. With well-meaning and plucky naivete, she refuses to give up. First, she goes to the principal, Ava, who has no experience in education—we find out she caught the superintendent cheating on his wife and later blackmailed him into hiring her—and is neither sympathetic nor competent.

Ava rebuffs Janine's request for a new rug. Janine decides to write a formal complaint to the district office about Ava. Then, later in the day, Ava announces that she's excited to share some big news. It turns out she applied for emergency funding from the district after Janine's complaint and received a $3,000 discretionary grant. But instead of essential supplies like a carpet, Ava spent the money on a huge gaudy sign featuring a picture of herself to hang above the school's front doors.

The episode ends with another longtime teacher securing new carpets from a construction worker friend building the new stadium project. The white construction worker drops the carpets off to the Black students and teachers in an unmarked truck, looking over his shoulder as though he is afraid of being caught committing an illicit act.

This narrative is a perfect illustration of the interplay between government structure and individual agency in school finance. In this case, they take the form of revenue and accountability, respectively. Abbott Elementary School needs money. Specifically, Janine's classroom needs a new rug. The district should be able to pay for that new rug, but resources are notoriously scarce. On the other hand, leaders like Ava spend an emergency grant on a terrible new sign that does nothing for the school except serve their own misguided interests.

This is what I'm calling the Abbott problem: Schools need revenue, and that revenue needs to be spent well. The insight shouldn't sound new or groundbreaking. It's pretty obvious. But in practice these two things get separated: The people calling for revenue are different from the people calling for accountability. To move forward, we have to think of structure and agency, revenue and accountability, together rather than separately, recognizing that both revenue and accountability are necessary for good schools.

For instance, the right and center insist that the problem with schools isn't money: It's accountability. This accountability imperative ignores that shameful scarcity (like the fact that companies building and owning stadiums don't have to pay property taxes that would otherwise go to the schools) and lays all the blame on principals. The way to make schools better, according to this argument, is not to spend more money, but rather to hire and fire the right people. While firing Ava and hiring someone who uses the stipend for a rug might solve Janine's problem, the larger problem of underfunding remains.

Plus, for right-wingers and centrists, the "right people" come from capitalist business and finance and push for market solutions (and increasingly ones). Privatize the public structures to get rid of terrible taxes on our businesses, they say. This tendency, which spans the Democratic and Republican parties, has set up a redoubt of think tanks, policy groups, research institutions, and lobbyists to disseminate and implement their ideas throughout the education apparatus. Justified by research done by the economist Eric Hanushek in the early 1990s, this pillar of the accountability imperative says schools can and should do more with less, blaming what they call the "money myth."

Hanushek's research has been widely disproven over the last decade, most recently by Hanushek himself. A group of educational economists including C. Kirabo Jackson and Claire Mackevicius have also shown that his claims don't hold up. Along with researchers such as Bruce Baker, they show that the money myth is itself a myth.[21] According to the revenue imperative, schools need money to do well. In other words, schools that have more money are better schools. Education is a human-resource-intensive process, and to do it well you have to spend. Schools can't do more with less. Given less, they do less. Further, calling for accountability without properly funding the school system blames the underfunded victim for the imperatives of the larger, structural forces over which they have no control. To attribute failure to school systems without providing the resources for success is to set them up to fail.

Thus, the revenue imperative says fund the schools. Give schools more money, particularly those schools serving populations who need more. If the School District of Philadelphia (both in the show and in real life) had the funding it needed, then a request for a new rug wouldn't be an issue. Even if there were a principal like Ava in charge, teachers and parents and students could organize and pressure her into finding the money, like Janine does, and hopefully hold her accountable if she doesn't spend it well. There might not even be a problem in the first place. Rather than emphasizing individuals' good or bad decisions independent of the structural context in which they work, the revenue imperative focuses on those structural policies. This imperative has a competing redoubt in the educational apparatus, advanced by entities like Rethinking Schools, the Network for Public Education, the Economic Policy Institute, the Shanker Institute, and others.

The predominant version of the accountability imperative comes from centrist and right-wing ideologies of personal responsibility, which are at work in the way that Marguerite Roza blames school officials for West Contra Costa's money problems. This focus on individual decisions at the school and district levels derives from an inherent distrust in "government"; specifically, the social democratic provision of public goods through taxation of private property. But there's a left-wing version of the accountability imperative too: Leftists want educational leaders to fund our schools equitably; treat students, teachers, and parents justly; and communicate transparently. And we will act collectively to ensure they do. This is what activists in West Contra Costa did to secure a bare minimum of resources to educate children.

But it could be that neither the activists nor Roza fully grasped both structure and agency. Roza leaves out the structure of the district's crisis entirely in favor of a punitive and myopic individualism, while the activists, wielding their collective agency against the structures undergirding the district's injustice, demanded concessions from that structure that only partly alleviated the issue.

How can we reimagine the structure? Consider the subtext of the *Abbott* pilot. When the veteran teacher coordinates with her construction worker friend at the stadium, we see hints at a different kind of structure: teachers and construction workers collaborating across racial differences, figuring out how to redistribute existing resources from the stadium to the school in a better way. My concepts tell me that this is how decisions about schools and money should be made across the board. Sadly, the reality of the distribution of money and resources in the American education system is far from that horizon. But we can get there.

2

The Tyranny of the Local Property Tax

In 1971, Citizens Action Program (CAP), a group of community organizers in Chicago, noticed something strange. They were researching U.S. Steel as part of a campaign to pressure the company to reduce its air pollution in Chicago. As they examined maps of U.S. Steel's properties, they discovered very low property valuations for all its steel mills.

Intrigued, they found that assessors employed by the Cook County municipal government had valued the factories far below what they were worth. Organizers estimated that U.S. Steel had gotten a 73 percent discount on the assessed value of their property compared to similar properties in other areas. This discount, at the behest of the city government's corrupt administration, had saved the steel giant more than $774 million in ten years in unpaid taxes. This $774 million (in 2025 dollars), a fortune in 1971, was revenue that was supposed to go to Chicago's public schools.

CAP changed gears. Instead of an air-quality campaign, the organizers launched a school-funding campaign. They got interested in systematic underassessment of property value in the Chicago region, going through records for other steel mills, racetracks, banks, corporate headquarters, and even suburbs. They found the same story over and over again: undervalued commercial property sapping tax revenues for public programs like schools. They also found overassessments of property in diverse working-class neighborhoods, charging everyday people higher taxes to compensate for the underassessments benefiting industrialists.

CAP organizers brought their findings to the county and ultimately forced a change in how property was valued. In her essay on school finance reform in Illinois, historian Tracy Steffes describes how the county replaced the young stooges in the assessor's office with new assessors who used fair market valuation, or sale value, calculated with computers, taking power away from the corrupt county officials. As a result, more money could flow to the schools.[1]

But a generation later, at the turn of the twenty-first century, the fat cats were at it again. This time, as education scholar and activist Pauline Lipman has argued, Chicago's ruling class pursued the same plutocratic ends as always—dislocating diverse working-class neighborhoods and pilfering property tax revenues at the expense of public schools—but in an entirely new way. This time, the beneficiaries were real estate developers. Instead of the assessment shenanigans that CAP uncovered, the Daley administration used tax-increment financing—a policy through which a city gives incremental increases in tax revenues to developers as an incentive to build in certain places. Whereas the scandal in 1971 was caused by underassessing property, the scandal in 2009 was in giving away municipal revenues in advance to private developers.

This is how tax-increment financing works: First, the city declares a neighborhood "blighted." Next, it creates a ceiling for tax revenues from property in the neighborhood. If property values in that neighborhood increase beyond a certain level, the city transfers any additional tax revenue from the property to developers, either to fund projects in the neighborhood or to pay off loans needed for the development. All of this, instead of funding city services like schools. In other words, the policy is a little like a city's government saying to a developer, "If you can turn this 'blighted' neighborhood into a 'good' one, we'll give you any extra taxes we collect if the property value increases." Over time, that takes money from schools, like the tax abatement in Philadelphia I mentioned. And this becomes a big problem.

When schools don't have enough money, there's much less to work with and it becomes easier to close them, for example. Though Lipman and fellow organizers won some protections, Richard Daley's successor, Rahm Emanuel, and his neoliberal administration ultimately closed fifty schools that the city deemed to be failing—a devastating loss for Chicago communities.

Like the rich whites in rural Halifax County, North Carolina, different iterations of Chicago's ruling class used different regimes of private property assessment and taxation to enrich themselves instead of fully funding education for all Chicagoans. And like the marchers and fasters in West Contra Costa County after them, organizers like CAP and the groups Lipman worked with took wealthy business interests and their political enablers to task for this indignity—offering a model for how we can analyze schools and money to push back against ruling-class austerity politics. Following their example, we now zoom in to schools and money at the local level

In this chapter, I outline some history of how the property tax went from working-class win to Pyrrhic victory via the transmogrifications of municipal home rule, tying in a quantitative measure I developed for analyzing super-expropriation in the present. I conclude by looking to the Twin Cities, Minnesota, to highlight a real-life, local-level policy that powerfully takes on private property's grip on school funding.

Funding public education through property tax revenue produces a fundamental tension. On one hand, it lashes the fate of public goods like education to the cruel vicissitudes of racial capitalist commodity markets. Indeed, organizers of Minnesota's landmark fiscal disparities programs—which I get into at the end of this chapter—called it the "tyranny of the local property tax."[2] On the other hand, as the progressive think tank Lincoln Land Institute puts it, the property tax—through which private property owners are forced to fund public services—is a "bulwark of public finance which must be preserved for the public good." In a 2023 report, the Lincoln Land Institute identifies this core tension. Property tax is tyranny; property tax is provision.[3]

Before we turn to a contemporary case, let's identify the source of this dilemma. Perhaps surprisingly, some historians argue that the property tax in the United States was actually a (white) working-class demand to force property owners to pony up for public education. Funding education through the property tax, then, was initially a kind of victory. But did the eventual losses suffered by the diverse working class from that victory overwhelm its benefits? Was it Pyrrhic?

Billy D. Walker tells the story of the property tax in a 1984 essay in the *Journal of Education Finance*. The first property taxes date back to Athens in 596 BCE. The first property taxes to pay for education were levied during the Reformation in Germany, when they were used to fund biblical study. At that time, Christian Germans were nation building and saving souls, and property taxes funded the project.[4]

Fast-forward to the Reformist Puritans of England, extremist Protestants following Luther, who left their homes after losses in the wake of the Reformation and colonized what would later become the Northeast of the United States. Walker says these Puritans couldn't tax property to fund their schools, even though they wanted to, because "land was so bountiful as to be practically worthless." The Puritans found other ways to tax themselves (on necessities like food and housing) to pay for teachers, eventually passing the Olde Deluder Satan Law, making it illegal for a town not to provide public education to all students—so they wouldn't be deluded by Satan.

A century later, Thomas Jefferson took up the idea of funding public schools through taxation, but for different reasons. Jefferson argued that taxes should be on people with too much authority, like priests and nobles, who, he said, "will rise up among us if we leave the people in ignorance." His idea was that taxing the powerful to educate the masses would mitigate the concentration of power among the elite few. Horace Mann, the famous framer of U.S. public schooling a century after Jefferson, took up this position too. Mann thought the people's property should fund the people's education, creating a "balance wheel" of opportunity and equality.

By the early nineteenth century there was some agreement in the United States that, indeed, there should be public schools and that they should be paid for by taxes on property. Budding technocrats argued for property tax revenue not from fear of Satanic delusion or from bourgeois (slave-owning) revolutionary sentiment but because it was the only tax that could be "administered locally with any degree of efficiency." And, because the economy was mostly agrarian, land was now considered a valuable asset. As historians of education like Robin Einhorn, Camille Walsh, Matthew Gardner Kelly, and Andrew W. Kahrl have shown, as education became more local and the United States confronted the legacy of slavery, the property tax for education didn't quite work out how Jefferson and Mann envisioned it.[5]

There's an inherent class conflict in using property taxes to fund schools for everyone. A tax on property within the boundaries of some territory, whose revenues finance education for everyone there, means that the property-owning class within that area has to pay for schools that serve everyone, even poor and working-class people. Rich property owners didn't (and still don't!) want to pay taxes on their property because (a) they didn't want to give up "their" money and (b) they certainly didn't want to give it to hoi polloi.

To complicate matters, there were also policies on the books left over from imperial England that the American bourgeoisie were happier with: rate bills to fund pauper schools and charity schools. Pauper schools with a rate bill worked like this: If you wanted to send your kid to a pauper school, you had to register with the state as a pauper. That is, you declared yourself poor. Then the state taxed you according to the rate that it set for the purpose; the money would go to the school. One can imagine how poorly funded these schools were and how poor people didn't want to publicly declare themselves paupers. Rather than a property tax policy, it was more like a state tuition program with the poorest members of society footing the bill. There were also networks of charity schools that the government encouraged rich people to donate to out of the goodness of their capitalist hearts.

This is why, in its early forms, the property tax to fund public schools was supported by working-class people, though it was a white working-class policy, since minorities weren't covered by the earliest property tax-for-education policies. (It would take Reconstruction efforts in the South post–Civil War for public education to become racially inclusive, though these efforts were fleeting and flawed.)[6] For example, Walker's history mentions there was an "inexorable" push for this tax in Ohio in the middle of the nineteenth century, "paralleling the desires of citizens for extended educational opportunities." In New York State there was a big debate between rate bills and the property tax. New York City abolished the rate bill in 1832, but the state kept the policy until 1867, when working-class advocates finally got the property tax enshrined at the state level. There was a more protracted fight in Indiana between its unique mixture of Northerners and Southerners around this period. After forty years, the Northerners and their progressive push for property taxation finally won in 1851, becoming the predominant way to fund schools in Indiana. Most other states followed suit.

But there's a second part of the story that complicates this victory, which made the property tax what it is today.

To understand how the property tax went from provision to tyranny, it's important to note that the battles over the property tax happened at the state, not the district, level. Working-class groups fought in Indiana, New York, Ohio, and elsewhere to get the *state* to collect a property tax to fund schools. Perhaps in response to this more redistributive approach to the tax, since state governments collected the tax and oversaw its allocation across rich and poor districts, the bourgeoisie and their allies got the policy to be more localized, changing it into a creature of "local control" rather than state distribution.

Matthew Gardner Kelly tells the story of how this happened in California in his book *Dividing the Public: School Finance and the Creation of Structural Inequity* and other research. Amid growing skepticism that states should tax everyone to provide public education, that it was more of a local thing, California abolished its statewide property tax in 1910 in its first-ever statewide referendum, Proposition 1. In the lead-up to that vote, there was a change in logic, which Kelly tracks in a report written in 1906. The authors argued that the state government should serve the local district, becoming an "agent for the districts" such that the property tax money it collected was only "nominally" state revenue. In actuality, they argued, it was local revenue.[7]

The campaign around Prop. 1, which would codify that logic into law, was successful—and not just in California. Only 8 percent of districts in the Bay Area collected a local property tax in 1890; by 1920 it was 60 percent of them. The local collection of the tax, rather than at the state level, spread quickly. Between 1870 and 1890, local property taxes accounted for less than 10 percent of school funding in North Dakota, Nebraska, Nevada, and Arizona. They were actually illegal in Indiana. After California abolished the statewide property tax, so did most other states.

It was this shift from state to local, along with home-rule chartering and zoning regulations, that transformed the school district into a racial capitalist fortress. Things started going downhill when the state government wasn't the one in control.

Whereas the property tax story starts in ancient times, the story of home-rule charters and zoning starts in and around American cities in the mid-nineteenth century. The big cities, sprawling from industry and immigration, spawned new residential areas called suburbs. While pretty, these suburbs were poor and couldn't control their own fates since they were connected to the big cities and governed by state governments.[8]

To make more efficient decisions about local resources and planning, municipalities began to write home-rule charters, kind of like local constitutions, that gave both cities and suburbs more autonomy from states. Missouri was the first to give a city this home-rule status, ratifying a charter in 1875. Nearly every state would do the same, and municipalities (including both cities and suburbs) got the ability to maintain their own streets, parks, and recreational facilities; provide police and fire protection; manage zoning and construction standards; and tax local residents to finance their projects. Between 1875 and 1950 tens of thousands of municipalities would establish home rule in the United States until the practice became routine.

As suburbs shifted from poor to wealthy, their ability to levy their own taxes reversed the working-class victory of the state-level property tax. This suburban dynamic produced some of the structurally racist and classed inequities we see today. In *Colored Property: State Policy and White Racial Politics in Suburban America*, David M.P. Freund writes that "home-rule provisions were by no means meant to segregate by race. Nonetheless they provided suburbanites with a means to separate themselves jurisdictionally from populations seen as socially and even racially suspect."[9]

With home rule, school funding now came from how municipalities taxed their property. How did the suburbs eventually manage to hoard their property tax dollars for their own mostly white schools? Dovetailing with the home-rule movement was a movement pressing to protect homeowners from the perpetually growing urban sprawl of industrialization in the early twentieth century. Key to this initiative was zoning, or mandating that certain parcels of land get used for particular purposes (whether industrial, commercial, residential, public, etc.). At the beginning of this trend was Benjamin C. Marsh, part of a group of nascent urban planners who took a trip to Frankfurt, Germany, and saw its zoning system. Marsh was impressed with the arrangement and advocated such a system in the United States. His group encouraged "scientific" thinking about "best use" practices for land during increasing industrialization. In 1914, the National Association of Real Estate Exchanges created a city planning committee that popularized the zoning concept.

Freund shows the way these planners conceived of zoning in explicitly racial terms: "Racial science figured prominently in the early planning movement because urban congestion and unregulated development were often associated with migrant Blacks, immigrant Asians, and immigrant Europeans, the populations whose cheap labor (and often squalid living conditions) made the era's rapid industrial and commercial growth possible."[10]

The Supreme Court of the United States agreed with urban planners and suburban residents who said that zoning was necessary to keep out the undesirables. In the 1926 *Village of Euclid v. Ambler Realty Co.* case, the court decided that local police could enforce zoning regulations. Citing the concept of nuisance as a factor in their decision, they said "a nuisance . . . may be merely a right thing in the wrong place, like a pig in the parlor." In the dissenting opinion, Judge D.C. Westenhaver wrote that "the result to be accomplished is to classify the population and segregate them according to their income or situation in life." That's exactly what happened.

After this juridical victory for the planners and real estate industry, zoning would spread to 800 cities by 1930. Ten years later, 1,500 counties, cities, and regions in the United States would be zoned. Municipalities could levy taxes for things like schools with home-rule charters. Those municipalities could adopt zoning ordinances to determine how land was used, sold, and built upon and, thus, taxed. The policies let localities build racist tax bases of wealth and property, which they now had more power to tax as they wished. Planners and real estate agents could generate proposals, legitimated by the "science" of the day, to parcel out that land according to the demands set forth by property markets and the prevailing racist ideology.

Home rule and zoning enabled residents to own homes in "good" neighborhoods where the property values were high and skin was pink, so their kids could attend good schools unblemished by the presence of those "pigs in the parlor" who were juridically and structurally airbrushed out of the American dream. This came directly to bear on schooling because it baked racism directly into the boundaries that municipalities draw for entities like school catchments and districts. Housing experts Tegeler and Hilton, in their 2018 report on the relationship between housing and school finance, confirmed, "Shared municipal authority over land use and school assignment . . . can exacerbate these patterns of segregation and school sorting, as school districts' local zoning boards practice exclusionary zoning to prevent the entry of lower-income students into affordable housing in the district, thus ensuring a higher tax base, higher test scores, and a well-resourced school system for local students."[11] Thus the current racial capitalist link between the local taxation of private property and school funding was forged. Instead of acting as Horace Mann's great equalizer or Jefferson's check on tyranny, the local property tax has become a kind of tyrant itself.

In a provocative article in the journal *Democracy* called "No More School Districts!" Kevin Carey calls school districts fortresses where "the wealthy and powerful huddle to keep their resources for themselves."[12] New America's *Crossing the Line* report from 2024 and its helpful interactive map that tracks school districts by race, poverty, and property value do an excellent job illustrating this fortress thesis.

Researchers Zahava Stadler and Jordan Abbott measured the degree to which school districts in the United States are divided by race and poverty by looking at the demographic percentage differences between districts that border one another. They found that "along the 100 most economically segregating borders, the average divide is a staggering 31 percentage points," while "along the 100 most racially segregating school district borders in the country, the separation is, on average, between a district that is 92.4 percent white and a district that is 86 percent students of color." On average, these district fortresses "serving more students of color collect $2,222.70 per pupil less in local revenue than their predominantly white neighbor districts." The cause of this problem? A system of school funding based on local private property values, a fortress whose walls demarcate an ongoing system of structural theft.

What happens when people try to cross these boundaries?[13] In Akron, Ohio, Kelly Williams-Bolar, a Black mother, was arrested in 2019 for trying to get her children into a school district where the property values were higher.[14] In Upper Darby, Pennsylvania, Richard Dunlap, a white veteran serving as superintendent for the school district, was fired after merely mentioning the idea of shifting school catchment boundaries heavily divided by race and class. The school board had even voted to give Dunlap a raise. But then he started talking about shifting those boundaries so that more students of color might attend predominantly white schools. When asked about the reasoning for this, the mayor talked about what concerned residents: property values.[15]

Some right-wingers have tried to argue that state funding more than makes up for the differences we see in race and class when it comes to school funding, and that critiquing local property values as segregating is anachronistically stuck in the past. This just isn't true. Stadler and Abbott mention the case of Nebraska, for example: "Nebraska is one troubling example: It is home to 11 of these most segregating borders. Along these borders, the districts serving more students of color raise almost $8,300 less per pupil on average from local sources than their neighbor-districts, and the state funding system provides less than a quarter of what is needed to make up the deficit." In states like this, and all over the country, districts are left to themselves to figure out how to generate the revenue they need for their students. It's a competitive, individualistic, and self-centered way to organize things when you consider how collective life can be across these boundaries, like when it comes to sports or transportation. Districts that border one another are in the same regions, follow the same sports teams, share cultures of food, religion, and identity (not to mention national citizenship), and create a social product together through their division of labor, industries, and production—and yet, across the district boundary between low and high property values, the schools have entirely different resources from which they can draw to provide for their students, which tend to fall along racial lines as well.[16]

These districts are in a society with one another, but the fruits of that society get divvied up disparately.

Notice how even my formulation, "divvied up disparately," is passive. It's a hard habit to get out of. While it's easier to say it that way, doing so absolves the individuals and groups perpetuating the policies and structures that create this inequality: the regional ruling classes and bourgeoisie that benefit from these structures, fail to challenge them, and then actively push back against counter-policies when they arise. There are truancy officers and neighbors and police forces, along with supporters of those individuals, and policymakers like school boards and superintendents, all creating and enforcing the structure that requires that a mother be arrested for trying to get her kids into better-funded schools across the district boundary. Those same apparatuses and groups are the ones that upheld a superintendent getting fired for trying to relax highly racialized catchment boundaries, potentially imperiling property values. This is all a more active, agentic, and choice-oriented situation than passive traditional framings of distribution would have us believe. There are people and groups that choose to do these things. In the cases discussed here, they enforce an arrangement where some people don't get the resources that they should because others take them by force. In other words, they steal, a brief history of which we've told in the last few sections.

Before I get to an example of the kind of policy that works against the tyranny of local property taxes created by zoning, home rule, and these other forces, I'll share a method for quantifying the racialized theft in school finance happening in metro regions across the country to make this more concrete.

Numbers are important in school finance, and leftists getting into policy need to be comfortable with using them creatively to express a vision for the world. It can get wonky, but we need to fight wonky. To express the racialized theft dynamic in numbers, I created a measure called the super-expropriation index.

For the index, I assume that each school district exists in a region that as a whole creates a social product, and that each district takes a certain amount of that social product for itself and its students. I begin by mapping the districts bordering a district of interest. I look at indicators of racial capitalist political economy of the region, like average racial and economic makeup of the student population; available resources from local, state, and federal sources; average property value; and student-teacher ratio; as well as debt per pupil that the district holds and owes to Wall Street.

From there, I calculate the coefficient of variation (CV) of each indicator, a common measure in school finance research a bit like the Gini index for inequality. The CV is a measure of spread; in other words, it shows how far, statistically speaking, certain entities are from one another in relation to each other. It's calculated by finding the average distance from the average in a dataset, then dividing that average distance by the original average of that set of numbers. The CV is typically used to calculate equity. The closer the entities are to one another, the lower their average distance, and thus the more equity exists between them.

But as education researcher and statistician Ben Brumley and I have argued, the CV is more sensitive to certain parts of the distribution, making it apt for measuring something like super-expropriation.[17] The CV lets us calculate the extent to which the school districts are sharing and cooperating. The more distance between them, the more they super-expropriate from one another; the less distance, the more they cooperate.

What I aim to show with this super-expropriation measure is that regional political economies create a social product, but people in those regions don't share that resource when it comes to education. They take from one another along racial lines. My index falls along a scale of low, medium, and high rates of super-expropriation. Any rating between .1 and .3 is low, between .3 and .6 is medium, and between .7 and 1 is high. Beyond 1 is very high super-expropriation. Generally, any rating above .5 means that, in a given region, white bourgeois districts are stealing from diverse working-class districts. I've found that the Seattle region gets .5; the Philadelphia and Buffalo regions get .6 on this scale; and New Orleans gets 1, for example.[18]

I came up with this measure based on my work on classroom discussion. Imagine a group of students having a discussion about something in a class. Let's say you want them to speak and listen to each other in turns, discourage them from dominating the conversation, and encourage everyone to participate together. The traditional way to grade discussion encourages the opposite: Give the students who speak the most the highest grade. This rewards dominance. Instead, you could count the number of turns they take, then give the person with the average number of turns A+, taking off points from those above and below that average. In this case, you'd be grading them socialistically, pushing them to share the discussion space and cooperate (I actually did this as a high school teacher).[19] When some students take way more than their fair share of turns, they steal the discussion resource from the group. When others don't take turns at all, they're not getting the space or encouragement they need, generally intimidated and exasperated by the dominators' continued commentary, the latter rarely leaving space on purpose to make sure others get their turn with the floor.

We can do the same thing with school finance, except instead of students around a table, it's a region of school districts bordering one another. If we think of districts across the dividing lines in Stadler and Abbott's map as students in the same classroom, in the same discussion, it's clearly the whiter and wealthier ones that are dominating the conversation, taking more of their fair share of the region's social product from bigger, more diverse, less wealthy districts.

In this chapter thus far, I've given a brief overview of how district boundary lines became battlement walls. They are constructed with the brick and mortar of zoning and home rule, which cemented the racial capitalist dynamic we inherit today with the localization of property taxes.

What's the best way to deal with the private property tyrant? For that, we look to Minnesota.

Frank Warren Preeshl was a municipal bond salesman with a civic bent. In 1968 he served as chair of the school board in his hometown of Burnsville, Minnesota, getting a detailed look at the district's finances. As part of his civic work in the region he was also a member of a small group of local policy wonks called the Fiscal Disparities Committee, part of the newly established Citizens League, a progressive nonprofit devoted to pursuing social justice through policy research.

On December 14, 1968, before the committee's monthly meeting, Preeshl met with fellow committee member Paul Gilje at a nearby pancake house and gave Gilje something auspicious: a three-page memo detailing the rudiments of a new municipal finance policy called tax-base sharing. The policy would redistribute a percentage of the growth in a municipality's taxable property value between local governments in a region. The proposal confronted the injustice of the localized property tax without resorting to raising taxes or relying on redistribution schemes at the state or federal levels, which historically have provoked cries of authoritarianism from local bourgeoisie.

Gilje added the tax-base sharing idea to a list of other policies the committee was considering for remedying inequities created by unequal property value. The Fiscal Disparities Committee had connections to state and local officials and wanted to find ways of combating this problem. The committee liked Preeshl's proposal, prioritizing it in their conversations with lawmakers. Gilje then took the lead on writing a report titled *Breaking the Tyranny of the Local Property Tax*, published a year later. The policy's journey into law is a rare story of bipartisan support for redistribution, with regionalism bringing together politicians who might otherwise have been at odds.[20]

Whereas right-wing and left-wing representatives within the metro region recognized the benefits the policy could bring to their constituents, representatives of more rural areas were opposed, since they weren't part of the region. Conservative Minnesota state representative Charles Weaver authored a bill in 1969 using the committee's language. The bill passed by a large majority but was not taken up in the state senate until 1971, where it faced a gauntlet. Two conservatives, Wayne Popham and Joseph O'Neill, supported the bill in the senate, though some liberal colleagues opposed it. The bill passed by one vote in the next legislative session. It was called the Minnesota Miracle; thus the Minnesota Fiscal Disparities Act became law.

Denigrated as metropolitan socialism by its detractors, the law still exists to this day and has succeeded in battling the tyranny of the local property tax, reducing inequalities between local governments in the Twin Cities region by 20 percent over the life-span of the policy. The policy has been effective, according to researchers who assessed it for the regional authority overseeing the programs. They showed that the program narrows "the gap between communities with the highest and the lowest commercial, industrial, and public utility property tax base per person. For communities with over 10,000 people, the difference [in tax base] is 4 to 1 with tax-base sharing and 11 to 1 without it."[21] I have found in my own research that, when compared to a dataset of ten other comparable metro regions, the Twin Cities have the lowest coefficient of variation, indicating more cooperation and less super-expropriation. While there appeared to be interest in the program nationwide after its passage, no other such program exists in the United States. It is therefore a model that researchers, policy analysts, and lawmakers should seriously consider replicating throughout the country.

In a retrospective on this system fifty years after its passing, Gilje described how Preeshl's idea worked using the American mythical figure of Paul Bunyan and a pair of scissors: "Imagine Paul Bunyan comes out of the North Woods with a big pair of scissors. Then he cuts pieces of certain industrial, commercial, and residential buildings here and there, takes those pieces, and puts them down in other municipalities in the region." The more technical version, as per the Metropolitan Council, whose remit is to oversee the program, is that 40 percent of growth in property values is put into a shared regional pool of money.[22] Participating municipalities submit the changes in their property values from year to year and receive funds commensurate with the fluctuation, compensating local governments for loss of revenue. This system draws from growth in revenues using a regional authority. Rather than allocating uniform amounts to municipalities, the program distributes funds according to need as indexed to fluctuating property values.

The protocol is far from a panacea. Inequities still exist in the Twin Cities region, and assessments of the program have shown that tax-base sharing masks underlying problems like wealth inequity. My own work has shown the same with debt-burden inequity. The international Black Lives Matter movement burst out of that metropolis in 2021 after the gruesome murder of George Floyd, indicating that fiscal disparities programs are no silver bullet for the brutalities of American racial capitalism. But on the same super-expropriation measure I used for other metro regions, the Twin Cities' index is relatively lower, at .45. When people ask me how school funding should be in this country, these programs are some of the first I tell them about.

We've seen here the sweep of schools and money at the local level, the ways that private property and its taxation have manifested a dialectic where, at certain times in its history, the tax was a way to expropriate the expropriators. But over time those expropriators hit back and neutralized the (white) working-class power of the tax, creating a maze of home-rule apparatuses to manage it so it wouldn't bug the bourgeoisie as much. Yet the dialectic keeps going and going, with organizers looking for justice continuing to apply pressure and win for the diverse working class, like Preeshl, Gilje, and the Fiscal Disparities Committee in Minnesota.

3
Unstable State Structures

Tara Yurichek was an elementary school teacher in Panther Valley School District, a rural district about an hour outside Allentown, Pennsylvania, and she was concerned. Her school's roof was cracking. Water came in when it rained and the floors and ceiling got moldy, threatening to make her first graders sick. But there wasn't money to fix it. Her school district joined a 2014 class action lawsuit, along with several suburban and rural districts represented by lawyers with the Education Law Center, claiming that Pennsylvania was out of compliance with the clause in its state constitution requiring that it provide a thorough and efficient education.[1]

Whereas the national average for state funding of public schools hovers around 47 percent, Pennsylvania was almost 10 percent below that, with 38 percent coming from the state, relying much more on local property taxes and their tyranny. Since the middle of the nineteenth century, states have had education clauses in their constitutions, obligating them to provide public education. Districts argued the commonwealth wasn't doing that. As part of her 2021 testimony, given when the case finally went to trial, Yurichek said, "In my first grade classroom you could see the sky. There was a hole in my ceiling, and you could literally look up and see the sky."[2]

It should be no surprise that, over the last fifty years, state court systems from Pennsylvania to Wyoming to Vermont to West Virginia have consistently found their school systems to be out of compliance with the public education mandates in their constitutions. In the wake of the long civil rights fight for equality in education, advocates have pursued educational justice through state court systems to win more resources for public school students, pushing state governments to rectify the disparities between districts given differences in property value.[3]

To address persistent inequalities and funding gaps, groups of districts have had to sue states in just this way. The pressure from the courts has improved states' efforts over the last few decades, compensating somewhat for the yawning discrepancies and unjust distribution of local property taxes by drawing state revenues from other sources like sales taxes. These cases are the subject of perhaps the most muscular and developed writing about schools and money.

But once a court has ordered them to pay up, how do state finance regimes actually do the paying? These don't get as much attention. Infrastructure policies are particularly underexamined. This is because schools' capital expenditures are often financed in ways that are Byzantine and hard to see in comparison to their yearly operating budgets, which contain high-profile and easily understood line items like teacher salaries. But if our children's health and safety weren't enough, we should be motivated to change our thinking about these policies as climate change wreaks havoc on every community, and as we flee to our school buildings to escape floods and rising temperatures.

In this chapter we'll look at a handful of state regimes: Pennsylvania, Indiana, and Virginia, focusing on how each state funds, or fails to fund, its supposedly public schools, with an emphasis on facilities. We'll finish by looking at the first few years of the best possible state school-funding policy under capitalism, Vermont's Act 60, as well as the more recent successful fight for a Millionaires Tax in Massachusetts.

The hole in the ceiling of Tara Yurichek's classroom should have been filled by the state long before, but there was a hole in the state's facilities funding policy. Pennsylvania's state government had been helping fund school infrastructure since the 1950s. The state is supposed to reimburse districts for infrastructure projects through a set of forms called the School Construction and Facilities Workbook, known as PlanCon for short.[4] If an elementary school needed a new gym, the district would submit the project and potentially receive partial state funding for it. Since 1979 the state has spent $8.1 billion on the program. The money for these projects came out of the General Fund, the big reservoir of state tax revenues.[5] But PlanCon has been unfunded for more than ten years, leaving districts like Panther Valley schools with holes in their ceilings. Why?

Everything went to hell in the wake of the 2008 financial crisis. Among his infamous budget cuts, then governor Tom Corbett took a knife to state government spending on education. In 2013, he put a moratorium on any new applications to PlanCon. In 2014, lawyers at the Education Law Center filed their class action lawsuit on behalf of six school districts.

Corbett lost his 2015 bid for reelection to moderate furniture magnate Tom Wolf. Under pressure from the ongoing lawsuit and his own campaign promises for more and better funding for education, Wolf opened up PlanCon for new applications. But in 2016, Wolf put a new moratorium on PlanCon projects. This wasn't any old moratorium: It was a pause during which Wolf reconfigured the program's financing structure—for the worse. Instead of appropriating taxpayer dollars from the General Fund, Wolf's plan financed it through bonds issued by state government entities Pennsylvanians have probably never heard of, like the Commonwealth Financing Authority.[6] So the state would go into debt for these projects rather than just fund them. The 2016 plan called for $2.5 billion in bond issuance, but crucially only for projects that had already been waiting years for reimbursement.

In a more promising move, Wolf's 2016 plan also created an advisory committee to figure out what to do with PlanCon. (Notably, Wolf also mandated a commission that would look at the state's funding formula and revise it—changes that did little to address underfunding on the ground.) Two years later, this committee issued a final report with lots of recommendations, many of which were adopted in early 2020.[7] They included streamlining the process for calculating reimbursement from an eleven-step protocol to a four-step process and creating the Maintenance Project Grant Program to provide up to $1 million for "roof repairs and replacement, heating, ventilation and air conditioning equipment, plumbing systems, health and safety upgrades and emergencies, as well as other maintenance issues." (This program then turned into the Whole-Home Repairs Act, which I talk about more in chapter 7.) Wolf was even planning to set aside $1 billion for lead and asbestos remediation at the outset of 2020. But then COVID hit and that initiative evaporated as the state government went into crisis mode. The moratorium on PlanCon funding was extended, and Wolf's plans never really went into effect.

In 2022, centrist Josh Shapiro beat neofascist Doug Mastriano. In a tumultuous upset, the Democrats, a state party controlled by moderates, took over the state house of representatives from Republicans—by one vote. By 2023, due to the assiduous efforts of lawyers, advocates, and communities like Yurichek's, the Pennsylvania State Supreme Court ruled that the state was out of compliance with its constitution and needed to do something about it. But the state senate remained squarely in the hands of conservatives. This was the cast of characters that was supposed to change the state's school funding for the better. And they did come up with something: They considered increasing public school funding for private schools![8]

This particular round of the education tug-of-war happened during 2023–2024 budget negotiations, which would determine how much money public schools got from the state. The house of representatives voted to increase funding for public schools by a respectable amount. But the Republican-led state senate, using its veto power, pushed a vicious new "scholarship" program that would route public money into parents' pockets to spend however they'd like. The moderate governor looked at the conservatives' proposal and supported it.

The proposed "scholarship" programs used state nonprofit tax law to reimburse parents who pay tuition to private schools through public tax credits. The tuition payments pose as charitable donations. Pennsylvania's private school parents, who on average make above $200,000 and mostly send their kids to religious schools, would "donate" to a nonprofit organization devoted to "charity" associated with the private school. These donations would then go to scholarships for students at the school. Which students? The donors' students! The charity wouldn't get taxed on this money; the state wouldn't tax the donors; and the scholarship program would even reimburse those donors some money as a tax credit for the donation. The chutes-and-ladders masquerade ends up being public money for private schools.

There were two programs like this in Pennsylvania already, each of which did something similar but used different chutes and ladders. But the conservatives' proposal in 2023 was new and even more brazen. With a kind of sinister humor, they called it the Lifeline Scholarship Program, targeting families living in areas with "low-performing" schools. The money was supposed to be a lifeline to these poor students drowning in their poor terrible districts. In Philadelphia, half the schools qualified because, as Pennsylvania's

Supreme Court would agree, they're underfunded. Not only that, but the Lifeline money would come straight out of public appropriations funds rather than arrive as a tax credit. Governor Shapiro, shamefully, supported the idea.

The scholarship proposal had some supporters among working- and middle-class parents, who have been disappointed and underserved by the public systems supposedly meant to serve them. At the same time, the rest of the diverse working class—the majority of it—are sending their children to public schools no matter what, either out of necessity or commitment to the system for which so many waves of civil rights advocates have fought. The scholarship program would have weakened this larger-scale initiative meant to serve everyone by appealing to individuals, in the short term. And all this was going to be pitched as the solution to the supreme court's imperative to make state school funding more just!

Fortunately, the powerful coalition that has been fighting for school-funding justice for decades in Pennsylvania got activated: Parents and students, organized through teachers unions and other groups, occupied the state legislature in Harrisburg; and policy think tanks and nonprofit advocacy groups launched a discourse offensive, writing op-eds, giving testimony, holding workshops, and taking to social media to call out Shapiro for turning his back on his own voters, which became a flash point in his unsuccessful bid for vice president in 2024.[9]

Shapiro ultimately relented, line-item vetoing the Lifeline policy in the final version of the budget, placing more than $100 million of funding in escrow. Some more funding went to facilities reimbursements, and there were big increases in state monies for public schools.[10] More could have gone to PlanCon to create a robust policy—but at least it didn't go to private schools.

One lesson here is that there's no telling what can happen when you win a state school-funding case. There's no way for the court to hold the state lawmakers accountable for what they end up doing to comply with the constitution. The state police aren't going to go to the state house and arrest every lawmaker for breaking the law. Some states did nothing, like Ohio, which collectively shrugged after their state supreme court mandated more funding for public schools. Some made excellent policies that should become the gold standard, though, like Vermont's Act 60 (which I talk about at the end of this chapter); others had middling successes that do make a difference but have been whittled down and diluted over time, like New Jersey, Wyoming, Texas, and more than thirty other states.

Another lesson in the Pennsylvania case is that states can be stingy when it comes to infrastructure, and, as Marialena Dawn Rivera argued in a five-state comparison, we desperately need critical analyses of this part of the apparatus when thinking about state school funding, particularly when infrastructure grabs everyone's attention on social media.[11]

A video that went viral on TikTok caught my eye.[12] Students at Carmel High School in Indiana were giving a video tour of their school building for an entrepreneurs club devoted to teaching students how to be good capitalists. As the video proceeds you see how shockingly huge and beautiful the school is. The student tour guides happily chirp their way through the multiple ceramics rooms, computer labs, cafeterias, and sports facilities. People across social media couldn't believe how great the school building was, many noting the kinds of school buildings they grew up going to, in places without as much money.[13]

One resident of a nearby district, Carlotta Berry, told NBC News: "I think that was the most appalling part to me. . . . At what point do you say, 'Let me stop throwing money at this high school and consider the other schools in the area.'" Berry asked, "If you've got a natatorium and three cafeterias, can we get all the schools within a 20-mile radius of the school to have one cafeteria? One gym?"[14] I got curious. How did this public school pay for all this fancy infrastructure? The answer has to do with complex debt policies at the state level and conservative incentives that benefit rich districts.

Given the realities of school district financing, it isn't surprising that Carmel High School is better funded than its neighbors. The school is part of the Carmel Clay School Corporation. (Indiana, weirdly, calls school districts corporations. There's nothing about the entity that makes it like a corporation in the private firm sense, but I guess they just like the term.) The district is a thirty-minute drive north of Indianapolis, what we might call an outer-ring suburb. Carmel Clay is wealthy and borders less wealthy districts to its south. Racially you can probably guess the composition: According to National Center for Education Statistics, it's about 70 percent white and 11 percent Asian.[15] According to the *Crossing the Line* map, median property value is a relatively high $372,100 as far as the region goes.

In the terms I explained in chapter 2, that meets many of the criteria for being a super-expropriator of school finances: a school that gains property value by its proximity to poorer districts, but then hoards that value for its own schools. The correlation with a predominantly white population is predictable too. I haven't done a super-expropriation analysis of the Indianapolis metro region, but I'd bet it's pretty high.

More surprisingly, Carmel Clay gets a high percentage of its revenue from state sources, at least on a national scale. On average across the country, about 47 percent of school revenues come from the state, while 8 percent come from the federal government. Carmel Clay gets 54 percent from the state. How does that happen in Indiana?

Reading an internal memorandum from Indiana's House Republican Fiscal Policy Department, you might think, based on what it says, that's due to Indiana's generous spending on education. The document proudly claims that state funding increased 21 percent between 2012 and 2021, with the basic foundation grant for per-pupil expenditure increasing by 33 percent in that period.[16] They might be right: Indiana ranked third in the nation, after Vermont and Kansas, for the highest percentage share of its state budget dedicated to K–12 education, according to the National Association of State Budget Officers.

And yet, there are flies in the ointment. I went over to a progressive source for statewide school finance data, the Shanker Institute's School Finance Indicators Database, led by Bruce Baker and his colleagues.[17] They paint a very different portrait of Indiana's state effort.[18] Contrary to the conservatives' rosy picture, they find that the state is a "low effort" state, meaning that it doesn't spend as much as it could. Indiana spent only 3.16 percent of its economic capacity on K–12 schools, making them thirty-ninth out of the fifty states in the measure.

Baker and colleagues measure state school finance according to adequacy (the dollars it takes to make modest improvements in test scores) and equal opportunity (comparing the adequacy of poor and wealthy districts). They find that Indiana is "severely unequal" when it comes to educational opportunity: "Spending in IN's highest-poverty districts is 24.1 percent ($3,755 PP) below the estimated adequate level, compared with 52.6 percent ($3,451 PP) above adequate in the state's most affluent districts." You can see this breathtaking disparity in the adequacy data, where we find something special about our friends at Carmel Clay.

Indiana has moderate adequacy, where about 39 percent of Indiana students attend schools that could be getting more to improve their performance. Fine. But check out the differences between the top ten most populous school corporations: Here we find Carmel Clay Schools, and nearby Hamilton Southeastern Schools, are off the charts when it comes to the adequacy threshold compared to their urban neighbors, Indianapolis and Fort Wayne. Carmel Clay is literally spending 100 percent more than it needs for adequacy, and 124.5 percent more than Indianapolis. Staggering.

What the fuck is going on in Carmel Clay?

When I want to know about the political economy of a district's facilities finance, I read bond documents. This is because in most states across the country, school districts sell themselves as fixed-income investment commodities on Wall Street (as I'll talk more about in part 2). According to recent research, more than two-thirds of schools sell bonds on the municipal bond market for their capital expenditures for facilities and other needs.

In doing so, the districts get credit ratings, go into debt, and pay big banks big money for the service.[19] The wealthier and whiter districts—seen as better investments—get higher credit ratings and lower fees and thus spend more on their buildings, making them safer and cleaner than both their urban and rural neighbors. The bond market literally designates these poorer and more diverse districts as junk investments. Debt Collective organizer and researcher Eleni Schirmer has called this situation the great unequalizer, playing on the famous phrase by Horace Mann.

Using the Electronic Municipal Market Access portal, I got the most recent bond statement from Carmel Clay. These documents tell you the material conditions of a school district better than anything else I've been able to find, particularly the appendices, where the borrower (the district) is convincing creditors (banks and their customers) that the district is a good investment.[20]

The bond I looked at was for $22.8 million, sold in 2022. It's got a very high, AA+, rating from S&P, with a high underlying rating of AA. The bond's purpose is to finance a ton of facilities at, you guessed it, Carmel High School, the subject of the viral TikTok. There are twenty-four points of specific projects they want to complete as part of a larger two-year facilities project. Some highlights for me include: planetarium improvements, renovation of varsity field press box, and expansion of the existing natatorium. I also see that Carmel High School is the district's only high school, and its oldest and most renovated school. It was opened in 1958 and had regular renovations, as well as a huge set of changes between 2014 and 2020, which seems like when the building became the beast it is now.

And here's the kicker. In the appendices, where the district tells creditors about why it's generally a good investment, it talks about employers in the area. The city of Carmel has a number of corporate headquarters, including Delta Faucet, CNO Financial Group, and Monster.com. The biggest employers in the city are (after the school district) Geico Insurance, Allegion Security, and CNO Finance. This is a ruling-class place where finance, insurance, and tech have situated themselves, thus the higher credit rating and better conditions for borrowing.

Not only do they already have plenty of money from their high property values; they also get state help in guaranteeing the bonds that fund their lavish facilities. The bond says that the state's Department of Local Government Finance has a state intercept program, which is when the state says it'll step in if a district can't pay back the interest and principal of the loan for whatever reason. A little less than half the states in the country have this kind of law.

But typically, these laws just say the state will step in to pay bondholders if a district can't. Indiana goes a step further, giving wealthy property owners a tax break. In the process of detailing that program, there are some numbers estimating how much the state would provide in grants in 2023, including $32 million to pay off previous loans. So the state is covering some debt payments, which is good to know (and not always the case), but there's more.

The state has a policy called the Circuit Breaker Tax Credit, which allocated around $8 million to Carmel Clay between 2020 and 2022. This policy is basically a tax cut for owners of valuable property. The program is supposed to reduce property owners' liability for property taxes above a certain threshold determined by a ratio of assessed value and approved taxes. Basically, the state will step in if the district taxes too much. Pennsylvania has something similar called the Act 1 threshold, which sets a ceiling for how high a district can raise its mill rate on property. But whereas Pennsylvania's Act 1 doesn't actually pay property owners or districts anything, Indiana's Circuit Breaker policy is an even more bourgeois policy that gives payouts to make property owners whole if the tax ratio passes the set threshold.

Using this complex-sounding state intercept and Circuit Breaker policies, the state provides incentives for Carmel Clay so it can have updates to its planetarium while other districts suffer.

As Rivera, who wrote the definitive critical take on school facilities finance in 2016, finds, the regimes of facilities finance in the United States provide very different experiences for students at different ends of the unequal spectrum of our society.[21] Wealthier, whiter, and ruling-class places might have a lot of debt, sure, but they get good rates and low fees and end up spending a lot more on their students than places that are diverse and working-class. Researchers Jason Wozniak and Frances Negron-Muntaner call this the extravagance-extraction of school district debt.[22]

Carmel Clay's students—whose parents work for insurance companies and financial firms, whose houses are worth a lot, who get help from the state, whose district spends double what it needs to—can show off their jewelry rooms and ceramics studio, while nearby Indianapolis and outlying rural areas struggle to get by. Indiana's right-wing state government can tout supposedly high spending numbers by using clunky absolute measures, getting backup from professional budget organizations, yet looking under the hood we find a state regime that supports places like Carmel Clay and leaves Indianapolis and Fort Wayne out in the cold (although, at the time of writing, Indiana is considering dissolving its public schools[23]).

Carmel Clay has gamed this system to get lavish facilities for its students, taking care of themselves as other districts flounder. That's why the TikTok went viral. Yet there are distinct differences between states when we look carefully at not only how much states give to their schools, but also how they give, and these differences can help explain why school buildings fall apart.

In Page County, Virginia, only the high schools had hot water in their bathrooms. Luray Elementary School didn't have air conditioning in its gym, didn't have enough electrical outlets, and apparently, "It's not uncommon that a teacher comes in to make copies and the room next door loses power," according to an assistant principal.[24] To put a finer point on it: Luray Elementary still had ceiling and floor tiles from when it was a segregated school. It was built in 1961 as a school for only white kids.

There are fearful financial stories too. The city of Charlottesville needed to rebuild Buford Middle School, which was also constructed in the early 1960s. But it was going to cost $70 million, and the city didn't know where that money would come from. It was like that all over the state. The town of Isle of Wight needed a new elementary school, which was projected to cost about $27 million in the late 2010s. That same proposal was set to cost them $40 million amid post-pandemic inflation.[25] How was the district supposed to close the $13 million gap?

Virginia's schools called for help from the state. A coalition of rural schools there made a big push for facilities funding by organizing a "Crumbling Schools Tour" in 2023, where state officials visited rural districts in every region to check out the school buildings.[26] They found some scary problems, like what was going on at Luray. For example, the computer room at King and Queen Elementary in Mattaponi flooded ankle-deep with water when rain got heavy.[27]

According to the American Society of Civil Engineers school infrastructure spending report card, Virginia had a $978 million expenditure gap in 2021, almost double Indiana's. That means they miss about a billion dollars of funding each year to keep up with their aging schools: Half of Virginia's school buildings, and more than half of its elementary schools, are over fifty years old. Meanwhile, the state government estimates that it would take $25 billion to replace everything that needs replacing. Not great. How did Virginia let that happen to their school buildings?

When you buy a house, people warn you that you'll need to keep up with it, meaning you'll need to fix things as they come up and maintain the building to live in it comfortably. You can do this more easily if have little or no debt, and a good income so you can save money for larger projects or improvements even as you fix smaller things along the way. The same is true for a school district.

But like school districts around the country, Virginia wasn't so lucky. Its districts (which it calls divisions) have to shoulder the burden of covering the costs of their school construction with very little help from the state. This is difficult, since unlike districts in some other states, Virginia's divisions aren't allowed to levy taxes themselves. Instead, they rely on local governments—counties and cities mostly—to do it. Those local governments need to tax their people's property to pony up the money, which means that poorer places—rural and urban—don't have enough for their school buildings.

The state government is not super helpful in filling this gap. It contributes less than 24 percent to school facilities. But it gets worse. Not only does the state not contribute much; it has decreased this support as Virginia's student population has increased since the financial crisis. According to a very helpful report produced by a commission specifically looking at school construction in Virginia, beginning in fiscal year 1999, $55 million per year was appropriated for grants to divisions for public school facilities.[28] That grant support was reduced to $27.5 million per year between fiscal year 2003 and fiscal year 2009. It ended completely after the financial crisis in 2008. Then, between 2010 and 2020, the state added 40 million new full-time students (or about 5 percent of the population), so as schools increased their need for newer and better buildings, state funding decreased across the board.

That's how you get a situation where there are a lot of local governments in high fiscal distress with a lower ability to pay for things like school buildings, as the report shows. There are a troubling number of districts that have low composite indices (a government calculation of how much they should contribute to per-pupil expenditure) and high fiscal stress. Basically, there are a lot of districts that contribute only a small amount to operating expenditures and can't afford to cover facilities costs.

Virginia does have some promising public financial policies at the state level when it comes to financing school buildings. It certainly has more than Pennsylvania or Indiana. We can see these policies when we look at where districts get their loans. Unfortunately, 53 percent have to go to Wall Street, but the fact that this number is below 100 percent means that there are other places districts can go. The biggest is the Virginia Public School Authority, which houses a loan pooling program with an interest rate subsidy.[29] This means school district leaders can take out a loan from the pooling bank at lower rates than they'd get by going directly to Wall Street since the authority's credit rating is high. (In addition to lower interest rates, one hopes they pay lower or maybe no fees, since those fees vary widely depending on school district size.) So that's cool. Even better is that 48.5 percent of districts use the loan pooling bank. Almost half of Virginia's districts—a respectable number—use this more cooperative financing model. (As we'll see in part 3, where I discuss pensions, pooling usually means more solidarity, which is better for the diverse working class.)

But there are other programs too, including the quirkily named Literary Fund. This is "a permanent and perpetual school fund derived primarily from criminal fines, fees, and forfeitures, unclaimed and escheated property, and repayments of prior loans for school construction." Before I say anything positive about the program, a few notes on it.

First, on the "criminal fines, fees and forfeitures" that states notoriously collect from exorbitant prison phone calls, seized property, and other unconscionable practices: Let's not make our public education money from mass incarceration, please. Virginia's kids' school buildings shouldn't be funded by oppressing their parents and extended families and community members. Second, in its current form the Literary Fund's scope and impact are small: Only 10.7 percent of districts use it, since it prioritizes projects that are capped at $7.5 million and projects that have interest rates tied to the district's composite fund.

But with these caveats, I want to point out that Virginia has an existing apparatus to blunt the force of Wall Street. Ideally, the state government would increase its grant money for school buildings on a regular basis—which it actually did with a new $1.25 billion program in 2023.[30] So we should support the concept of the Literary Fund (except for its current funding sources—let's find others). We should aim to have the Virginia Public School Authority lending to two-thirds of divisions rather than Wall Street, which will create savings for local taxpayers, increase the cap on project cost from the Literary Fund to $10 million, decouple the interest rate from the composite index, and make it a no-cost loan program. Oh, and advocate for a national investment authority that would basically do this at a national level (more on which in chapter 7).

Of course, ideally, I'd like Virginia's workers to own the means of production and for their worker-owned firms' leadership councils to appropriate funds directly from their revenues for schooling. That's not going to happen soon, but it's entities like the public loan pooling program and Literary Fund that we'll want to strengthen, build out, and build up to get a more just (and socialist) policy for school buildings, hopefully something like what Vermont did in the late 1990s.

Carol Brigham's family stopped talking to her. The superintendent of her school district got his tires slashed. A father had to explain to his daughter why their neighbors were calling them sharks.[31] The popular fiction author John Irving, who felt his children were being threatened by "trailer-park envy," pulled them out of their public schools and started his own private school using the money he'd made from his books about quaint New England culture.[32]

It's Vermont in the late 1990s. An inspiring school funding system has been put in place by the state government. Brigham and others took on the state's wealthy property owners (including, apparently, John Irving) and won a rare victory. But the intense reaction shows the class struggle in school finance, how private property is at the root of so many of our issues, particularly at the state level, and how Vermont made a real working-class policy that takes up and takes on that force. It's a policy whose equal I haven't found elsewhere.

A few years before this big kerfuffle, the local elementary school that Carol Brigham's fifth-grade daughter attended, called the Whiting School, couldn't afford a new roof. It couldn't afford the extra teacher its small group of rural students needed. It couldn't afford them because it couldn't wring enough revenue out of the district's low property values.

Just across the Green Mountains, Killington schools had more money than they knew what to do with. That's because Killington was a ski town with high property values. It could spend 25 percent more per pupil than Whiting. This was characteristic of inequalities across Vermont, where average per-pupil spending was nearly $15,000 in rich towns and less than half that in poor towns, $6,500.

So Whiting's superintendent worked with a coalition of other districts to sue the state government for being in violation of its own constitution, which guarantees an education to all its students. Carol's daughter Amanda agreed to be a plaintiff, and the case was named after her: *Amanda Brigham et al v. State of Vermont.*

The court found in the school districts' favor. Judge John P. Meaker skipped the appeal stage and wrote a scathing opinion. It's worth a read.[33] The best line, I think, is when he calls local control a "cruel illusion," since districts where property values are low don't have control over the education they provide. "Local control" is only for the rich districts. This is still true (see chapter 2).

As happens with successful school finance court cases, the judge ordered the state legislature to come up with a new funding structure. Unlike Pennsylvania, where lawmakers dragged their feet and threatened to publicly fund private schools, Vermont legislators got busy and passed what I think is the best state-level school-funding structure in U.S. history.

They called it Act 60.[34] People in rich towns called it Marxism, leftism, and Robin Hood gone wild. And they were kind of right. Here's how it works.

Similar to most states, in Vermont every district levies a property tax to fund its schools. Left to their own devices, districts with high property values can tax a lower proportion, get more, and never consider their neighbors with whom they share space and culture and a social product. Districts with lower property values have to tax a higher proportion to get less. Siloed into the dog-eat-dog, individualistic illusion of "local control," it's everyone for themselves. Act 60 changed that.

Each district got a ceiling for the spending it needed based on the state's calculations. It was the state, not the district, that decided when enough was enough in terms of school money. Any amount of revenue a district raised above that state allotment went into a statewide pool and got distributed to poorer districts. For instance, a rich district couldn't keep adding more gyms, like it did in Carmel Clay, when other districts around it couldn't afford a new roof. This is brilliant because it forces the rich districts to tax their property at a relatively (though not outlandishly) high rate, and then, given the state allotment, captures excess revenue to redistribute.

Act 60 set a state standard for property tax rates. Every district had to tax their property at about $1 for every $1,000 of assessed value. At the same time, the state calculated funding allotments to each district based on adequacy measures. It milked the rich districts. It also ensured that poor districts didn't have to tax their property overmuch. They got what they needed in terms of school funding. Rich districts became "giving towns" and poor districts became "receiving towns."

At the height of its powers, Act 60 equalized the tax burden. Before Act 60, average town tax burdens varied from .1 to 8.2 percent on assessed property. After Act 60, they ranged from 2 to 4 percent. Average differences in per-pupil spending between districts fell from 37 percent to 13 percent. Districts that had historically spent less increased their spending at a greater rate than districts that had spent more. And, according to education researcher Jane Fowler Morse's analysis of the policy, Vermont's achievement gaps closed between 1998 and 2001.[35] Turns out Marxism—to each according to need, from each according to ability—is good, actually.

But history is a struggle, and as you'd expect, the king came for Robin Hood. When you confront wealthy property owners, they come at you.

Rich people went bonkers. They slashed superintendents' tires, put up ropes blocking roads to their neighborhoods, and called towns like Whiting shark towns. Ruling-class blocs don't mess around. They get creative and get organized. In the giving towns, wealthy people formed private foundations and donated "voluntary levies" for their schools. This meant the money couldn't be recaptured by the state and shared. They basically created a parallel privatized funding structure to maintain the luxury of their public schools. They formed alliances, initiatives, and organizations that supported these foundations. One example was the Freeman Foundation of Stowe, which promised to match any district's private fundraising each year. In all, they matched $20 million with private voluntary levies.

The Freeman Foundation was a powerful organization in Vermont. And guess who was too scared to stand up to it? Then governor Howard Dean. He ended up saying Act 60 "didn't work" and sided with the Freeman Foundation. After his second term was up, his lieutenant governor, Doug Racine, supported Act 60, though. In 2002, when Dean did not run for reelection, he called Racine a misguided whiner, even though they were in the same party and worked together. Come on![36]

Act 60 was at the center of the 2002 gubernatorial election in Vermont. It was very close, but the Republican, Jim Douglas, won on a promise of making "struggling taxpayers" whole. Act 60 was largely gutted when Act 68 reformed it later that year. The new law got rid of the sharing pool, its most class-confrontational protocol. It left some things in place, so Vermont's not awful in terms of school finance, relatively speaking. Act 60 in its original and strongest, and I think best, form became a thing of the past.

But losing a battle doesn't mean we should stop fighting. Act 60 gives us a vision of what we could press for as policies that make our schools actually public. Organizers in Massachusetts have also given us an inspiring victory recently, which shows us we can win the state structures we need.

Massachusetts has a remarkable 4 percent tax on individual yearly income over $1 million. Using this tax, it redistributes $2 billion more a year for education and public transportation across the state. It's called the Millionaires Tax, and it wasn't easy to get.

There was lots of coverage of the tax itself during the policy fight over it in 2022.[37] There are even pages for law firms and wealth management websites telling rich people what to expect now that they'll be taxed at this rate—and plenty of pearl clutching from the ruling class.[38] While you can get basic information from the headlines and some technical details from the analyses, what you don't get is the story of how public educators and organizers across the state fought bitterly for twenty years to win this redistributive tax.

I learned about the organizing history behind the Massachusetts Millionaires Tax from Eve Weinbaum at the University of Massachusetts Labor Center. With her permission, I retell that story here.[39]

In the early 2000s, Massachusetts had a string of conservative governors (most famously Mitt Romney) who at various points pursued austerity agendas for public programs, like the university system. At the University of Massachusetts, this austerity meant cutting programs and merging departments like languages and literature. It also threatened the existence of the Labor Center, where Weinbaum worked.

In the face of those cuts and mergers and threats, Weinbaum and colleagues at Umass Amherst got together and agreed something had to change. Being labor organizers, they wondered why their union wasn't doing much about these cuts. They thought to themselves, this institution should reflect our values. They got organized and ran for leadership under the banner of Educators for a Democratic Union and agitated for the sclerotic Massachusetts Teachers Association (MTA) gears to grate and grind toward action.

The main goal of their efforts in the MTA at Umass Amherst was to respond to the cuts by pushing back austerity. The problem, as always, came down to money. Where did the money come from and how could they get more of it to prevent cuts? Their answer was to tax the rich.

Before the Millionaires Tax passed, Massachusetts had a flat tax written into the state constitution.[40] A flat tax requires every resident of the state to pay the same percentage of taxes, rather than a tiered income tax where the rich pay more because they earn more. Pennsylvania has a similar policy in its constitution called the uniformity clause.[41] It's really annoying because you can't tax different incomes differently. If there are richer people, you can't tax them more because you have to tax all people uniformly, or flatly.

But getting a millionaires tax in Massachusetts required more than just a legislative victory, more than just passing a law. Since the flat-tax clause was written into the constitution itself, organizers had to amend the state constitution to tax the rich. In Massachusetts, amending the constitution requires a multistep process including a ballot initiative as well as a two-part legislative assembly where representatives in the state government form a constitutional convention and vote to make the change.

So the battle Weinbaum's little band of unionists faced was daunting. But it didn't stop them. They took a step-by-step approach, scaling up, getting lucky, fighting and winning smaller battles, maneuvering internally, and finally taking on the big fight—and winning.

Here's how they did it. A group of faculty in the Massachusetts Society of Professors, the Umass Amherst local of the huge state union of teachers, the MTA, got together to take on the funding problem. They knew they had to get in the driver's seat of the whole union, not just the part of the union covering public higher education. Meanwhile, a parallel effort to organize the whole union into a more fighting stance to take on the rich emerged in the Educators for a Democratic Union (EDU), a progressive caucus within the educators union.[42]

Typically, the left faces immense opposition in these kinds of formations whose goal is changing the union's leadership. In terms of teachers unions, we've seen recent victories in Chicago and Los Angeles, but continued struggles in places like Philadelphia and also much of the country is still under the shadow of right-to-work laws preventing educators from having unions at all.

Together, the professors' chapter and the progressive educators' caucus were making sure the MTA worked for them. But the sprawling bureaucracy was intimidating, to say the least. One common method to build up a caucus's power is to run candidates for leadership, whether identifying individuals for top positions or running slates of candidates for every position. The election creates an opportunity to clearly articulate your program, have conversations with rank-and-file members, and make a concrete ask: Vote for us. So Weinbaum and her fellow organizers wondered: Who could we run for a long-shot presidential run? Someone popped up on their radar: Barbara Madeloni.

When I was a graduate student at Teachers College, Columbia University, in the 2010s, one of the issues we organized around was to stop Teachers College from supporting the privatization of teacher certification. At the time, the education conglomerate Pearson had developed something called edTPA, a service it could offer colleges of education to certify its teachers.[43] Traditionally, state governments developed their own programs for certification rather than private firms. But neoliberalism was in full tilt, and Pearson was making moves.

So when we heard the story of Barbara Madeloni organizing with student teachers at Umass Amherst, we were in awe.[44] Madeloni was a former high school teacher who had been fired in the early 2000s for her outspoken lessons against the Iraq War. She got other teaching jobs, however, and became a veteran classroom educator. By 2012, she was adjuncting in a teacher preparation program at Umass. In her capacity as professor, she was part of an effort, led by student teachers working toward certification, to reject Umass Amherst's use of edTPA. She made national headlines when the students refused to take the assessment on principled grounds, and she was fired.

The professors' union chapter and the EDU caucus saw these headlines and thought maybe Madeloni would be their long-shot candidate. Madeloni agreed. They all knew what they were in for: a zigzag slog across the state, visits to towns and boards of education and union chapters, talking to everyone who would listen about making the MTA a democratic union and a fighting union. They expected this to be Madeloni's first attempt and prepared to run again and hopefully win two or three election cycles later.

But they won. In a huge upset, Madeloni beat the anointed candidate.[45] It was the first time in decades that the sitting vice president of the union hadn't succeeded the president. It was a big win. But it was a mixed victory since the EDU hadn't won other leadership races, leaving Madeloni alone at the top. I've heard from Barbara about this situation and it sounds extremely tense and difficult.

But the organizers kept their eyes on the prize: fighting for more money for public school budgets. Before they could get the Millionaires Tax, they had to protect public schools' existing resources from an incursion by charter school operators. Madeloni showed her prowess as a leader in adverse circumstances by heading up the opposition to Ballot Measure 2 in 2016, which would have increased the number of charter schools in the state.

The MTA came out staunchly against this measure and beat the odds, defeating it, creating a glimmer of light in an otherwise dark landscape on Election Day in 2016.[46] During this process, EDU did more organizing to shore up support across the state. Finally, they were in a position to go for the Millionaires Tax. They called their proposal the Fair Share Amendment.

The more conservative MTA leadership, a majority, spent tons of money on polls to demonstrate that there wasn't support for such an initiative. But these expensive polls kept coming back positive. So in 2019, they couldn't be sticks-in-the-mud anymore and took their shot as part of a broad coalition called Raise Up Massachusetts.[47]

After they'd gotten far more than enough signatures to get the initiative on the ballot, the state supreme court struck down the ballot initiative.[48] The judges said the initiative was illegal because of a policy on the books stating that such initiatives can only be about a single issue rather than multiple related issues. They determined, in their legal wisdom, that the Fair Share Amendment actually was about two issues: taxing and spending. Organizers had tried to make sure that the amendment they proposed would go to public infrastructure like schools and transportation. A ballot initiative can't make demands about both taxing (Millionaires Tax) and spending (on public goods).

But as the Worcester legislator who'd proposed the amendment said at the time, "this gets us on the right path." The coalition organizers on the Millionaires Tax campaign knew what to do next.

The other way to amend the Massachusetts constitution starts with a legislative process where the legislature itself writes the amendment. Then a majority of lawmakers has to pass the amendment in two consecutive sessions. That means that the house and senate have to vote for the proposal twice. Importantly, the supreme court could not rule the ballot initiative illegal if it came from the legislature itself.

So the organizers all got working again. There had been a huge coalition behind the first amendment that had failed, so they leveraged that toward the next struggle along the legislative path. They got their first up vote in the house in 2019 and then they got the other one. Technically, this second path through the legislative assembly approves another ballot initiative. After a bitter fight, the legislators approved the new ballot measure in 2022. It was a squeaker: 52.3 percent of voters approved the measure.[49]

In a presentation she gave about this fight at a workshop on radical pedagogy at Yale in 2022, Weinbaum emphasized the constant pressures and tensions both within the union and between the union and the ruling class throughout Massachusetts. The conservative unionists were against taking on the ruling class, and the ruling class was against anything that would take their money. Despite these challenges, the band of union organizers forged ahead, doing the work of power analysis, campaign strategy, and the organizing of thousands of conversations, spreadsheets, emails, meetings. And they prevailed.

What was novel to me in Weinbaum's presentation was the arc of the story. She started it in the classrooms of Umass Amherst, with the immediate impacts of austerity in the departments and programs at her university. The discontent born from that experience galvanized a small group that snowballed itself into larger and larger formations, keeping the eventual target in mind and jostling over the various vicissitudes of the Massachusetts state regime, until the formation was big enough, strong enough, and well-formed enough to take on its original target successfully. They fought for and won more state funding for public education, and instead of a legal strategy where you take the state to court, they used a social movement strategy that changed the state constitution.

You don't get many stories like this in school finance organizing, not to mention social justice union organizing. But they're out there. Recounting them highlights the uneven dialectic in which we're all working and the stop-start ways that victories are won. With enough focus, commitment, energy, will, agency, and luck, we can change state structures for the better.

4

One-dering About the Federal Government

In school, I learned that there are two kinds of people: math people and non-math people. The math people are smart and the non-math people aren't. The main lesson I took away from my math classes was that I was a non-math, non-smart person. Then in college I discovered that I had a knack for logic and studied the philosophy of mathematics, including set theory and mathematical logic, and started to work through the intense layers of ideology and bullshit that math education had left in my psyche.

After studying Marxism more carefully, keeping my experience with math in mind, I saw that numbers have an intimidating power. They shut people down. They bore people. They're abstract and rigid in certain ways, and while they appear to run the world as some kind of natural measure of objective truth, deep down, numbers are just language. Math is a formal language, yes, but it's as slippery formed by struggle as natural languages like the one you're reading right now.

My favorite passage in Marx's *Capital*, volume 1, is the chapter on the struggle over the working day, which is a great example: Workers' hours, pay, and benefits are the result of class antagonism.

These numbers are literally caught up in the fight. But it can feel like the numbers are set in stone, determined by a market that has naturally and immutably set the price of labor and benefits at whatever the innocent and well-meaning bosses have stipulated. But they're not. When we fight back, those numbers change.

The intimidating authority of quantification, combined with its malleability, has made math an effective tool in pushing agendas for centuries. Indeed, the power of numbers in education now is unquestioned. Everything must be data driven (which of course only ever means numbers), and we all know numbers don't lie.

Oh, but they do. This chapter is all about the confused role the federal government plays in school finance policy. I want to start off by telling a story about one of the most maddening cases of mathematics' ideological potency in federal educational policy, which can serve as an entry point for this federal terrain.

Maybe you've heard about the infamous *A Nation at Risk* report, authored by the National Commission on Excellence in Education, published in 1983. It was a watershed moment for U.S. education. After a landslide victory consolidating a new and vicious right-wing hegemony, the Reagan administration set its sights on America's schools.[1]

Until that point, there had been at least twenty years of incisive civil rights struggle, mostly in federal courts, to get schools to integrate. The big question in education policy wasn't just whether schools were succeeding or failing in some decontextualized or traditional way; they were understood to be excellent. The question was whether they were equal or unequal, fair or unfair, just or unjust, segregated or integrated.

Reagan's administration changed all that, exemplified by this bombshell report. The thesis of the document was that American schools were failing, and thereby threatening the position of America's power in the world. The nation was "at risk," its authors argued: If students in our schools don't perform well, then how can America continue to be the most powerful country in the world?

The report was based largely on a calculation of average student performance on the SAT. There was a big scary graph at the center of the propaganda: a downward-sloping line showing how average scores on the test had been sinking. The authors argued this downward trend was the symbol and cause of America's sinking power overall: a graph of the loss of American greatness.

Deployed in the conservative froth of the 1980s, *A Nation at Risk* reset the terms of national educational policy debate that we still have today. The question became how to make schools excellent rather than equal, setting these two goals against each other rather than pursuing them together; how to hold school people (teachers, boards of education, superintendents, parents, policymakers) accountable for their decisions, in terms not necessarily of equity or integration or justice, but rather efficiency and evaluation. At the heart of the tendency was a skepticism that the solution to the problem of education was spending more money, which economists of education conveniently justified in their research. There was a crackdown on compensation of all kinds, physical and social. We won't spend more on schools; we don't try to compensate for inequalities. The high-stakes standardized tests that students take today have their policy origin in the discursive din this report caused.

Most conversations over the last generation about schools start from a presumption, stated or unstated, that our schools are "failing." The next step of the dialogue then becomes some kind of blather about data, evidence, and averages of scores generated by kids filling out bubbles on a test produced by some billion-dollar corporation, followed by merit pay, charter schools, vouchers, and so on.

A Nation at Risk manufactured that presumption of failing

schools, juxtaposing that failure with efforts to integrate, and crystallized the conclusion that evaluation and testing was the ticket to solve the issue. It was used to justify all kinds of irrational, punitive, and miseducative practices to get schools to "succeed" at being "excellent," from supplanting critical consciousness with more apparatus-oriented critical thinking, to abandoning progressive pedagogies and bringing back chalk-and-talk readin', writin', and 'rithmetic. Its shadow can be seen in the neoconservative-neoliberal consensus on No Child Left Behind, the George W. Bush administration's flagship centralization of federal education policy in favor of high-stakes testing, as well as Race to the Top, the Barack Obama administration's program that incentivized charter schools and other big-time neoliberal reforms.

This is all a well-known story in education policy. What's less well-known is that the numbers behind *A Nation at Risk*—the numbers that kicked off the whole terrible epoch—were deep, profound statistical bullshit.

Sandia National Laboratories, under the direction of the secretary of energy James Watkins, raised its institutional eyebrow at *A Nation at Risk*. A handful of researchers at the nonpartisan think tank took a second look at what the report was claiming. Ten years after *A Nation at Risk* was released, these Sandia researchers published a report in response, whose innocuous title belied its punch: "Perspectives on Education in America: An Annotated Briefing."[2]

The report found that, when it came to SAT scores, the reality was the opposite of what *A Nation at Risk* said. Scores during the period under consideration were actually "steady or improving." After a couple of decades of successful civil rights struggles, "declining average SAT results underscore that a more diverse mix of students is taking the test." Of course, researchers admitted that "average performance of minority and urban students remains low," but this was "despite improvements over the last 20 years." Reading their conclusions now is scandalizing:

> Our investigation of the SAT data revealed that the much publicized "decline" in average SAT scores misrepresents the true story about student SAT performance. Although it is true that the average SAT score has been declining since the sixties, the reason for the decline is not decreasing student performance. We found that the decline arises from the fact that more students in the bottom half of the class are taking the SAT today than in years past.

So what was actually happening was that more and more diverse students were taking the SAT and doing better and better on it. The Sandia Report, as it became known, demonstrated that when you broke down the average decline in SAT scores by subgroups (like racial demographics) every subgroup showed steady performance or improvement. The trend lines were all going up.

But how could it be that the overall average of SAT scores went down while all the subgroups had gone up? The Sandia authors attributed this quirk of the SAT data to a statistical phenomenon called Simpson's paradox, which "shows that an average can change in a direction opposite from all subgroups if the proportion of the total represented by the subgroups changes."

What the Sandia Report revealed is that the right-wingers had manipulated the numbers to make it seem like the schools were failing and the nation was at risk. But it actually wasn't. In fact, the nation was doing well! At least when it came to SAT scores, there had been increases in the number and kind of students taking it, and their scores had improved. Excellence and equity were happening together.

If anything, the number told a racial and class equity story. The whole narrative of America's failing schools and thus declining power relied on a statistical mirage exploited by right-wing zealots bent on erasing the gains of the civil rights movement, which was then seared into the national imagination and survives as an ideology plaguing public education to this day. Sam Abrams, in *Education and the Commercial Mindset*, points out that the material conditions of this furor around schools had much more to do with the Japanese auto industry than student performance on tests. Starting around 1980, Japanese car manufacturers—using new juiced-up management efficiency practices called lean production—started outselling American companies. The schools were actually doing fine; it was the car companies that weren't keeping up.[3]

There was a racialized element to the panic also. The SAT scores showed a more diverse student population taking the SATs, and making improvements, which to white-racialized interest groups and their hangers-on perhaps felt like an incursion, where nonwhite populations were gaining ground. These successes looked like failures to those more disposed to spit at the nonwhite students getting bused to their "nice" white schools from the other side of the tracks.

There's a labor story here too. The ideology of failing schools, accountability, and standardization was mobilized to attack teachers unions, educational expenditure writ large, and the entire public school system. Rather than a statistical finding that led to action points, the move to average those SAT scores and leverage Simpson's paradox was actually to launder an already existing set of right-wing demands through objective-looking data.

History was written with *A Nation at Risk* on top. We don't talk about the Sandia Report today in the same breath. That was intentional. When the Sandia authors brought their report to Congress, David Kearns, the deputy secretary of education at the time (and former CEO of Xerox), reportedly told them, "Bury this, or I'll bury you."[4] There's some disagreement about whether Kearns actually said this line, but the Sandia Report was effectively buried. Yet the two reports should be taught side by side, rather than ceding the historical ground to the right-wing agitprop. The more general lesson, though, is that numbers and quantitative methods are ideological, caught up in the wider class struggle. Socialists have to engage with them properly as we organize for a better world, specifically when it comes to federal education policy.

The last time the Democrats had a presidential primary, in 2020, and we could actually debate policies, I noticed something weird. Bernie Sanders was obviously the leftist candidate, Joe Biden the moderate, and Elizabeth Warren somewhere in between. The gap between Sanders and Biden was obvious in almost every way, except federal school funding. Both Biden and Sanders said they'd triple Title I funds on their education platforms. Warren even said she'd quadruple Title I funds at one point.

As a socialist, I felt my ears perk up. Biden saying the same thing as Sanders made me wonder what was happening there. Why would a moderate and a socialist both take this position? Is there something they're not telling us about Title I? Specifically, what does "tripling" Title I funding really mean? If we believe the politicians' rhetoric, it seems like Title I refers to the money that schools in poor districts get from the federal government. If your school gets X amount of Title I money, then tripling it means they get 3X. So, that's what would happen, right? Students in poverty would get triple what they're getting now? From what I can tell, the answer is: I don't think so.

Meanwhile, Donald Trump won the presidency in 2024 promising to dismantle the Department of Education, something that Ronald Reagan started saying in 1979 when he was running what he thought was going to be a close race against Jimmy Carter, who had created the department in the first place. It was a provocative thing to say for Reagan, who won in a blowout, and Republicans have been repeating the demand ever since as a kind of battle cry. Since Trump won and, at the time of this writing, has tapped the head of World Wrestling Entertainment, Linda McMahon, to run the department, there's been an understandable freak-out about whether, if they abolish the department, this would end Title I programs in general. Is that true?

So far as I can tell, the answer to this question is also: I don't think so.

To understand how Title I operates, let's begin by looking at the law itself. "Title I" refers to the first big part of the Elementary and Secondary Education Act.[5] This whole law with its eight titles was passed as part of the Great Society legislation in 1965.

Title I of the law is called Improving the Academic Achievement of the Disadvantaged. This title has eight parts, labeled A through H. Part A is where the action is. This part "provides financial assistance to local educational agencies for children from low-income families to help ensure that all children meet challenging state academic standards."

At first, this looks great. From the language, you might assume that the federal government gives money to districts or other local bodies (referred to as local education agencies) and that those local agencies disperse the funds to schools that need them, based on poverty measurement in the census. But looking at how the money is spent shows differences across states. A 2019 study mandated by the Obama administration's flagship education law, the Every Student Succeeds Act, found that average per-pupil Title I, Part A funds were $1,227. Compare that to how much is spent per pupil in the United States, which is a little more than $12,000 on average, and you get a sense of how this money, while qualitatively important, is quantitatively small relative to the costs and needs of diverse working-class districts.[6] It's also unevenly allocated. According to the 2019 study, Idaho spent only $984 of Title IA money per pupil, whereas Vermont spent $2,950.[7]

The reason is that the money doesn't just "go to districts with poor kids." Instead, dollars flow from the federal government to the states, which distribute funds to districts based not only on their need, but on accountability criteria too. This is one of the worst legacies of No Child Left Behind: the use of "adequate yearly progress" measurements to punish or reward schools. If a school made adequate yearly progress, great. If it didn't, it could get sanctioned, restructured, or even closed. So it's not as simple as increasing money for Title I means more money for all kids—there are strings attached.

Adequate yearly progress requirements persist in Title I. Under the section on accountability, it clearly says that state education agencies can include sanctions and rewards according to annual yearly progress on standardized tests. There's also a whole level of considerations within the district here, at the level of the district budget office that puts budgets together for individual schools: which principals get what money, what they do with it, and so on.

The Democratic candidates' promises to triple Title I funds, then, did not mean that high-need districts would receive enough funds to plug spending gaps left by unstable state structures and the tyrannies of the local property tax. Not only are Title I funds dependent on your district's successful application to the state; there's no guarantee from year to year whether you get money for the funds, since they are dependent on adequate yearly progress.

To be blunt, Title I is not achieving its stated purpose of providing federal support for the disadvantaged. A 2018 report by the U.S. Commission on Civil Rights confirmed this with trenchant analysis.[8] Reporting to Congress on the success of this legislation, the document concludes that "the longstanding and persistent reality is that vast funding inequities in our state public education systems render the education available to millions of American public school students profoundly unequal. . . . Low-income students and students of color are often relegated to low-quality school facilities that lack equitable access to teachers, instructional materials, technology and technology support, critical facilities, and physical maintenance." Of course, I repeat, this Title IA money is important, but it's not nearly enough, and focusing solely on the amount, and specifically the amount of appropriation, obfuscates the causes of school funding inequality and the tools available to us. We need a rationalized distribution protocol for Title I spending, a new pot, rather than more money in the existing cracked and uneven pot, which is what Biden and Bernie just wanted to keep adding to (and Trump wants to get rid of).[9]

What may be the most frustrating aspect of Title I has to do with the authorization amount, money that the law says can be spent on a given item, versus appropriations, which are the amounts Congress actually sets aside for the law. For Title I money, the authorizations matter just as much as the appropriations. If the federal government appropriates more, then districts maybe do get more, but only relative to their authorized amount.[10] This is why the amount each state gets varies widely. There are differently sized spoons that dole out the money from that cracked and uneven pot. Apologies for the clunky metaphor, but bear with me: The pot amount is the appropriation, whereas the spoon amount is the allocation, decided by the soup-giver authorizing the latter while considering the former.

The authorization gets calculated through four formulas, which then apportion four types of grants: basic, concentration, targeted, and education finance incentive grants. Here's how each works.

The basic grant, which was the first created and the largest, is calculated using a state's average per-pupil expenditure and the number of poor children in the state, as measured by the census (and determined by the Bureau of Labor Statistics and the Department of Commerce). The federal government pays 40¢ for every dollar the state spends to educate poor kids. There are also thresholds for minimum and maximum basic grants, to make sure every state gets a percentage of the national average per-pupil expenditure.

The concentration grant is calculated by factoring the number of poor kids in a population that are above a certain rate of poverty into the basic grant, making it more sensitive to increased poverty.

The targeted grant is calculated by weighting the concentration grant differently according to geographic distributions of poverty and proportion of poor students, capturing not just the number of poor kids but where those poor kids live. This grant is one of the fastest-growing grants over time. The education finance incentive grant is calculated based on "measures of state effort and equity in funding public education." Importantly, these four grants are categorical grants whose amounts get calculated according to the law, rather than block grants, lump sums given to the state to allocate as it sees fit (this becomes important later).

The authorized amount of Title I funds is what a state is entitled to according to these formulas. But the authorized amount doesn't take the total appropriations into consideration. A state could be authorized to get a whole bunch of money, but if there's not enough in the pot for every state to get what they should get, then you have to make changes accordingly. When you put the authorized amount in relationship to the total appropriations possible for Title I spending, you get the actual allocation made to each state. By the same logic, tripling the money available doesn't necessarily mean tripling the money sent to any given district. If your district's poverty level stays the same as it was, then you won't get more money just because there's more Title I funding available, which is why what Sanders and Biden and Warren were saying is misleading. You'd need to triple the allocation to get that result. The way money gets doled out depends on how much the formulas say you're entitled to get.

The history of the formulas is a history of how to quantitatively interpret the concept of poverty in school districts. Is it neediness, income, number of poor families, percentage of poor families, absolute number of poor students . . . ? When the Title I program began, funds were distributed only according to the basic formula, which relies on each state's per-pupil expenditure and numbers of poor children based on the poverty line set by federal agencies.[11]

After a few years of the program, in the late 1960s, policymakers and researchers noticed that "the 20 wealthiest counties in the nation . . . were allocated almost twice as much as the 10 poorest counties."[12] Some lawmakers called the formula "patently foolish" because it reflected a "political decision" to spread the funds as broadly as possible, rather than concentrating them in the areas of greatest need, to build a "powerful lobby for the continuation and expansion of the program." While there had been a program proposed for "special grants to urban and rural schools which would provide additional funding to areas where there were high concentrations of disadvantaged children," it was not until an analysis of the basic grant in 1978 that researchers demonstrated that "per pupil Title I expenditures were higher in predominantly urban and suburban districts" than rural districts.[13]

The urban/rural divide, along with the push-pull of spend/don't spend ideologies from Republicans and Democrats, rendered the weird (and mostly anemic) mosaic of distributions used today. In the back-and-forth between small government, suburban-rural conservatives, and more social-democratic urban moderates over the last sixty years, people kept making new formulas. That's how we got four. It's the absurdity of bourgeois deliberation: just keep tinkering, adding on, and making little changes as part of the art of compromising.

The 2018 civil rights report found that the basic grant still has the same problem that lawmakers noticed in the late 1960s. There are two ways this problem manifests in the formulas. First, there are areas with low populations but relatively high concentrations of poverty that still need more resources. Second, there are areas with much larger populations that have bigger absolute numbers of formula children, or poor children who are eligible for the funding (yes, they're referred to as "formula children" in the policy world). Thus it was that the concentration and targeted grants were born, but we more or less have the same problems as before—and overall the program doles out so little money generally that it can be a difference that doesn't make a difference.

That's where socialists might come in.

What matters most in approaching this mess is the allocation: how much each state actually gets. That's the bottom line. This is the amount that states distribute to districts and local education agencies (which include charter schools) and thus the amount that gets into the school budgets. It's a given that schools need more money. Schools in districts with low property values in ungenerous states need it especially, which includes districts in both rural and urban areas.

What do we want schools to have at the end of the day? Federal funding of education increased dramatically during the pandemic as a result of three waves of relief policies. Those pandemic programs showed us what's possible, and increasing federal funding along those lines would be a start. The federal government typically provides something around 8 percent of public school funding, and Title IA ends up being about $1,227 per pupil. In the pandemic relief programs like the CARES Act, we saw big federal infusions of dollars that districts used for all kinds of things. It's easy to do! And it makes a big difference!

So next time, instead of saying we should double or triple or quadruple the appropriation, let's get that national average per-pupil allocation of Title I funds up to $5,000. If that means making appropriations $100 billion, quintupling the appropriation, then so be it. Limiting our demands to appropriation limits the imagination. Maybe we need to shift the proportions of the minimums and maximums in the basic grant more. Maybe we need to add some coefficients to targeted and concentration grants. Whatever we have to do to get that average up, then let's do it. But right now there's a much different set of issues we have to consider.

As I was writing this book, Trump got elected again and was fond of saying that he'd abolish the Department of Education. This is, again, highly unlikely and difficult to do, but since the new administration doesn't appear to give much of a shit about precedent or protocol, we should take it seriously. So what would this mean? According to the infamous Project 2025's proposal, it would involve moving the department's programs to other departments. One thing the department does is oversee all that federal spending from Title I that I just talked about. Trump and McMahon can't just get rid of this law by getting rid of the department that oversees its programs. They might fire everyone in charge of doing this work, yes, but to really abolish it they'd have to change that law like other presidents and congresses did. Unless Trump reissues the law, the funding protocols themselves stay the same. But he can underfund it and make it more disorganized. How would that work?

Certainly, getting rid of the Department of Education would impact the quantity and quality of coordination around calculating and then distributing these grants, the largest of which go to school districts who educate lots of poor students. If the Department of Health and Human Services administered the grants for special education, for instance, while the Department of Commerce disbursed the grants for poor students, there'd be all kinds of ways for things to get messed up. But without writing legislation that undoes Title I itself (which the Republicans couldn't do without a sixty-vote majority in the Senate, which they don't currently have), they can't just get rid of the grants.

The right-wing proposals for federal education go beyond just weakening coordination of getting money to districts with a lot of poor kids, though. They also want to change the very structure of the grants themselves. This particular idea is actually older than the idea of getting rid of the Department of Education, and more pernicious.[14]

Right now, federal Title I education spending, specifically Title IA, comes in the form of *categorical* grants: the four formulas I talked about before. A *block grant*, on the other hand, would consolidate these four grants into one. Then this big grant would get passed on to the state itself to disburse however it wanted, rather than the federal government saying who should get what.

Changing federal education spending from categorical grants to block grants makes it more difficult to account for nuances in what it means for the federal government to provide money for poor students. For instance, there's a big difference between saying that your district serves a lot of poor students *relatively* and saying that your district serves a lot of a poor students *absolutely*.

A district of 10 students, where 3 are poor, has a 30 percent poverty rate. But a district of 100,000 students where 10,000 are poor only has a 10 percent poverty rate. The current categorical structure for Title IA accounts for this by looking at concentrations of poverty, targeting specific poverty rates, and providing grants for particular aspects of poverty.

A block grant wouldn't do any of that. On the front end, it would take out any subtle criteria for appropriating and authorizing the grants by state, probably doing it by student head counts. (It would also be much easier to decrease and zero out the grants in general, which the right-wingers want to do, by the way.) The block grant flattens out the categorical nuances.

On the back end, block grants would leave it up to the state to dole out funds to school districts however it wants. What if right-wingers in the state capital disdain their diverse working-class town and city dwellers? They could systematically underfund the school districts even more.

I think there's a fair socialist critique of the four Title IA formulas, focusing on increasing the allocation rather than the appropriations and authorizations, as I wrote earlier. I think they could be more generous and more efficient at the same time. And I'm not entirely opposed to block grants. But block grants in the hands of far-right-wingers who want a techno-authoritarian / free market education system are a dangerous weapon that we should be working against vehemently, along with other issues.

★ ★ ★

Parents in Wyoming Valley West School District in Pennsylvania were terrified and angry. The district sent a letter threatening to send their children to foster care. Why? Students in the district's schools had increasing school lunch debt.[15]

School lunch debt, believe it or not, is a real thing. It's when students can't pay for lunch and the school has to spot them. Typically, parents have to put money into accounts for their students, who swipe cards or give their ID numbers when getting food in the cafeteria. If a student's account is empty, then they technically can't afford the meal. But the district is obligated to feed them. It's a loss for everyone. Districts lose money and students get shamed. A blog post by American University's School of Education on this phenomenon of lunch shaming tells more harrowing anecdotes:

> Imagine a high school cafeteria in which a student's meal is taken away and thrown in the trash in front of his peers because his lunch account had an outstanding balance of $4.95. In another school, a student's breakfast was thrown away due to a 30-cent debt. And one school denied a child breakfast even though the child's mother told the school over the phone that she was on her way there to pay for it.[16]

One case that made national news was in Warwick, Rhode Island. The district said students with lunch debt would only get a peanut butter and jelly sandwich for lunch.[17] After pressure campaigns against this lunch shaming, they reversed that policy.

Why is this happening? Who benefits? And how do we change it?

Let's start from the ground up. How does school food finance work? Most school districts have a food service department that manages meals. There are two ways this department can approach its work: in-house or outsourced. No matter which way you slice it, this is hard to do (the food puns in this literature are to die for). The School Superintendents Association, in a very thorough summary of the outsourcing debate, puts it this way: "Operating a school district food service department is anything but simple. Even in the smallest districts, food service operations are businesses that must comply with many more rules than those in the private sector. School food service departments must operate as nonprofits, yet they need to make enough money to be self-sufficient. There are federal nutritional guidelines to follow, and the meals have to be attractive to hard-to-please consumers who are inclined to complain about 'mystery meat.'"[18] It's a tough job. The districts also set school food prices. These meals are way cheaper than lunches that you or I might get at our workplaces. A few years ago, the School Nutrition Association, which tracks this kind of information, found the average price of an elementary school lunch was $2.48, and only a few cents more across middle and high school. Meanwhile, there are federal programs for free or reduced-price lunches, but districts have to apply to participate, and many districts don't apply.

Like most public programs, government funding for school meals has been slashed repeatedly. Laws have made it easier for private firms to provide school food too. I'm sure you'll be shocked to hear that over the last ten years school food service has become more and more privatized, with departments opting to contract with big corporations to handle their food. According to a CDC report from 2000, private companies were doing this work in 17 percent of U.S. schools then. That was twenty-five years ago, and the laws have only made it easier to go to the private sector for everything. There's a whole history here, which Jennifer E. Gaddis tells well.[19]

Basically, the ruling class doesn't want school meals to be free. They want them to be subject to capitalism like everything else. That's why there's school lunch debt. But it's not that simple. There are government programs that reimburse schools for their food service costs, particularly schools that serve poorer communities. Like everything else in the Reaganite fever dream we've been living in for forty years, these programs are insufficiently funded, decentralized, and not conducive to helping people.

The U.S. Department of Agriculture manages the National School Lunch Program, whose Community Eligibility Provision provides reimbursement for schools and districts serving a certain proportion of poor students, as defined by their families' participation in programs like SNAP or TANF.[20] The program serves about 30 million kids nationwide.

But you have to be super poor to get these. The School Nutrition Association says that children from families with incomes at or below 130 percent of the poverty level, or $34,060 for a family of four, are eligible for free meals. Meanwhile, those with incomes between 130 percent and 185 percent—up to $48,470 for a family of four—can receive reduced-price meals.[21] Schools and districts have to formally register students for these programs, which requires a certification process to prove that they need it, which can sometimes go awry or not work.

When it comes to lunch debt, these regulations are, well, out to lunch. The USDA makes school meal policy, which the Food and Nutrition Service administers. And right now, the law of the land is that districts can make their own policies to address school lunch debt.

The USDA says it is "sensitive" to the issue of unpaid meal charges and provides guidance, reports, and talking points for districts to deal with the problem, including how to prevent lunch shaming.[22] The legal scholar Ilana Linder, in her article "'Hangry' for School Lunch Guidance," calls this a "hands-off" and "decentralized" approach to the problem.[23]

And hypocritical. Schools are on the hook for food costs, like I said, and the budget item is quite different from other expenses. For example, get this: According to legal researcher Anique Aburaad, the USDA does not allow schools to use federal funds to directly pay off meal debt, but it does allow such funds to be used to contract a for-profit agency to collect the debt.[24] In a 2014 study, the USDA's Food and Nutrition Service reported that 6 percent of schools sent unpaid bills to collection agencies. These numbers may have risen as a result of the USDA's 2017 requirement for schools to collect unpaid lunch debt.

So districts can use federal money to pay private companies to handle their food service, but they can't use the same money to pay off the debt parents accrue when they can't afford food. Some districts even end up sending these debts to collections agencies. Yuck.

Lots of policies have targeted lunch shaming, like laws in New Mexico and California. And some district leaders make the decision not to enforce any lunch-debt policies that might be on the books (like withholding grades or graduation). But these are treatments of a symptom rather than the disease: poverty and the inability to pay for food. People should be able to afford food for their kids. Probably the best way to address this would be to transfer control of the means of food production to cooperatives of working-class people, who would then allocate grants and credit and resources to schools according to democratic procedures.

That's a tall order, for sure. As we work toward that revolutionary policy solution, what kinds of reforms might we pursue? The problem at hand is that schools don't have enough money to pay for food. What can be done about that?

At the start of the pandemic shutdowns, the federal government passed a law that covered all student meal costs independent of students' ability to pay. The USDA extended this policy through spring 2022.[25] Not surprisingly, Bernie Sanders and Ilhan Omar want to make this permanent policy.[26] These bills look good. At the state level, Texas legislators wanted to cancel the debt in 2021, and North Dakota actually did pass a free lunch bill in 2023, which socialists had fought for.[27]

For leftists generally, this is a winning issue. The Debt Collective's Pennsylvania chapter has been working to get a lunch-debt cancelation bill through the state legislature, which is a particularly inspiring story.[28] Debt Collective worked with a coalition of democratic socialists and progressives from Bucks County and got the Bristol Borough School District to cancel $20,000 of school lunch debt.[29] Nick Marcil, an organizer with the Debt Collective on this campaign, told local news outlet WHYY that "we have the power to make sure that every single kid has school meals for free, as I think it should be" and that the campaign "is a great win." I'll have what they're having!

In 2017, a funny little article came out in Politico comparing two unlikely things: the Trump Organization's purchase of the old postal service building in Washington, DC, and the state of U.S. public school buildings.[30] The common thread here is financing updates to old public buildings. The article explains that, thanks to a Reagan-era policy, Trump got big tax credits for taking over a historic public building and redoing it for a private purpose.

You could do the same thing with public school buildings, the authors point out, but there's a clause in the policy that says you need to change how you're using the building to get the tax break. It's called the prior-use clause.

Trump changed a post office building into a hotel, using it for something new. So he got a tax break. But if school buildings are going to keep being school buildings, then school districts doing projects on them can't get that break. If the clause wasn't there, school districts could contract with private companies to take over their school building construction and maintenance through public-private partnerships (nauseatingly called P3). Another way to do this would be private activity bonds, where a local government takes out a loan, but all the proceeds go to a private company. This is as close as the federal government gets to helping school districts with their facilities, aside from not taxing income from municipal bond interest payments (which I get to in chapter 5).

Republicans campaigned to get rid of that prior-use clause in

2016, and Trump talked it up when he tried and failed to do infrastructure legislation in his first term.

The editor of *The American Prospect*, David Dayen, reminded us awhile back that getting rid of the prior-use clause and expanding the tax credit program for historic infrastructure was a Trump policy, a "stalking horse for privatization."[31] Dayen calls it asset recycling. This Republican stalking horse ultimately made it into the bipartisan infrastructure deal that Democrat Biden signed in the form of private activity bonds.[32] There are school districts around the country that have been privatizing their school buildings in various forms already.

In Prince George's County, Maryland, the school board voted in 2020 to approve a $900 million project to build six new school buildings.[33] There was a taxpayer gasp at the news. People were concerned about the cost of this project. But the CEO of the school district calmed them with soothing tones. There's no new money being spent on this project, she said. We won't need to raise taxes, she said. Some money, about $211 million, is coming out of a fund already dedicated to school buildings. So how can the district afford to do this without dipping into operating costs? The stalking horse of asset recycling.

The district entered into a public-private partnership with construction companies who won the bids for these schools. The companies will own the school buildings for thirty years after their completion. The school district will pay them rent during that time. In exchange for ownership of the buildings, the private companies don't ask for the full amount of capital up front for the projects and get to charge the district whatever they want for maintenance and other costs along the way. In local reporting on the issue, the district leadership called it Alternative Construction Finance. With Biden's infrastructure legislation, there's now federal backing for this kind of move. I wonder if districts will follow Prince George's lead.

There are other ways to privatize public school buildings. One of them is to force school districts to sell vacant or underutilized buildings to charter operators or private schools. The Wisconsin state government, run by Republicans, tried to do this in 2015–2016. Their methods were somewhat different. Rather than permit districts to enter into partnerships with private companies, who would then own the buildings, or let districts issue bonds whose proceeds would go to private companies, they passed budget legislation to force a district—Milwaukee—to sell its buildings.[34]

In another fun application of high-stakes testing, the law created an independent board of state officials to make key decisions about "underperforming" schools, including what happens to their buildings. It was called the Opportunity Schools and Partnership Program, specifically the Surplus Property Law. But the district wasn't exactly motivated to do so, since opening more charter schools would weaken its own revenues. Conservatives huffed and puffed about it (and they still do), but their top-down use of force hasn't really worked.[35] It did get the district to do something about the buildings. It has a website where it lists buildings for sale for other uses, buildings for sale to education operators, and sales pending.

School buildings are fixed infrastructure serving a public good that's locally funded. In a society where neoliberal austerity has been the dominant policy framework for more than forty years, where schools are funded through a racist regime of local property taxes and state taxes and school buildings are financed through state and local streams without federal backup—this is a perfect storm. The whole country's school buildings are in bad shape. It's a massive failure.

I understand this failure, along with the failure to address school lunch debt and provide meaningful federal support for education generally, as a failure of capitalism. School districts have to take out big loans, most of the time from private credit markets, to cover their buildings. It puts them in debt. Parents have to go into debt to feed their kids at schools that are supposed to provide food for them. The confused Title IA formulas are part of the same problem. But like the state and local levels, where I've suggested policies that could make things less shitty, it doesn't have to be this way in federal funding either. It was Richard Nixon, of all people, who proposed what I think is probably the best sort of viable reform to get the federal government to be more generous in its spending on education.

There was a brief moment in the early 1970s when federal school funding in the United States could have changed for the better. After decades of court cases challenging *Brown v. Board of Education*, federal district judges were finally putting muscle into desegregation efforts. Busing took center stage as a tactic to enforce *Brown*'s call for equal education. While it pissed a ton of people off (mostly white, but also some nonwhite) and probably wasn't the best way to achieve equal education across racial difference, busing was what Marxists would call conjunctural: It found one of the weakest links in the chains of U.S. oppression and hammered on it, hard.

Meanwhile, civil rights lawyers were going for the throat. They kept bringing school finance cases to state courts, showing how educational resources were illegal because they were so racist and unequal. Then a big decision came down in 1971. The California Supreme Court decided in *Serrano v. Priest* that the state had to provide equal school funding to every district no matter its property values. It was amazing.[36]

Across the political spectrum and across the country, people in positions of power were racing to figure out what to do. Busing was creating enormous social pressure. They also didn't want more *Serrano*-like decisions. There was an urgency to think transformatively about school funding systems. Enter Richard Nixon.

A conservative known for enigmatic approaches to big social problems (that sometimes feel left-wing to this day), he wanted to stop the busing pressure and saw school finance as a way to do it, establishing a more robust federal funding program for public education. According to Mark Brilliant's article "From Integrating Students to Redistributing Dollars: The Eclipse of School Desegregation by School Finance Equalization in 1970s California," even Derrick Bell Jr., civil rights lawyer and founder of critical race theory, agreed with Nixon.[37] Bell said the better way to integrate would be to desegregate the dollars, not the bodies.

The question was how. Nixon created a commission to study school finance. The plan they came up with—and that he strongly endorsed—was to replace the main source of school funding in the United States. Instead of municipalities collecting taxes on property, the federal government would collect a tax on products at every stage of production. Every time a firm added value to the product, they had to pay a small tax. (This is different from the retail sales tax, which is collected at the point of sale and entirely shouldered by the consumer.)

The value-added tax (VAT) was a German idea from the beginning of the twentieth century.[38] This VAT would slightly increase prices, too, of course, since firms would have to do markups to account for the charge, but unlike the retail sales tax it would be deductible on their own taxes and, Nixon thought, would generate a ton of money to pay for schools.[39] Most countries around the world have a VAT in some form.[40]

Ultimately, right-wingers without Nixon's penchant for controversial proposals shot down the idea.[41] The report they published in response to his proposal, which was very ungenerous, stopped the initiative in its tracks. Like Greenland, North Korea, and Saudi Arabia, the United States doesn't have a VAT at the national level. We're definitely behind the times. All OECD countries have one except the United States. Some states have tried it, though. The Brookings Institution recommended that Alabama and Iowa adopt it in the 1950s (they didn't), but Michigan did in 1958, only for it to be repealed in 1967 in favor of corporate and personal income tax.

I think socialists should consider backing a VAT for schools. Just imagine pulling the rug out from under the whole local property tax / school finance situation. Using a VAT to fund schools removes a keystone from the fortress of white supremacist real estate markets that determine so much about social and political life. For the people who believe taxes fund programs, it could cover whatever gaps in the four formulas to get to $5,000 per pupil, at least for the time being.

Furthermore, the VAT undercuts the prospect of taxpayer revolts at the state and local levels. Plus, right-wingers hate the property tax! They're always talking about getting rid of it, lessening it, weakening it. Their proposal is vouchers, which are basically property tax reimbursements for private school families. Why not take them up and take them on and say, okay, if you don't want to tax property to fund your schools, then don't. We've got the VAT. The fact that it's a Nixon policy is pretty juicy too, given the way moderates love to punch left. It'd be easy to say to the moderates of the world: Hey, listen, this was Nixon's idea!

Instead, what we have is a confusion at the federal level that leads to sclerotic provisions for poor schools, lunch debt, and poor buildings. The federal government could be doing so much more, as could the state governments. But if we zoom out and think about this entire part of how school funding works and the policies we deserve, we can see that even if the federal and state governments did more, there would still be that structure of racial capitalism thriving off the property markets at the district level. The whole apparatus needs to come down, get reassembled, so education can be as public as possible.

Part II

School Bonds: The Hidden Force Behind Education Injustice

5
Toxic Finance

The Debt Collective organizer and writer Eleni Schirmer, writing for *The New York Times*, said we're piling debt on our kids, just not how you think. Rather than student loans for college, she was talking about municipal bonds for K–12 school districts. According to recent research, two-thirds of U.S. school districts sell bonds directly on the municipal bond market to get the money they need for things like their facilities, but also to fill budget gaps. The other third rely on state governments, which have to do the same thing. In 2022, public school districts held about half a trillion dollars of private debt.[1]

It was this debt that got Marialena Dawn Rivera knocking on doors. Rivera, interning with a school bond consulting firm, found herself stepping awkwardly over chicken coops in high heels, a farmer yelling at her not to raise taxes. It wasn't how she imagined her research on school infrastructure financing would go. The internship was part of her groundbreaking dissertation research in education policy, critically looking at how schools fund their facilities. For her job, she had to convince California residents to vote in favor of their school districts taking out huge loans from Wall

Street, which would increase taxes for property holders within the district boundaries. When these votes fail, schools don't get what they need. So districts have to pay consultants to help them make the case for these loans to taxpayers. America!

Rivera had driven two hours to that particular rural district to get yelled at by the farmer, and along the way she noticed something.

> As I traveled around the state, I was surprised by the disparity in the quality of school facilities. . . . For example, when on a trip to Napa Valley, along with other private contractors and consultants on the facilities team, including architects and polling consultants, we visited a school with many outdated portable buildings. A teacher talked about how she lost some of her school supplies when rain leaked through her portable classroom's ceiling. That school was sharply juxtaposed to the stunning new school facilities we passed in American Canyon while driving back to the Bay Area. This pattern—of touring or hearing about leaky portables and then visiting new, state of the art facilities—repeated itself throughout the summer.[2]

We've already seen these kinds of differences, from the hole in Tina Yurichek's ceiling in Panther Valley, Pennsylvania, to the high school in Carmel Clay that has a planetarium. But few people have researched why this is and how it all works. Rivera's dissertation adviser, Jeff Vincent—one of the foremost experts on school facilities expenditure in California, and director of the brand-new National Center on School Infrastructure—working with economist Eric Brunner, found a clue to understanding the racism in the situation in California.[3] Focusing on the state, Brunner, Vincent, and their colleagues found that districts with the highest number of Black and Hispanic students take out fewer of the loans they need to build or fix schools. Or, to use technical terms, these nonwhite districts issue fewer general obligation bonds and thus have lower total revenue per pupil for capital expenditure (I promise I'll explain those phrases).[4] School facilities funding is thus substantially lower in these diverse districts.

This connection between school bonds and crumbling buildings in diverse working-class districts is not just a California problem. Schirmer, I, and the econometrician Sebastian Anti recently found, using census data for around 13,000 school districts, that a 1 percent increase in a district's white population yields a .3 percent decrease in the approximate interest rate the district pays on its bonds. In states where there's high racial animus (a measure used by finance researchers to uncover racism in the market for bonds sold by historically Black colleges and universities),[5] a 1 percent increase in white students in your population comes with a 1 percent decrease in borrowing costs. The whiter your district, the less you pay.[6] Schirmer writes, in her article for *Rethinking Schools* called "School Debt: The Great Unequalizer": "Paterson, New Jersey's public schools, which enroll 95 percent students of color, pay more than 60 percent more in fees than the neighboring, predominantly white school district of Fair Lawn. In Mississippi's Claiborne County, where 55 percent of children live below the poverty line, the school district pays 94 percent more in borrowing fees than the neighboring Hinds County, where merely 14 percent of children live below the poverty line." Confirming the dynamics in these findings, finance researchers Nicole Boyson and Weiling Liu have found that "less wealthy districts pay higher yields and third-party fees to issue bonds, even after controlling for factors including credit quality," and that districts borrowing on the municipal bond market creates educational inequality.[7] Others have shown that historically Black colleges and universities pay more than other universities when borrowing from the bond market.[8] Researchers at the Brookings Institution proved that there's racial discrimination in municipal borrowing generally.[9] What's going on here?

Historian of finance Destin Jenkins, in his book *The Bonds of*

Inequality: Debt and the Making of the American City, calls the municipal bond market the spider in the web of urban segregation and racial injustice at the infrastructural level, including schools.[10] The municipal bond market is the problem, underwriting all the sticky tendrils of mold and asbestos and malfunctioning ventilation in our school buildings. Political scientist Alberta Sbragia, whose work is some of the clearest at explaining what she calls the "municipal money chase," has said that this arrangement is a debt wish for local governments like school districts, an arrangement that saps life from cities rather than providing it.[11] Municipal finance researcher Tom Sgouros called this system predatory.[12] As Camika Royal and I claim, it's toxic.[13]

According to census data as of 2022, public school districts in the United States had about $544 billion in debt outstanding. This is likely an undercount given the wide variety of methods districts use to take out and pay back their loan. Chatham County, Georgia, for instance, reports zero interest on their debt in national census data, but their penny sales tax policy for financing capital needs shows the district holds at least $47 million in debt obligations.

That's just one example of how little is known about the actual amount of money that school districts devote to their debt service as a percentage of their overall expenditures. Still, the rule of thumb in research circles is that it's usually between 8 and 10 percent. Every year, nearly a tenth of public school district budgets go to paying Wall Street loans back, which includes fees and interest. The fees go to credit rating companies, consultants, lawyers, and big banks. The interest goes to wealthy investors who park their money in municipal bonds because the profit they make from that investment is tax free at the federal level, and even sometimes the state level. This isn't some neoliberal policy. It's been true since at least the early twentieth century if not before.

Municipal bond researcher Marc Joffe found that school districts pay about 1 percent of school bond principal just in fees on average, with high variability depending on income, wealth, and where the district is located.[14] A rural district like the one Rivera visited will sometimes pay upwards of 10 percent, which, when a loan's principal can be in the hundreds of millions, adds up. Camika Royal and I calculated, for instance, that between 1993 and 2021, the Philadelphia school district paid about $3.65 billion in interest and fees, and about $145 million of that was fees associated with selling the school bonds. A staggering number when you consider that in 2017 an independent assessment of the district's facilities found about $4.5 billion in maintenance backlog.

Districts lose a lot of money in this municipal money chase. In the wake of the 2008 financial crisis, as Sgouros notes, Philadelphia schools lost $330 million selling risky variable-rate bonds. Public finance researcher Amanda Kass and her colleagues found that selling a similarly risky kind of school bond cost Chicago Public Schools $100 million for the same reason.[15] There are so many stories like this—but because the municipal bond market is so hard to understand, outside of the small group of officials who do the lending and borrowing, and the researchers who study them, there isn't a lot of public conversation about it.

In this second part of the book, following Jenkins's idea that debt is the spider in the web of problems like segregation, I do some spider-watching and look at this largely hidden cause of school-funding injustice: the relationship between schools and the municipal bond market. Rather than an explainer, I approach this subject with scenes and analyses, digging into certain details that zigzag across cases and features of the landscape. This first chapter offers a bird's-eye view of bonds and a few specific scenes of the bond market, whether it's the television show *Billions*, Jim Lebenthal's municipal bond commercials, or the life and times of Bill Gross, known as the Bond King, I want to gently ease you into the world that school district budget officials have to deal with every day to figure out how to get the students, teachers, and other members of their school community the resources they need. After that, I present some of the fees school districts have to pay and how bonds fail through oppressive bond ballot initiative laws (which is what forced Rivera to knock on farmers' doors), and I get into other fun specifics—like a connection to crypto, Build America Bonds, and more—in chapter 6.

Jim Lebenthal started his career reporting on celebrities for *Life* magazine in the 1940s. When his father died, his mother asked him to come home to New York City and help run the family business: a municipal bond company.[16] He left the glamour of interviewing John Wayne in Hollywood for getting on the phone and selling bonds to rich retirees trying to find a place to park their money. Lebenthal made a name for himself and his family's company by making quirky commercials that aired all over New York, wanting to help people understand municipal bonds so they'd buy more of them. He was a municipal bond evangelist.

One famous commercial opens with a teacher in an elementary school addressing her students, saying, "Alright kids, we have a very special guest today, he's a celebrity that everyone knows, he's kind of like a superhero, and you're meeting him today! Mr. Lebenthal!" A kindly old man steps in front of the blackboard, the camera zooming in, and says:

> We may sing of purple mountains majesty and amber waves of grain, but everything in this country—its roads, its buildings, its Subways, its schools, in a word, its infrastructure—didn't just come to be. They were built by bonds. You can't get up in the morning, take a shower, take a subway, a bus, go over a bridge or under the river, without a municipal bond touching your life.

The camera zooms out to the kindergarten classroom, little kids sitting on the floor looking up at Lebenthal, their colorful drawings hanging on the walls around them in their classroom, which was built by bonds. Sitting cross-legged, one student raises her hand. Lebenthal calls on her and says, "Yes?" The student asks, "Who are you?"[17] Lebenthal looks at the camera, frustrated.

Municipal bonds are the most powerful political and economic force you've never heard of. The political strategist James Carville, while advising Bill Clinton in the 1990s, famously said, "I used to think if there was reincarnation, I wanted to come back as the president or the pope or a .400 baseball hitter. But now I want to come back as the bond market. You can intimidate everyone."[18] This is true in schools. Freda Anderson, a public high school teacher in Philly, wrote in a 2023 reflection on teaching "debt pollution" in schools that "I didn't even realize a school district could be in debt until well after years of wading through its disastrous effects. The very air we breathe and water we drink as educators and students . . . is polluted with indebtedness."[19]

A bond is a "debt security," which, again, is a loan. It's an obligation for someone to pay someone else back with interest at a later point. It's widely accepted that the oldest bond is about four hundred years old. In 1624, some ice broke a dike on the Lek River near Utrecht in the Netherlands, and builders for the town needed money to fix the problem. So they promised a local businessman they'd pay him 5 percent interest every year if he lent them a thousand guilders for the project. The businessman took the deal, lent them the money, and collected the interest. While contemporary bonds have terms for when they're paid off, that bond is still paying out to this day.[20]

Because the bond was for a local municipality, it was a kind of municipal bond. The town went into debt to the businessman and set aside money every year to pay him back with interest. Like Lebenthal said, you can't take a shower or go to school without a municipal bond touching your life: According to the National League of Cities, municipal bonds finance 80 percent of America's infrastructure.[21] Private credit for public infrastructure is a huge market. The U.S. market for municipal bonds was worth about $4.1 trillion in 2024, the bulk of which goes toward education. According to a leading bond research firm, as of April 2024, education bonds (which include everything from day care centers to graduate schools to research) were 27.3 percent of the market.[22]

Public school districts have to sell bonds to get money for all kinds of things. There's no national program for school infrastructure, so when an elementary school needs to be rebuilt or a high school needs a new heating system or a playground turf needs to be fixed or hackers have broken into the district's system and they need new cybersecurity software, the school district sells a bond on Wall Street (they also go into debt between budget cycles and refinance previous bonds). Public schools are therefore in the business of selling themselves on the municipal bond market. And this business has a long history. While there's no history of the school bond that I've been able to find (I'm working on that now), the first mention of a bond for education—a loan that a district had to pay back—is from Kentucky in 1837.[23]

Bonds are an outsize part of the material conditions of education, but they're difficult to understand. So I'm constantly on the hunt for relatable texts, images, and narratives that can explain all this. I think if people knew more about how it all worked, there'd be a better chance of changing it. And sometimes I find something good.

There's an episode of the television show *Billions* that might be the only popular culture treatment of municipal bonds that gets at how they work and why they're so bad, particularly for school districts. In season 2, episode 7, of the show, we get a very clear look at this direct touchpoint between capitalism and public schools. If you don't know the show, it's about the rivalry between a charismatic investment banker and the lead public prosecutor for New York's Southern District. They're at each other's throats and in the push-pull you get a pretty pulpy picture of the dialectic between the repressive state apparatus and capitalist mode of production, specifically finance.

The banker leads an investment firm called Axe Capital. At one point, the firm sees an opportunity to invest in a small town in Upstate New York called Sandicot that's slated to get a casino. Axe Capital buys the town's municipal bond to finance the project. That means the town is deeply in debt to the investment firm and has to pay back the loan with interest. The money that'll come in from the casino once it's finished will more than cover the cost, so it seems fine to do the deal. Until things go bad.

The lawyer's father is an older investor who's involved in state politics. In a vindictive move to support his son's fight against Axe Capital, he gets the state government committee in charge of approving locations for casinos to change the casino's location to a different town, leaving Axe Capital with Sandicot's debt. Since the casino will no longer be built there, the town has no way to pay it back, leaving the investors to figure out how to deal with collecting what they're owed. As *New York* magazine summarized the episode when it came out,

> the brain trust at Axe Capital has to figure out how to salvage the Sandicot situation. The only real idea on the table is the one that makes it hardest to sleep at night—austerity. What that basically means is that the city will have to pay back Axe Capital before they pay anyone else. Think about that on a city level. It will gut schools, city jobs, utilities, and public funds. Crime goes up. Schools will close. The police force will be cut. It has a viral effect that could go as far as to turn Sandicot into a ghost town—just so a hedge fund gets paid back.[24]

There's an amazing scene where all the people working at the investment firm are figuring out what to do about this situation.

They have the power to decimate the town. It's in their legal right to lay waste to it by collecting their principal and interest payments, draining it of every resource, including its schools.

Some of the traders can't stomach ruining an entire town just for the meager profit. But then a character named Taylor advances the libertarian position that the town must fail, that it's better for the town and its people to face the consequences of their decision to take out the loan in the first place. Basically, Taylor says the town mismanaged its own funds and should either dig its way out or die, like an animal in nature, and that the firm should continue to pursue its own profit seeking and collect the debt without a thought.

At the beginning of the monologue, Taylor says, "In many ways, a town is like a business." That's the key here. For this whole arrangement to make sense, you have to understand something public—a town and its schools—as something private: a for-profit entity competing on a market. You have to imagine towns and school districts in a constant battle to survive.

Of course, we don't have to imagine reality that way. There are many other, kinder, more generous ideologies available. In a market socialist version of this world depicted by the television show, it would be the worker-managers of local firms gathered together trying to figure out how best to allocate resources to their people's education, not a group of capitalists looking to make as much profit as possible on the hope that, as they pursue their self-interest and the town does too, the best allocation of resources will emerge magically as everyone acts as selfishly as possible.

While the example of Sandicot is fictional, it illustrates a rule of school finance in the United States, which is that public school districts themselves are beholden to private investors who loan them the funds they need for their infrastructure costs and other kinds of budget financing. These public school districts are always already in a fight for their lives due to the interest and fees these private entities charge them, a fight that manifests in the constant fear of impacts to the district's credit rating. If anything goes poorly—a late payment, a drop in enrollment, a dip in property value, a charter school opens—the district could get bumped down a notch on the scale of creditworthiness, making it harder and more expensive to borrow.

Like the example from *Billions*, investors can and will collect their debt payments on the bond, which ultimately shackles districts' ability to fulfill its mission: to educate kids. Sometimes a state or other authority takes out the loan for districts; sometimes districts take them out themselves. It varies from state to state. But the logic is the same: The bondholders must be paid, or else.

Whoever does the legwork, the loans are generally subject to unreasonably harsh credit ratings, expensive legal and consultant fees, and higher interest rates than loans made to private companies. Marc Joffe, drawing from analyses conducted by the Securities and Exchange Commission, found that rating companies like Moody's give corporate bonds higher ratings than municipal bonds, despite more frequent defaults, because the credit raters view private firms as doing more "significant business." These onerous ratings cost districts about $2 billion annually in interest. On top of that, on average, school districts pay 1.02 percent of the cost of issuance in fees. Paying these fees saps school district budgets, sometimes to an absurd degree.

In 2010, Joffe notes, the West Haven School District in Connecticut sold a bond for $45 million. To get this loan, the district had to pay credit rating agencies to secure a rating of the district, a measure to indicate to creditors the district's likelihood to repay the funds provided by the bond. The district was also going through a budget crisis. Just prior to issuing the bond, it laid off more than fifty teachers as a cost-cutting measure. According to Joffe, citing reporting at the time from Bloomberg, West Haven "paid S&P and Moody's combined fees of $31,700," an amount that "would have covered nine months' salary for one teacher."[25] The credit rating for their Wall Street loan was about as expensive as a teacher's salary. The district fired the teacher and chose the credit rating.

Alongside the material toxicity of lost education dollars and cents that go to Wall Street instead of teachers, there's also a spiritual toxicity, an immorality in this system. As part of a course on law and finance in a principalship program, where teachers train to get their certifications to become administrators, I took my students to the university's Bloomberg Terminal lab. The terminals are like a finance Skynet. They have constantly updated information on all kinds of data relating to investment, by and for investors. It's how Michael Bloomberg made all his money. All the finance bros are glued to these screens because it's where you see the prices of things go up and down in real time, but with ready-to-hand context, news, background data, and historical trends. They have their own screen style (black screen, white and yellow text) and their own unique keyboards. It costs $26,000 for an annual subscription to the service.

But most universities have a Bloomberg lab for students interested in learning about investing. So I went to my university's lab—I got a lot of weird looks from people at every step of the way—and I looked up school districts I knew, like where I lived and where I grew up. Then I brought my students, and they all found their public school districts too.

It's jarring to see your public school district, as a public servant, listed like a company on the stock market. It undermines all the messages you get about public school as a public good. Every school district has a unique page with local, state, and federal demographic information and pricing conditions. You can graph historical data on housing price indices, population increases/decreases, and credit rating shifts across multiple rating agencies and levels (insured credit rating, underlying credit rating). You can dig into individual bond deals or zoom out on all bond deals. We could see up-to-date volumes of trades, tranches of debt, the details of the deals, with helpful breakdowns of everyone involved in making the bond happen: consultants, law firms, banks, depositories, underwriters, etc. You can also see which big investment firms and banks hold the most municipal debt (last I checked, it was Vanguard). Seeing this bonded reality of their school districts with my class was like the episode in *Stranger Things* when the characters saw the upside-down world for the first time.

Ultimately, the fact that we rely on the municipal bond market as the source of revenue for schools is a policy choice. It's a decision we collectively make to treat school capital expenditures, for example, those lumpy and bumpy costs districts accrue when they need to build facilities, as a credit problem and, beyond that, a private credit problem. This whole arrangement is a way of allocating resources, and some people—namely, the bankers, consultants, and others who benefit from this system—think that it's a good way of allocating resources, letting the market determine which school districts should get what kind of liquidity for their infrastructure at what cost. The municipal bond market is also really big and it can be hard to imagine other sources of liquidity that match what's needed. I disagree, and so do a lot of others when they find out how it all works.

The research I have listed here all points to this system of credit allocation as being the reason why the best-cared-for school buildings are in districts with high credit ratings, high property values, and largely white populations. In 2020, Pennsylvania students highlighted this disparity when they marched the four miles from Overbrook High School in West Philadelphia to Lower Merion High School, just over the district border.[26] At that time, Lower Merion spent about $12,000 more per student than Philadelphia did. Lower Merion's student population was majority white, while Philadelphia's district was majority nonwhite. Philadelphia's credit rating, according to Moody's, was Ba3 (just above junk). Lower Merion's is Aaa (investment grade). While the racial disparity in the ratings is clear, what's less obvious, and perhaps more profound in terms of the municipal bond regime, is the immorality: the actual risk of default is equivalent between the two districts. School districts barely default, if ever. Bond marketeers would likely tell you that there's a "risk premium" in Philadelphia, a jargony racial capitalist euphemism for "this city isn't worth it."

Like Anderson said in her reflection about debt pollution, the connection between the bond market and toxic infrastructure is literally in the air students and teachers breathe, which the pandemic highlighted with a terrible clarity. Before the pandemic, Lower Merion's schools' ventilation exceeded standards, and they were further updated with advanced technology such as MERV 13 filtration and bipolar ionization. Philadelphia's schools got rickety-looking window fans, which made national headlines. Students were fed up, and actions like the one in Philly happened all over the country during the pandemic.[27]

This wave of student strikes highlighted the stark reality that the Omicron variant of COVID-19 broke through the supposed firewall of vaccinations even while leaders as high up as President Biden and Secretary of Education Miguel Cardona, along with a bevy of experts and pundits, insisted that schools were safe for in-person instruction. According to the students walking out—and the teachers agitating nationwide—they weren't. It didn't have to be this way. The spread of COVID-19 in classrooms was and is an infrastructure problem. If the air in a classroom is stagnant and not refreshed frequently, the risk of infection and spread can increase (not to mention that it's terrible for learning).

The inefficient, inadequate, and unequal school-building finance system is a result of the tendency in the United States to trust private finance with social services in the relative absence of the federal government. There is no federal law or policy that calls for the regular study and funding of school infrastructure. There has been a law on the shelf for years, the Rebuild America's Schools Act, which proposes to spend $100 billion on physical and digital school infrastructure. When it was brought forward in 2019, it didn't pass, and an updated law that came out in 2021, the Reopen and Rebuild America's Schools Act, currently sits in limbo.[28]

The Biden administration's recovery package, the American Rescue Plan (ARP), was not enough to overcome the problems with the way the United States funds its schools. The ARP's numbers looked impressive: By January 1, 2022, the program distributed $122 billion to schools.[29] Yet because the money was not intended for facilities exclusively, it was also spent on other priorities, such as transportation, mental health services, and internet connectivity. Georgetown University's FutureEd found that most districts spent this money on hiring and teacher training.[30] While at least half of districts receiving ARP funds will spend some of the money on ventilation, school leaders were so concerned about completing these ventilation projects by 2025—when the ARP funds ran out—that in January the School Superintendents Association formally asked the Department of Education for an extension on the funding.[31] It was not granted.

The complexity of the projects, combined with the short-term funding infusion and supply-chain issues with materials, made it difficult to get the jobs done. That's because the bond market is a gross way to finance public schools.

All these issues are notoriously difficult to grasp. Unfortunately, besides that *Billions* anecdote, there are very few engaging ways to learn about bonds. This lack of comprehensible material that explains municipal bonds is a big pedagogical problem since school district officials have to spend so much time issuing and then managing their bonds, yet they get little to no training about this until they get into their positions (which is why I bring my students training to be principals to the Bloomberg lab). Plus, there's no way for anyone—practitioners or researchers—to think beyond the status quo. How can outsiders transform a system that only insiders understand?

A search for general audience nonfiction books about municipal bonds yields very few results. I was looking for books as readable, narrative, and character-based as possible. One of them was Lebenthal's *Confessions of a Municipal Bond Salesman*, which I recommend for its silliness and down-to-earth tone. As I was looking, a more mainstream book was published that was super helpful and really interesting. *The Bond King,* by Mary Childs, is about Bill Gross, the chief investment officer of the investment management firm PIMCO.[32] He is known, like the title says, as the Bond King, for his historic transformation of the bond market from a sleepy place for slow fixed-rate profit to a roiling go-go market.

The Bond King is focused on corporate bonds, which are loans that private companies take out to finance their operations. But the book provides a lot of fine-grained dynamics about bond markets and helps set the scene for school bonds. It's a dirty ruling-class story, like *Succession* or *The Big Short*, a genre of infotainment that gives a look into the lives of the most filthy-rich people and how terrible they are. These are the kinds of people who control whether or not schools get the money they need for their playgrounds.

Childs tells how it is that a life insurance agent at a place like Pacific Mutual gets into bond trading. It turns out the rhythms of bond trading and death are similar enough to be profitable. The business of life insurance necessitates knowing generally how many customers will die each year, how much an insurer will need to pay out, and when-ish these things will happen relative to one another. Usually it's not for a while. So Pacific Mutual, and every other insurer out there, could take its customers' life insurance premiums and invest the money in bonds that threw off interest payments until they matured (and returned the money), approximately when the insurer expected to need it back. Investors could pretty safely buy a thirty-year bond and earn the interest with money from customers who most likely wouldn't die for another thirty years.

People pay into their life insurance policies over the course of their lives. While they pay those premiums, the insurance companies turn a profit by putting that money into bonds, which mature over long periods, just like human lives. They're long-term investments. When you look at a general obligation bond statement, for instance, it's usually broken up into sections of yearly payments going ahead fifteen, twenty, thirty years. Gross came upon this system as a young trader and amped it up.

What Gross realized is that he could make these investments more frequently, more riskily, and more differentially as interest rates vary, thereby getting a ton more interest payments (and then sell derivatives on these bonds). Rather than a sleepy forest of slow-growth trees bearing fruit and seeds at their own pace, Gross grafted new plants to the old trees and used new fertilizers to generate exponentially more yields. His approach followed a more general trend after 1975 in finance, which was to do anything to increase the client's profit, even at the expense of entire governments. Childs writes, "If pushing governments and companies is okay if it is done in service of the client, arguably people with money invested at private money managers outranked taxpayers. The public pays to serve capital holders. But this wasn't Pimco's problem. Its interests stopped with the client. The rest was society's concern."[33] Indeed, bonds are the way that local, state, and federal government entities get financing. Gross, following this client-based ethos, whipped the market up into a frenzy that contributed to the huge crash in 2008.

And speaking of crashes, I couldn't pass up this portrait of Gross as a college student literally losing his scalp while going on an errand for his fraternity: "On a Saturday night in 1966, Gross's Phi Kappa Psi brothers sent him out to get donuts for potential recruits—'nobody trusted me to do anything but buy donuts'—

but, speeding, he lost control of his Nash Rambler and smashed into oncoming traffic. He went through the windshield, which sliced off three quarters of his scalp, detaching it entirely."[34] There's something gruesomely poetic about this anecdote. First, the fact that this fraternity couldn't trust Gross to do anything other than get donuts. He was clearly reckless in a number of ways, including speeding. And during the one mundane task he tried to accomplish for them, he lost his head in a crash. It's a pretty good metaphor for what he did for the bond market, which is a place where many school districts have to go to finance their budgets. Wall Street is a reckless place where people are constantly crashing and losing their heads—and this is where the money for our school buildings is supposed to come from?

Whenever we think of how our school buildings are crumbling, for instance, we have to think of this bond market as the place where districts and states are supposed to go for the resources to maintain them. Do we really want to trust our school buildings to the market that Gross built?

It's a place that clearly takes advantage of our public school districts. Fees are a good concrete example. The researcher Marc Joffe wrote about those fees in a pair of jaw-dropping reports for the Haas Institute at UC Berkeley, both titled *Doubly Bound*.[35] After analyzing 812 municipal bonds (no easy feat, as data on bonds can cost tens of thousands of dollars to acquire), Joffe found overall that 1.02 percent of bond issuance money goes toward the fees required for issuing it, totaling potentially around $3.5 billion annually across the country. But these averages cover up a lot of difference among those municipalities that shoulder high fees. Indeed, "these costs fall disproportionately on small issuers—which are often poorer rural districts that could undoubtedly use every extra dollar not consumed by financial industry interests."[36]

This makes sense: If it costs a certain amount to take out a loan, then those fees are going to be roughly the same whether you're taking out a big loan or a small loan. So small municipalities taking out small loans have to pay relatively more. A Salt Lake City bond only had .13 percent going toward these fees. But a small school district in rural central California, like where Rivera was working, had a whopping 10.62 percent go toward fees.

These fees include the financial or municipal adviser or consultant fees and expenses, bond counsel fees and expenses, underwriter's counsel fees and expenses, rating agency fees, bond insurance premiums, verification agent fees, trustee fees, cost of issuance agent fees, paying agent fees, escrow agent fees, printing fees, CUSIP fees, contingency costs, or other costs such as fees paid to state treasurers, payments to the attorney general, costs associated with the municipal employees' time working on the issuance, or appraisal fees. And then there's underwriter's discount, a sum paid to the private banks (which doesn't even get invoiced). What are these costs?

The underwriter is the investment bank doing the deal on the lender side. It's putting the whole thing together to make the sale.[37] They take a piece that they call an underwriter's discount. These can differ from their legal expenses, since the underwriters hire lawyers too. The borrower also needs lawyers and agents for the deal, whom they have to pay. There are financial advisers who guide the lender and borrower through the process, who take a cut. Lawyers called bond counsels check the legality of everything. They get paid. A different law firm prepares the actual bond statement, giving a 10b-5 opinion, which is when they say the bond is all kosher, free of errors and omissions.

The ratings agencies collect fees too. Joffe did a study just on this aspect of the whole apparatus and found that these agencies, which rate the creditworthiness of issuers and bonds, take $2 billion annually from municipal borrowers.[38] He proposes a much more streamlined, public, and formula-based rating system that could save borrowers money. But you can imagine there's not a lot of incentive, energy, or popular consciousness to make that change.

In that report, Joffe also looks at an industry that's emerged around the overly harsh credit ratings that municipal borrowers get. If you can believe it, people make money by selling insurance policies to municipal borrowers to make sure they don't get a bad credit rating. That costs money too. This is just one reason the financial researcher Tom Sgouros called this "predatory finance."[39] When you look at it, remember that neoliberals across the spectrum think that private markets are the definition of freedom. More like feedom!

There are ways to help districts with these costs, but the costs never fully go away. A common one is state-level programs. The Virginia Public School Authority, which I mentioned earlier, helps with this, a version of which other states have too. In his report, Joffe notes that one reason a Missouri bond's fees were lower is because of a program at the state level. Cole County appears to have achieved lower issuance costs and a higher bond rating because the state of Missouri offers a "direct deposit program" through its Health and Educational Facilities Authority. Under this program, the authority pays bond investors directly and deducts debt service costs from state aid payments remitted to participating districts. Massachusetts and Wyoming have something similar. A national investment authority, would basically do this kind of thing but for the whole country as I'll discuss in chapter 7.

Generally speaking, state programs are helpful in taking the burden off local governments like school districts. But a state program doesn't guarantee the state will fund the program, as we saw in the case of Pennsylvania's PlanCon, nor does it really address the root cause of the problem. Instead, these programs pass along the debt to state governments, which, while they have higher credit ratings, still bond themselves to the private credit market. State programs move the problem around rather than solving it. And the problem isn't just fees.

In 2023, a group of parents in the Alpine School District in Provo, Utah, sued the district because it was looking to close five elementary buildings that were listed on a state registry pointing to public structures that weren't earthquake safe.[40] A few years before that, when the state of Utah found that the five elementary schools there were not built to withstand an earthquake, the district quite logically took steps to put together a facilities plan to update the buildings so they wouldn't collapse and kill the people in them. But they had to contend with the bond market, which, along with all the things we've already talked about, also means contending with cantankerous taxpayers.

As in most districts, Alpine officials had to consult its local residents before it could take out that loan. This is what Marialena Dawn Rivera was doing stepping over chicken coops in her high heels in California: trying to convince property owners in a school district to vote in favor of taxing themselves higher to pay back Wall Street so the school buildings would be safe. Because the district would have to increase its property taxes by some amount to pay the loan off, they needed to put it to a vote of taxpayers in the district. If the voters agreed to pay a little more in taxes to fund the project, then the district could take out the private loan and make their buildings earthquake safe—and make some wealthy investors tax-free income.

I generally think voting is great; it's democratic, I completely support it and think we should do more of it everywhere. But when a school district needs buildings to be safe from earthquakes, and to do that it needs to get approval from a local group of taxpayers thinking about their property values to take out a private loan from Wall Street that benefits the rich, I just can't get excited about the arrangement. While school bonds and the referendum process is so normal as to be unquestioningly accepted by district officials and communities all over the country (one of the only systematic textbooks on school bonds is basically just an explainer on how to plan and then pass the referendum vote[41]), I don't think we should just accept it. When it comes to making sure public schools won't collapse in an earthquake, private property and its value, the extent to which owners think they should pay taxes on their property, whether the private credit market has investors willing to front money to the district for a good return—the profit motive generally—shouldn't have anything to do with it.

What happened in Alpine School District is a case in point. The voters rejected Alpine's bond referendum. The district asked if they'd pay a little bit more in property taxes to make the buildings safe and the taxpayers said no. This is bad for all kinds of reasons, not least of which is that the district's enrollments have been increasing incrementally over the last decade and they need to update their facilities. They've got more students and now they have even less space for them. Believe it or not, this all happens pretty frequently. The data is ten years old, but Ballotpedia reports that, for the forty states that require these school bond referenda, success of the bond votes was 72 percent in 2012.[42] That means that about 30 percent of the time, the district wouldn't get the money it needed for its school facilities.

This whole system leads to some perverse outcomes, like the case of the Boundary County School District in Idaho whose kindergarten students were playing on playgrounds with nails sticking out of the ground. The Idaho state constitution doesn't have any programs to pay for school buildings. The local property taxes the Boundary County School District gets its operating revenue from couldn't handle the playground expense. Districts there needed a two-thirds supermajority to pass bond elections, not just a simple majority over 50 percent. The bond vote failed, meaning the district couldn't even get the go-ahead to get fleeced on the municipal bond market to get the money to fix the nails sticking out of its playground.[43] The situation was even more extreme for the Gervais School District in Oregon. It lost so many bond votes that, in April 2024, school officials said they might have to dissolve the district. They needed a bond vote so badly that it was literally life or death for the district itself.[44] More like referendumb.

These school bond referenda make the infrastructure of public education sensitive to the wrong whims. While technofascist Christian nationalism aiming to decimate public education in the United States looks like a new phenomenon now, when it comes to school bonds, there have been initiatives on that front for a couple of decades. Take the Iowan evangelical financial consultant Paul Dorr, for example, who made it his goal in life to thwart school bond elections and prevent school districts from getting the money they need.

Dorr founded Copperhead Consulting in the early 2000s to do the opposite of what Rivera's firm was doing. Instead of promoting school bond votes and trying to get people to vote in favor of them, Dorr tries to get people to vote against them. At a 2013 religious conference he spelled out his motivation:

> I work at this because I have a deep passionate abhorrence of government schools. . . . I'm dedicating my life to see . . . that institution one day be gone. . . . Let me give you one reason why. . . . Wilhelm Reich was born in 1897 in Galicia to a Jewish family. Reich, who had his first sexual experience at the age of 11, went on to become a psychoanalyst in the footsteps of Freud. His scholarly work, if you will, the sexual revolution, became the foundation for America's sexual revolution in the 1960s, the primary conduit of which in the United States is the government school.[45]

Dorr goes on to detail how public schools influence children to act "contrary to the Christian church's morals" sexually, making them become suggestible. "The total sexualization of children means the total destruction of the church, and the state, based on God's law." There's so much here to untangle—the veiled antisemitism, the logical leaps from Reich (an antifascist Marxist psychoanalyst, actually) to public schools being Reichian, to the mentioning of Galicia (where my great-grandmother was from!)—I don't even know where to start. I include this snippet of Dorr's motivation to give you a sense of the energies to which bond votes make public schools' crucial funding streams vulnerable. Dorr goes about his epic task of destroying public education by making sure districts across the country lose their bond referendum votes. In 2019, it was reported that he'd defeated forty-three of the sixty-six bonds he's fought against across ten states in the Midwest.

Alex Baumhardt, reporting for American Public Media, tells the story of Worthington, Minnesota, where the school district needed a new high school and athletics facilities in 2014, since the district's enrollments had been growing steadily. The nearly $80 million bond would have raised taxes by about $26 per acre of land. The district had to put it to a vote. At the town's annual Turkey Day Parade on Thanksgiving, residents noticed young people handing out fliers arguing that voters should vote no on the bond referendum. "It claimed the school board was mismanaging money and was incompetent, even deaf. The committee encouraged people not to eat at restaurants where school bond information was displayed and wrote critically about business leaders who supported the new school."[46]

Dorr had been hired by a local group to kill the bond vote, and along with the fliers, he organized critiques of local officials on Facebook that created fights among otherwise peaceful neighbors. It worked: The bond was voted down four times between 2016 and 2019.

This shouldn't be possible. School districts should get public money for their facilities as they need it. They shouldn't have to be entangled in private property relations and the perverse religious fantasies of those who know how to manipulate arcane finance policy. The Alpine bond failure, and sheer existence of policies like Idaho's and people like Dorr, are failures of American capitalism. It's structural—and structurally important—not just for public education but for American society more broadly. These bond votes can have larger social impacts, and they've always been lightning rods.

In the early 1960s, Marvin Pickering was a high school science teacher in Township School District 205, Illinois, outside Chicago. The district needed to do a lot of maintenance on its buildings, including the construction of two new schools and finishing Pickering's own classroom.[47] District officials had to get voters' approval before selling a bond that would get them the money they needed. They held a bond referendum in 1961. It failed. Over the next three years, they'd hold several more votes, all of which failed. The voters kept saying no. Pickering, who still had to teach in an unfinished classroom, was frustrated with the district's fiscal leadership and in 1964 wrote a letter to the editor of his local newspaper taking the district to task for its financial decisions.

Pickering was particularly pissed that the district was giving student athletes free lunches and building new playing fields while leaving classrooms like his unfinished, as well as refusing raises to teachers. Going line by line, analyzing certain expenditures, Pickering's letter was detailed and must have hit a nerve, because the district fired him soon after it was published.

He sued them for a violation of his First Amendment rights and the case went all the way to the Supreme Court, which handed down one of the most famous cases of workplace freedom of speech rights in *Pickering v. Board of Education*. The court found in Pickering's favor, Thurgood Marshall writing for the majority that the problem before the court was "to arrive at a balance between the interests of the teacher, as a citizen, in commenting upon matters of public concern and the interest of the State, as an employer, in promoting the efficiency of the public services it performs through its employees."[48] While the decision was a momentous one for free speech by public employees (and was reeled back in 2006 in another case), the school bond vote was the occasion for the challenge. School bonds are very sensitive and powerful social practices.

So much so, school bonds were also the occasion for the birth of neoliberalism.

A common idea about recent history is that neoliberalism began more or less with the turbulent economic environment of the early 1970s and the unstable combination of high inflation and unemployment, giving rise to a tax revolt, most prominently in California around the state's infamous Proposition 13. This proposition froze property value assessments in place at the time of purchase, reducing property taxes that would go to public school districts, and passed in an effervescence of property-owner frustration at the high cost of living. Many see the success of Prop. 13 and the tax revolts behind it as the swelling of the wave on which Reagan rode to his 1980 landslide victory against Jimmy Carter, shifting the country's politics rightward.

But a 2020 article by historian Josh Mound published in the *Journal of Policy History* tells a different story. Mound argues that it was an earlier revolt among a more diverse group of voters—many of them working-class—rejecting school bond referenda that created the conditions for the later, more conservative tax revolts. The successive bond vote failures happening in Township School District in Illinois, Alpine, and Worthington were happening nationally. Mound focuses on the case of Youngstown, Ohio, which voted down its school district bond referendum six times in a row, causing a national stir.

Between 1950 and 1978, Mound shows that school bond

approval rates fell nationally from 100 percent to nearly 45 percent, a sharp decline that took its most intense fall between 1954 and 1964, years before the Proposition 13 vote. How did this happen? Mound tracks how, after the 1960 presidential election, the Kennedy-Johnson administration abandoned FDR-style economic policies in favor of early versions of supply-side laws, giving a break to big corporations and zeroing out New Deal–era programs. School bond referenda votes therefore became an outlet for diverse working-class people to express their outrage at this new political-economic reality.[49]

As a result of these failed bond referenda, school buildings didn't get the investments they needed, of course, but across municipalities a dissatisfied energy grew into the better-known tax revolts of the 1970s, ushering in a tectonic shift in the country's political economy toward privatization. School bonds were at the beginning of that story. Perhaps we shouldn't be surprised, then, that in 2024, as school bond votes from New Jersey to Minnesota were failing again, another extremely right-wing carnival barker, riding a wave of populist dissatisfaction with the status quo, has won office with a shockingly high margin in the Electoral College.[50]

Back in Utah, the parents in Alpine were rightly pissed. The school buildings weren't earthquake safe. Their only other option was to rezone their existing catchment boundaries to use the safe school buildings they had, which was not a good option given their rising enrollments. In an ironic turn, the school district had to spend money on legal counsel to resolve the court case. If the case exceeds their allotted budget for legal defense, they may have to raise property taxes to pay legal fees in the court case resulting from the failed bond referendum, the very thing residents didn't want to do to pay for the bond in the first place.

This snake eating its own tail gets even scarier when you consider its connection to school shootings.

6
Nightmare Ouroboros

Police in Uvalde, Texas, falsely blamed a teacher for not properly shutting a door through which Salvador Ramos entered the school with an assault rifle, killing nineteen children and two teachers in 2022. In fact, the teacher shut the door but did not realize it could only be locked from the outside; and the door to the classroom the shooter entered was also unlocked. In the horrible crucible of the news cycle after the rampage, the national spotlight was on law enforcement. At the same time, there was another story just as nefarious—if not more so. Indeed, if we follow the money, the assault rifle and the school door share a common denominator: private banks and their thirst for municipal bonds in Texas—something the state's Republicans have used to force banks to keep the credit flowing to gun manufacturers.

In chapter 5 we took a bird's-eye view of the municipal bond market and school districts and slowly zoomed in. We saw the negative impact of our collective choice to fund public education using private credit allocation. In this chapter we look at just a few ways the bond market is embedded in and exerts influence upon educational trends we see in the news: school shootings, the new fascism creeping into school board elections, cryptofinance, and federal budget dynamics in the midst of crisis recovery. The spider of private municipal finance is there in all these webs, creating looping flows of resources in and against our values, like the ouroboros that eats its own tail.

According to 2024 figures, three of every ten bonds issued on the municipal bond market have to do with education, just above the capacious category of "general purpose," and double those issued for transportation, utilities, housing, health care, and electricity. This by itself is astounding. When local governments take out loans from Wall Street, they do it mostly for educational purposes. Conversely, to educate, the United States relies heavily on private debt, and more heavily than any other municipal provision.

What does this have to do with the shooting in Uvalde? Here's how it works. So, in principle, if the banks cared about gun control and preventing school shootings, the chance to make money by financing gun companies that profit from selling automatic rifles, like the one used in the shooting, wouldn't tempt them. They'd say to themselves, "We know there's money to be made in Texas municipal bonds, but we want fewer school shootings, so we'll stick to our guns and not do business in guns in Texas or any other state." In fact, some banks did make these kinds of statements after the Parkland school shooting in Florida in 2018. Bank of America said it wouldn't finance Remington if it kept producing assault rifles for sale on the mass market. Jamie Dimon, CEO of JPMorgan, was fond of decrying mass shootings publicly too.[1]

If banks actually did conduct a thorough boycott of the gun industry, it would matter. Even profitable industries need access to bank credit sooner or later—to pay for a new factory or a big supplier expense, or to paper over a bad turn in sales, and so on. If gun companies were locked out of credit sources, they would be forced to cut back on sales or even go out of business entirely. If there were fewer gun sales, there would certainly be fewer shootings on the margin.

This happened to some degree. In 2019, Guns Down America put out a scorecard called "Is Your Bank Loaded?" rating where certain banks stood when it comes to the gun industry. The best bank on the list was Citi, which got a B. While most others got Cs and Fs, it could have been worse, and Citi is one of the biggest banks in the world. If this had been sustained for years, it might have seriously bitten into the gun business.[2]

However, Texas fought back by passing a law in 2021 that blocks banks from doing business with state and local governments if the bank "discriminates" against the gun industry.[3]

Texas is a large state with a large municipal bond market, second only to California's, with around $50 billion worth of municipal bond deals happening there every year. There's a lot of business to be done in Texas, which gets the bankers' mouths watering.

The Texas law favors banks that do business with gun firms—and it worked. Citi, the second-largest municipal bond issuer in the United States, is now ninth in Texas, and still falling. *The New York Times* reported at the time that part of this law requires banks to make official statements declaring that they don't discriminate against guns.[4] Banks had to get on their knees and apologize, kissing the gun industry's ring, to get in good with Texas's municipal bond market.

First, JPMorgan sent a letter saying they do business with gun firms. Then so did Citi, issuing a statement that it did not "have a practice, policy, guidance, or directive that discriminates against a firearm entity or firearm trade association." *The Times* put it plainly: "The stakes are high for big banks. If a bank states that it is in compliance with the law and is found to be otherwise, it could face criminal prosecution. It could also be shut out of the state's giant municipal bond market. . . . Texas generated $315 million in fees last year alone for financial firms."

Texas has thus created a truly appalling set of financial incentives. Just a few years ago, the Uvalde school district spent $69,000 on security upgrades—from a state grant, but no doubt many similar upgrades are financed through bonded debt.[5] The same financial industry that makes money on loan deals for school districts also makes money doing deals for the gun industry. They make money lending to school districts to install security upgrades that manifestly do little or nothing to prevent mass shootings, and then make more money lending to the companies that make AR-15s, the weapon of choice for mass murderers of school children.

It's not just the same money: Since the banks are the common denominator here, these flows of revenue are dependent on each other. If schools didn't need private credit markets for facilities, banks might be considerably more willing to stop financing the gun industry, which after all is not very big. This particular network of banks, industry, and public education couldn't exist. Conversely, if school districts like Uvalde just got public financing for their credit needs, then banks couldn't chase after the profits to be had in Texas school bonds. Given the size of Texas's municipal bond market, and the proportion of bonds that go to education, public credit for public schools might go some way toward neutralizing that law punishing banks for limiting credit to the gun industry. If there weren't so many bond deals in Texas, Citi wouldn't throw its principles away and give up its pursuit of gun control.

If Uvalde didn't need to pay for that door with private credit, the assault rifle company might not have gotten the financing to make and sell the assault rifle to Ramos. But everyone's got to be loaded in the United States, and the shootings keep happening.

In 2022, Central Bucks School District in Pennsylvania made national headlines when it approved a policy that required the superintendent and his designees to review books before school libraries offer them.[6] Pennridge School District was considering an even more authoritarian policy.[7] The purpose of these policies, we should be clear, was to prevent whole communities of children from receiving the nourishing recognition they need to survive and thrive in our society. While venues like the *Bucks County Beacon* and groups of parents and students were speaking out against the book bans, there was a powerful echelon of Bucks County society that was silent: capital.

According to public documents, the Central Bucks School District did a $13.8 million bond deal the previous year.[8] A lot of money changes hands when school districts do deals like this on the municipal bond market. In the most recent bond deal, PFM financial advisers, JPMorgan, and Wells Fargo were banks and financial consultants involved, while Begley, Carlin & Mandio LLP and King, Spry, Herman, Freund & Faul LLC did legal work for it.

In total, the consultants and advisers made $114,204.45 from the deal. Due to the secrecy of private credit markets, we can't know exactly how much JPMorgan and Wells Fargo made by serving as the go-between for the district and its lenders. Nor can we know the names of the wealthy fixed-income investors who stand to make tax-free 5 percent coupon payments in this deal, with interest on this loan totaling around $700,000.

While we tend to think taxpayers are the ones that pay for public schooling, it's actually finance capitalists that provide and circulate the necessary funds up front to finance budgets—taxpayer money just pays these capitalists back for the service. These wealthy elites provide the district with its financial lifeblood. I imagine if JPMorgan, Wells Fargo, PFM, and Begley and King really disagreed with the new fascism in Bucks County, they would have refused to do business with the district. If there were such a capital strike, I also imagine the fascists in the district would think twice about banning books. However, no statement or op-ed or even private communication was known to the public along these lines. I've never heard of a municipal market capitalist protesting a school district's neofascist turn. Will big banks and regional financiers stand for fascism in their midst?

At nearby Pennridge School District, there was a 2022 bond deal that went down for $8.3 million.[9] PNC Capital Markets was the banker here, while Dinsmore and Shohl, LLP were the bond counsels providing legal advice. They made $104,088 on the deal with a $978,000 premium. The whole vignette is a local window into what's happening in school districts all around the country. As Pennridge decided to surveil student communications with an eye toward excluding whole communities of students from our shared social life, did the bankers and lawyers keep taking their money?

I would have hoped not. But it's hard to turn down millions of dollars in fees and tax-free interest payments, even if that money comes from a school district systematically oppressing its own kids. As communities stand up and fight back against this tide of immoral, unethical, and mis-educative educational policy, we should remember this crucial choke point if the region's elites won't stand up and do the right thing.

A Trump tweet inspired blockchain-based mini muni bonds. This sentence isn't something I ever thought I'd find myself writing, but here we are. Apparently, when fascy provocateur Milo Yiannopoulos was deplatformed at UC Berkeley in 2017, Trump threatened the city's federal funding in one of his infamous tweets. The city government got to thinking: Um, maybe we should be looking at alternative sources of revenue.[10]

In 2021, a local politician, city council member Ben Bartlett, was big into crypto and made a proposal: What if the city sold minibonds to our own residents using the blockchain?[11] The blockchain, at least in terms of money, is a bunch of computer code that provides something to trust when you can't trust any of the parties involved in a transaction. This code guarantees the legitimacy and ownership of cryptocurrencies, for instance, giving these currencies their libertarian appearance of unregulated freedom. On a crypto podcast, Bartlett said this proposal was a kind of democratic liberation.[12]

The city of Berkeley said yeah, okay. So they went and did it.[13] Municipal bonds are a key source of revenue for school districts, and even though Sam Bankman-Fried is in jail, the Bored Ape non-fungible token went bust, and Hawk Tuah Girl's HAWK coin was pump-and-dumped, Donald Trump has significant ties to the cryptocurrency markets, so this whole business seems to be here to stay. It might even get more fully integrated into the economy in the coming years. This Berkeley thing portends a new frontier in school finance. So let's take the idea to do crypto muni minibonds apart piece by piece.

What's a minibond? Remember that "buying a bond" means lending a locality money (it can be other governments or firms, but let's just stick with the city for this example). The money you lend to the city comes with a price that the city has to pay: interest. So the city promises to pay you back with interest later, which gets you a certain yield as an investor. The city has an obligation to do this. The municipality is bonded to you because you lent it your money.

It's mostly really rich people who buy municipal bonds, because the minimum amount you have to put in to get in on the deal is so high. You need to pony up at least $5,000 to get in on most muni action. It's worth doing because the interest payments you make when you lend a city money are tax-free and pretty reliable, which is great business for big banks and the ruling class.

The minibond, or microbond, is when a city says, "You know what, we're gonna get rid of that $5,000 minimum. Folks can buy our bonds for $100 if you want to!"[14] The basic idea is to let people get in on bond deals in very small amounts and then get the money back with interest, tax-free. Why not have the people benefiting from the infrastructure also finance it—and benefit from the returns the regime provides?

We should keep in mind that interest rates on bonds are usually somewhere around 4 percent, and yields are usually a little lower, which means that if you put in $100 you might get back something south of $104. So it's not a massive windfall, but the program can and does make a difference. These bonds last for twenty-five years sometimes. Little payments over a long time add up and could mean extra income.

One of the most cited minibond programs started in Denver in the 1990s.[15] Only residents of the state could buy the bonds. In 2014, the city sold $12 million of these bonds in twenty minutes, which was understood as a good thing, indicating the bonds were popular. They could say their city government's financing was coming from Colorado's own people rather than nameless, faceless ruling-class investors. It also meant the interest payments might possibly be going into the bank accounts of more middle-class (even working-class?) people rather than the superrich.

Berkeley's crypto program was like this, except with lasers coming out of its eyes. Instead of relying on banks to record deposits in their ledgers, digital currencies like Bitcoin run on the blockchain. The basic idea behind blockchain is that it's a digital ledger. Rather than being guaranteed by governments and private institutions, the digital currencies are backed up, protected, and made available by decentralized computers. In our current banking system, banks are largely private institutions regulated and backed up by public government in the form of laws, reserves, and protocols, which, in turn, are enforced by the whole repressive state apparatus (police, courts, prisons). Because of this, the libertarian fantasy of blockchain is that the crypto ledger is "independent" of "government" and can thus be truly "free." Fantasy indeed.

Berkeley wanted to sell its low-minimum microbonds using the blockchain, rather than through traditional banks. On that crypto podcast, Bartlett used the language of social justice to justify this project, saying these crypto micro muni bonds are meant to be a "fund for equity." Bartlett talks about families getting micro-returns for decades while funding playgrounds using this micro-bond: "We're solving for poverty and the nation's infrastructure needs." He sounds like Bernie Sanders sometimes, saying "we're creating a slave class" with "how much money gets sucked up to the 1%." Bartlett also argues that you don't need as many consultants, lawyers, banks, and investment firms on the deal since the computers do a lot of this work. This means the bond itself is less expensive because the fees are lower.

On the face of it, the proposal sounds at least interesting and at most promising. Municipal bonds are exclusive and fee-heavy. Everyday people need more income. People need better infrastructure. From a schools perspective, it sounds kind of nice for working-class people to make extra income on the side by putting a bit of money toward their schools. Rather than shrouded in secrecy, public finance becomes more open. Rather than a ruling-class tax haven, public finance becomes redistributive.

But the interview Bartlett gave is almost pure techno-optimism. In the parlance of our times, it's cringe. Right off the bat, it turns out that Bartlett is a crypto lawyer who represents crypto firms. He obviously stands to benefit from this deal no matter what happens. Ew.

And there's so much more that's wrong with this proposal. There was some local pushback.[16] One critique has been accessibility: People don't really know how to do this crypto microbond buying; is it really available for everyone? Indeed, it's complicated. It's hard to imagine a domestic worker taking some time after a long shift, going to a public library, and buying a crypto bond while checking email (without, perhaps, more money and time to do so). Another critique is about the environmental impact of the computing needed for blockchain. Bitcoin's carbon footprint alone is equal to New Zealand's.[17] Both of these critiques were launched at a public comment session in the city.

In financial terms, there's been some sobering research on microbonds. Analyzing Denver's five minibond projects, financial researchers Ely and Martell found in 2016 that the minibonds were actually more expensive to issue than traditional bonds.[18] In terms of cost as a share of the principal, these minibonds cost the city up to 7.8 times more money than traditional bonds. That's not cheaper at all! They observed that minibonds got higher interest rates than traditional bonds too. In general, they found minibonds were on average 21 percent more expensive than traditional bonds.

Okay, so maybe they're more expensive. But at least regular everyday local people were buying them, right? No. In 2007 and 2014, less than 35 percent of purchasers were from Denver. Oh, and the average price people paid was way higher than the small denomination made available. Despite lower denominations ($333 to $500) for minibonds, the average purchase amount exceeded the standard $5,000 municipal bond denomination in four of the five issuances. In 2007 and 2014, minibond purchases averaged $11,506 and $14,118, respectively, suggesting that much of the minibond principal was purchased by relatively large buyers who may be able to access the traditional municipal bond market in other ways.

So even though the denomination was lower, the average amount purchased was above the traditional $5,000 minimum. In the latter cases, it was much higher. At least in Denver, the democratizing dream of microbonds was just that—a dream, not reality. (It could be that the averages are hiding a democratic reality. Maybe there were a ton of small purchases and a few really big ones? But I just don't think that happened.)

I can't imagine the crytpo angle on microbonds helps the exclusivity. If anything, the tech element will make it harder to understand. If Denver is any indication, people who already have access to muni bond markets and/or have an interest in crypto will buy these bonds. As media studies professor David Golumbia argued: Blockchain is garbage.[19] It doesn't do any of the things its advocates say it does, including this democratic promise.

So it's not as democratic as Bartlett says. Will the crypto bond be less expensive? The Denver experience says no, but remember that Denver wasn't doing crypto—just regular bonding. Will the interest rates and fees be lower for a crypto muni bond?

The answer is no one really knows, but probably not. Imagine the patrician, stuffy, and bloated municipal bond market trying to price a crypto municipal microbond. They're not going to say, "By golly, that's innovative and it sure sounds like a good bet that isn't risky at all, we'll rate it high!" Nope. Muni bonds are already punitively rated because public governments are compared to the private sector. A new product on the market will most definitely be viewed as risky, which means a higher interest rate, which means it's more expensive (and ultimately raises taxes!). What interest rate will Berkeley get on this bond?

A distant precedent is when the government of El Salvador issued a government bond in Bitcoin.[20] It was priced at 6.5 percent. *Forbes* notes that there's no real guarantee the rate is reliable. (Another case to look at is in France.[21]) In retrospect these worries were well-founded: Crypto lost billions in value within a few rocky months, and the excitement of those heady days turned into a series of crashes.

The fees part is questionable too. Why would a micro muni bond on the blockchain have lower fees? Berkeley had hired a crypto firm to do the bond deal. I can't imagine the cost of that contract is going to be less than that of typical bond contracts. If anything, there'll be more legal oversight, more consultants necessary, and more labor needed generally to roll out the deal (again, this is something Ely and Martell found in Denver).

The Bond Buyer, a publication that largely represents the interests of bond market participants, was optimistic about the streamlining of muni bond contracts.[22] This feels right: All the information would be in one place, it would be easier to verify tons of information about lenders and borrowers, and there wouldn't be a fragmented cloud of legal languages, styles, and data like there is now. The French government said it reduced the wait time to issue its crypto bond from five days to one day. Okay. But even the efficiency-loving capitalists in *The Bond Buyer* are careful to point out that this will be complex and take a long time to really figure out and scale up. And Golumbia dispatched most of the premises they rely on as garbage. So . . . not democratic, not less expensive, maybe more efficient, not revolutionary.

Ivana Nedyalkova at McGill wrote a master's thesis on urban blockchain projects looking at Berkeley, Denver, and Miami. She's got a good critical take. Crypto municipal finance, like Bartlett's plan in Berkeley, is yet another attempt by capital to automate, alienate, and exploit. There's no real plan for redistribution in the crytpo microbond vision, just a vague promise of democratization. Research like Ely and Martell's supports her reading. She points out that techno-libertarianism has been around for a long time and very little of its dreams have come true.

Generally, Nedyalkova sees the crypto turn in muni finance as a new chapter in the neoliberal story. It might entail some changes, like which lawyers and consultants are the ones advising cities on the deals, but ultimately it's just an addition of a zero in terms of justice. "Under this light, endorsing urban blockchain initiatives seems like less of a political decision than a marketing one. . . . The proliferation of these technologies can only serve to accelerate the dispossessive processes."

Right. Neoliberalism with another code.

You can't dress up the municipal market regime in shiny new clothes and convince us it's a different thing. Even when the federal government tries to help, we see the same disappointment.

In a great paper on state credit enhancement programs by Lang Yang at George Washington University, something about

Pennsylvania caught my eye.[23] Some context: Wang was measuring the impact that state credit enhancement programs have on school district capital spending. Credit enhancement means that the state will "promise to repay district debt when a district cannot do so." When the state has a program that will divert its grants to the school district to cover the district's expenses if something goes to hell with its debt payments, does that make bonds less expensive for the states' districts? Do the districts take out more bonds when the state assures bondholders like that? Do the districts spend more on capital expenditure?

The paper is helpful because it uses a kind of natural experiment. There are twenty-four states with credit enhancement programs. These programs lower interest rate costs by 6 percent and increase capital spending by 7 percent. Small, yeah, but not nothing.

But that's not what caught my eye. In Wang's literature review, she notes that the only time in recent history that a credit enhancement program was actually triggered—these policies are largely there as safety nets; districts rarely actually fall into them—was in Pennsylvania, where I lived for eight years.

This surprised me because I didn't actually think that my former state had any programs for school district capital expenditure. As I described in chapter 3, the reimbursement funds have been closed for years. But Pennsylvania has an intercept program called Act 150, which means that if shit hits the fan in a school district's debt service, then the state will redirect state resources from that district to repay a debt.[24] As one presentation explains, "If a school district fails to pay debt service, state aid payments can be intercepted and used to pay debt service due to bondholders."

Apparently the one time Act 150 was used—which also happens to be the only time any state credit enhancement program has been used in recent history nationwide—was when the state had to step in and cover for the Penn Hills School District in 2015. The story is a great example of how the municipal bond market creates a myopic framework, not unlike Marguerite Roza's article that I talked about in chapter 1. The reporting and narratives swirling around the incidents distort how we think about school district finances. Not only that, the case of Penn Hills and the intercept program also shows the limits of federal interventions that rely on the bond market.

The Bond Buyer covered the story in detail when it all went down.[25] The state auditor, Gene DePasquale was doing an audit and found some apparent shenanigans in Penn Hills, which is fifteen miles east of Pittsburgh in Allegheny County. (As an interesting sidenote, the city is half an hour north of Braddock, where John Fetterman was mayor for many years. This becomes important later.) The big thing that caught DePasquale's attention and ultimately triggered Act 150 was a huge increase in debt the district had to pay back. Debt obligations went from $11 million in 2009 to $167 million in 2015, increasing more than ten times in just five years.

According to *The Bond Buyer*, the subsequent audit claimed that "stunning financial mismanagement and illogical business decisions" got the district super-heavily indebted. *The Bond Buyer* is pro–muni market so it titles its story "Debt Gone Awry," but the story the article tells, and I'm pretty sure the audit itself revealed, doesn't quite add up. Again, the claim is that the district—specifically, its finance officer and secretary Richard Liberto—mismanaged the district's finances so badly that it wasn't able to make debt payments, causing that debt service number to explode, triggering the intercept.

Indeed, DePasquale found some corrupt-looking shit happening in Penn Hills. First off, you probably shouldn't be finance officer and secretary of a school board at the same time. But also Liberto oversaw "$424,000 in . . . credit-card spending [that] included doughnuts for meetings, lunches at local restaurants, sports equipment, hotel rooms for district consultants and even a residential water heater for $358.98. The district issued twenty-four such cards, even though only four people were authorized to use them." Okay, while this sounds bad, some of the spending could be defensible, like take the water heater: it could be, for instance, that the only retailer supplying water heaters was selling residential water heaters, and it was the only one the district could find in time. It's not necessarily corrupt. The article also mentioned $384,500 of lost fuel money due to lack of attention to its transportation contracts and $22,000 of missing revenue from sporting event tickets, along with tons of missing records. Okay, doesn't look great, but again, could be an honest mistake.

But even if these were corrupt expenses, the numbers tell a different story.

The reporting makes the doughnuts and restaurants and water heater seem like a smoking gun. The implication is that the district officials were using money for personal purposes, lining their pockets, and losing huge sums. But this narrative is flimsy when you look at the numbers. The total expenses attributable to the corruption don't even get to $1 million. That can't possibly account for the tenfold increase in debt service responsibility between 2009 and 2015, which gets up into the hundreds of millions. The story there is actually much different than the article lets on. While these little things like the water heater reflect poorly on the financial judgment of Liberto and others if you tell them in a certain light, it's not the whole story behind the debt balloon that triggered Act 150 at all.

The story actually started in 2010. The district needed a new high school and a new elementary school to replace its old buildings. So like any upstanding American school district, they went to the municipal bond market and sold themselves as a commodity investment for ruling-class bond investors to borrow $130 million for the new schools. It was a lot of money.

Apparently, the architect consulting on the building project recommended that to afford his plans, the district would have to consolidate three elementary schools into one, increase taxes on its residents, and reduce staff throughout the district. In other words, they had to close buildings, fire people, and ask their residents for more money. Rents would increase. Property taxes would increase. People would lose their jobs. This was going to be bad for the people of Penn Hills. The district leadership didn't do this. They kept the buildings open and didn't fire people. This prompted DePasquale in the audit to say that the architect gave better business advice than the district's business manager, but is that really what's happening here?

Come on, everyone, helping people out and keeping schools open isn't bad advice! It's just bad business advice in capitalism, where profits and the bottom line trump everything else, which, for public education whose bottom line is educating everybody, makes things worse. Schools shouldn't be treated like this, but I suppose it was very de rigueur then to be unquestioningly neoliberal about everything. Besides an austerity narrative tainting this account of what happened in Penn Hills, there's more.

I wanted a little more info, so I went to the bond itself.[26] Yes, Penn Hills sold a series of big bonds in 2009–2010. At first, I was wondering if they, like Philadelphia and districts around the country, had gone in for some yahoo go-go bonds that were all the rage in the 2000s and crashed big and hard during the 2008 crisis, which I mentioned in chapter 5. Penn Hills didn't do that exactly, but there is a crisis story here that sheds light on their thinking, and a dynamic that's formed around the federal government and municipal bonds.

The lion's share of this $130 million bond—$104 million, in fact—was sold as part of the Build America Bonds program created by the Obama administration's response to the 2008 financial crisis.[27] It was a milquetoast tax credit program that I mentioned in a previous chapter as well, whose provisions reimbursed localities like school districts for 35 percent of interest payments on bonds issued under the program. It's right there in the bond document.

So the Penn Hills people were thinking, let's take advantage of this federal program to build our schools. Federal support is largely absent when it comes to school buildings, so maybe they thought: Let's go big. The recovery program will cover more than a third of our interest payments. Maybe we don't have to fire people and close schools. That's what the recovery package is all about, right?

In principle, yes. In practice, the U.S. federal government was in the process of lurching to the far right. The Build America Bonds program was torpedoed by libertarians when the Freedom Caucus was born and discovered it could use an arcane policy called the debt ceiling to bully moderate Democrats into giving up modest social programs.

Remember that Obama came into his first term controlling both houses of Congress. Democrats passed tepid response packages in the wake of the 2008 financial crisis, including the American Recovery and Reinvestment Act. In 2010, the Freedom Caucus emerged out of wild right-wing fantasies and protests, eventually getting Koch funding to elect a bevy of congresspeople who came to Washington, DC, raving, looking to take no prisoners. They consolidated into the caucus and rode the frenzied libertarian wave to power in Congress, financed by people like the Kochs who thought Obama was the second coming of FDR and Lenin simultaneously and that after the 2008 crisis, the moment was some kind of historical Frankenstein of 1917 and 1930.

These libertarians combined a colonial bloodlust with fiscal and parliamentarian expertise to fight tooth and nail on behalf of the capitalist ruling class instead of the diverse working class. One thing that makes 2008 different from 1917 was nearly a century of ruling-class consolidation of power. But in their fury, one of the new conservatives' moves was to take the debt ceiling hostage and make sure there wasn't any socialist revolution, or, at least, that the first Black president couldn't have success with a moderate program. What was once a procedural vote that no one really cared about became a life-or-death threat for the United States' credit rating and thus the world's economy, only two short years since the worst economic crisis we had seen since 1929. Right-wingers played this game in the 2010–2011 budget negotiations for the first time, winning a significant weakening (through a process called sequestration) of some of the programs in the federal relief, including Build America Bonds.

As part of my attempts to understand school finance, specifically for facilities, I've had a bunch of off-the-record conversations with school district finance officials. A couple of years ago, while I was trying to see whether the Federal Reserve's pandemic-era Municipal Liquidity Facility would or could lend to school districts—and whether school districts would or could borrow from the Federal Reserve (which I talk more about in chapter 7)—a district official said something jarring.

He told me that he prefers the private credit markets for municipal bonds to federal financing programs when it comes to school finance. He trusted the market more than the government because, he said, the government could change its approaches to its programs in volatile ways, making it hard to rely on for fiscal planning. I asked him what he was thinking of specifically and he mentioned Build America Bonds but didn't explain. I noted it down, tried to find some histories or analyses of the program, couldn't find much, and lost track of it for a while.

Then I was researching the story of how the country's only state intercept program got triggered in Penn Hills School District, Pennsylvania, in 2015, and lo and behold Build America Bonds were a main character. What the district official told me made sense. Penn Hills—far from being a corrupt and wasteful school district, as the state government and *The Bond Buyer* had portrayed them—had made the mistake of . . . relying on a legal, available, and valid federal program meant specifically for this purpose, the Build America Bonds program, for their new elementary and high school construction projects.

They were just taking advantage of a public program, which ultra-capitalists in Congress, most likely with support from the good people at *The Bond Buyer*, blew up in the sequestration fight. And wasn't it go-go capitalists who blew up the secondary markets for mortgages that created the 2008 crisis in the first place? It's the capitalists who are corrupt in this situation, not the public school district. Public borrowers like the University of California are actually using this logic in court, suing for relief on Build America Bonds payments on the grounds that their being taken during the debt ceiling fight qualifies as an extreme circumstance.[28] Some, like Maryland's public transportation system, are actually winning.

Ultimately, DePasquale's audit concluded that the Penn Hills district didn't "budget properly" to cover the resulting debt payments. Their inability to cover those payments was supposedly their fault, but they'd been relying on the Build America Bonds program to cover a third of them! The audit tried to make it look like they were making bad business decisions, but all those little accusations about the water heater and gas bills and doughnuts, even if true, pale in comparison to the debt the district incurred from relying on Build America Bonds. How were they supposed to know that the Freedom Caucus would hold the debt ceiling hostage and sequester those payments?

Zooming out and looking at this district's political-economic history also favors this interpretation. We know that the Pittsburgh area heavily deindustrialized in the 1980s. Between 1970 and 2010, Penn Hills lost a third of its population. It was the steel industry that kept the whole area afloat. After that industry collapsed, property values sank. Indeed, it was a wolf that came for Pittsburgh like John Hoerr's book said, characterizing deindustrialization as a dangerous creature that hunted and killed regions like Penn Hills.

Senator John Fetterman staked his national political career on being a champion of downtrodden towns hit by this overwhelming social force of deindustrialization. He was mayor of a place near Penn Hills, Braddock, which had to deal with the same issues. He's clear evidence that this trend is politically meaningful. Not to mention that the Commonwealth of Pennsylvania has failed its school districts time and again over the last several decades. Remember PlanCon had been cut by Corbett in 2008, so there was no state money for facilities. And also remember that the Pennsylvania Supreme Court found in 2023 that the government had been out of compliance with its constitutional obligation to properly fund schools. The districts have been left in the dust and, this Penn Hills story shows, blamed for their situation.

Maybe Penn Hills would have been able to pay their loans if the deindustrialization hadn't been so severe; if the federal response to the 2008 crisis had been more generous; if confused libertarian billionaires hadn't seen the ghosts of Lenin and smothered the meager programs that were put into place to help public programs by a centrist technocrat who happened to be Black; and if state government did more to take care of school districts and their facilities needs in the wake of the crisis, like funding PlanCon and following its own constitution. Penn Hills' debt balloon can't just be explained by corrupt mismanagement; there are structural features of the situation, centering on school bonds, that account for the astronomical debt in which it found itself.

But that's what the municipal bond market does to people's brains and material conditions. It exerts this individualizing, market-oriented, rapaciously capitalist force that casts a kind of shadow over everything, making it look like Penn Hills did something wrong, when in fact it was the victim of these larger structural circumstances. Certainly, if all those conditions I just listed were true, then maybe Penn Hills wouldn't have been blamed. But what about all the other school districts throughout the country that have to deal with the plague of the municipal bond market? What about the banks that keep making their money financing school bonds and gun companies? What about the financiers who keep working with fascist school boards? What about the crypto bros who try to cover this all up in their false techno-optimism? They're all still around, weaving this nightmare ouroboros policy sapping the energies of public schools everywhere.

What we need is an entirely different kind of policy.

7
Constructive Politics

In 2020, when I started the newsletter that would eventually become this book, I was helping organize a campaign in Philadelphia that I thought could change school finance for the better. It was a turbulent and transformative time, with schools and everything else closing to protect people from the novel coronavirus, while policymakers were creating unprecedented possibilities for how schools might be financed.

Under the bond market regime, for the past thirty years, Philly's school district had spent $3.65 billion on interest and fees rather than on its buildings, whose poor ventilation systems were becoming centers for spreading disease. When my partner and I were living there, our local elementary school needed at least $100,000 for its out-of-date ventilation system. In the pandemic, how could students at this school—almost 100 percent African American and working-class, in our neighborhood of West Philly—enter this building without intense risk of infection?

Cash rules everything around this problem. If there was money to fix the schools' infrastructure, then schools would be safer. If there was money, the public system could pay for needed updates.

If there was money, the school district could even hire thousands of people to fix the dilapidated infrastructure. But there wasn't money, for all the reasons I've talked about in this book. Philly's property taxes just hadn't been enough to meet the need, and the state had historically underfunded the district (proved legally in the state supreme court case in 2023).

But then something sort of magical happened, at least in terms of school bond finance. In this final chapter of the part on bonds, I go through policies and organizing campaigns that I think we should fight for, which together form what I call constructive politics: the grassroots organizing around the Federal Reserve's Municipal Liquidity Facility, socialist state senator Nikil Saval's Whole-Home Repairs Act, the Inflation Reduction Act, the national investment authority, and the Green New Deal for Public Schools.

As the pandemic hit the United States and it became clear that mass shutdowns were necessary to protect the population, the Federal Reserve Bank of the United States (the Fed) leapt into action. Having learned from the slow recovery of the 2008 financial crisis, the approach under Chairman Jerome Powell was to do as much as possible as fast as possible, creating an alphabet soup of public programs to protect the economy from going under. One part of its suite of rescue programs was to create lending facilities: special programs to provide various kinds of credit opportunities through the federal government.

In crises, the markets for loans on which public and private entities' budgets depend can crash as potential lenders, scared of the uncertainty, pull their investments. Runs on credit markets spell doom for whole sectors of the economy, including public entities like school districts. So the Fed, within the purview of section 13(3) of its charter, created special-purpose vehicles to provide credit if and when it became necessary.[1]

These vehicles took the form of facilities that could issue loans through specific Federal Reserve districts, thus providing liquidity support to private and public entities. Lines of credit came directly through the government, rather than the private markets, which were in danger of crashing. Along with corporate lending facilities for big business, and a main street lending facility for small businesses, for the first time, the Fed created a facility to provide liquidity to local governments: the Municipal Liquidity Facility. The new facility's stated goal was to "help state and local governments better manage cash flow pressures in order to continue to serve households and businesses in their communities."[2]

Two main views emerged on the Municipal Liquidity Facility: a conservative view and a progressive view, manifested dramatically at the oversight hearings checking in on its progress, perhaps most vividly at the congressional oversight committee meeting on September 17, 2020.[3] The conservative view, best represented by Senator Pat Toomey of Pennsylvania, understood municipal liquidity to mean backstopping private municipal markets. Providing a backstop in this case meant preventing a run on the municipal bond market, ensuring local and state governments could still sell bonds there. The facility in this case is a safety net for the markets. This view is all Wall Street: The existing markets for municipal credit, and the lenders who stood to gain from them, were the top priority.

The progressive view, represented best by Bharat Ramamurti, held a starkly different perspective on each of these issues. Rather than a backstop for existing private credit markets, the progressive view of municipal liquidity was the provision of support to local and state governments in the form of direct lending. Progressives noted that providing this support was in the Fed's mandate and was much needed in the pandemic crisis. Indeed, rather than succeeding in its stated goal, progressives claimed that the Municipal Liquidity Facility was failing to enact its mission. Ramamurti pointed to whole sectors of the economy threatened by the shutdown, leading to decreased tax revenues.

Rather than end the program, the progressive demand was to ramp it up, lower the interest rates, and extend the limits on repayment. They saw the facility as a public option for public finance; others on the left understood it as a way to "cancel Wall Street."[4] It would cancel Wall Street because the Federal Reserve, through its public program, would create a public alternative to the municipal bond market regime for school districts and other governments.

As progressives noted at the hearing, there was precedent for the Fed shifting the terms and conditions of Municipal Liquidity Facility's loans. Several months into the program's existence, the Fed dropped the basis points for their Municipal Liquidity Facility interest rate scale by fifty to fit New York's Metropolitan Transportation Authority's needs (it was one of the first and only entities to take advantage of the program, along with the State of Illinois). This contingent space of possibility created an opening for political pressure. Nothing like that program had ever existed before. In this country, we treat municipal governments like businesses and make them compete in markets for the credit they need to maintain their infrastructure. It's always about preserving the profit motive. Like with health insurance, a public option for municipal liquidity had never been available. Until that moment.

In other words, the Federal Reserve was making extraordinary decisions in that extraordinary crisis. Nobody in finance or economics could quite believe it. The modern monetary theorists, who have known for decades that the Fed could create programs that provide public credit for public programs, were jumping for joy, yelling "I told you so!" at every opportunity: The federal government, with its Treasury and vast reserves, could always lend directly to the people at whatever rate it decided.

Those of us working on this area wondered: Could school districts apply for support from the Municipal Liquidity Facility? The loans, potentially at no cost and due whenever the Fed agreed, could go to infrastructure improvements during the shutdown. A new school finance imaginary formed: Flush with the Fed's extraordinary lending support, school districts could take this opportunity to hire unionized trade workers to fix up schools, using green technologies to lower the amount of carbon the buildings put into the atmosphere. Philadelphia's school ventilation systems, for example, could be one urgent project given the relationship between the virus and air circulation. Plus, having good air to breathe in classrooms is correlated with all kinds of improved learning outcomes.

Drawing from the outpouring of Black Lives Matter organizing in the moment, we thought: Let kids breathe! Fix the ventilation! Use the Federal Reserve's new special-purpose vehicles to finance it! It was a new era.[5]

I imagined what would happen in school districts, particularly urban and rural districts, if there was a flurry of employment, improvement, and progress around school buildings. It would be exciting. Public schools could be places of positivity, progress, and hope. Trade unions in the city receive contracts for work and start hiring more workers, normalizing green infrastructure and development. The workers would arrive at the school and start hauling out the decrepit ducts and dusty fans and asbestos-ridden walls and floors, and replace them. New conductive windows that gathered solar energy like a solar panel would replace the old ones that wouldn't even open. It would be a Green New Deal.

Community leaders and elected officials would set up parties to watch the progress and cheer the process. Parents, teachers, students, and community members would feel a sense of pride. Excitement would build to go back to school once we got the pandemic under control. Given the right messaging campaign, public schools could become dots of light in a dark time. Might the same logics of austerity, failure, and destruction weaken in this shining hope?

Would charter schools be able to sell their snake oil? Would advocates of private school tax credits and "scholarships" to encourage segregationist-theocratic-capitalist school choice schemes hold as much sway? Maybe not.

We worked for that green dream, and things happened.

I was with a socialist group called LILAC, which in turn worked with the Action Center on Race and the Economy as a coalition partner (and we were both members of a larger coalition, Our City Our Schools). We did political education and a pressure campaign where we emailed Philly Fed president Patrick Harker and board member John Frey to demand that they support those two proposals: Open the eligibility criteria for the Municipal Liquidity Facility to school districts, and make those criteria generous. Our slogan was Cancel Wall Street.[6]

Applying to the Municipal Liquidity Facility for loans could be a political act. It meant engaging in a practice that stretches our imaginations when it comes to municipal finance.

But it wasn't to be. As part of a deal with Democrats, Pat Toomey forced the Fed's programs closed and tried to salt the earth so nothing like them could ever grow again. Toomey said the deal achieved his four goals: to sweep out $429 billion in unused CARES Act funds allocated for Fed lending and repurpose the money, to shut down the four lending facilities, to forbid the reopening of those facilities, and to ban future clones of the program.

It was unequivocal: The facilities were shut down on December 31, 2020. Toomey dismissed the progressive interpretation of the Municipal Liquidity Facility: "These facilities were put in place for a specific purpose. The purpose was to restore the normal functioning of the private lending and capital markets, not as a general all-purpose salve, fix-all for the economy," he said. The thing is, we still need something new and different. The private lending markets aren't doing what they need to do about school infrastructure.

But Toomey didn't get a complete win. The sticking point in the negotiations, apparently, was Toomey's demand to ban programs "similar" to the current facilities. Democrats pushed him back to "clones," meaning that in principle the Fed could do something similar if needed. The Democrats' won the ability to set something similar up if the need arises. But the language in this bill means there would at least be a debate about the Fed's legal authority to do something like this again under section 13(3) of the Federal Reserve Act.

Another silver lining in all this is that one of the chief proponents of the progressive interpretation of the Municipal Liquidity Facility was Bharat Ramamurti, who became an economic adviser in the Biden administration, which would go on to entertain a Green New Deal for Public Schools and ultimately pass the Inflation Reduction Act, which contained echoes of the dream we all dreamed with the Municipal Liquidity Facility. As Toomey went crawling back to some expensive private sector hole, we kept imagining and organizing.

To use Eve Weinbaum's term, the organizing we'd done was a successful failure. Those organizing energies for a new political economy of school finance, at least in Philly, manifested in the Safe Air Campaign of the Philly Democratic Socialists of America (DSA). As this campaign got off the ground in Philadelphia, a sort of economic awakening occurred, and new ideas about public finance started getting more popular, getting more airtime, and even in certain cases taking root. In this last chapter of part 2, I describe these policies and the movements around them as a kind of constructive politics, examples of what can be done to fight the excesses of the municipal bond market in public education as climate catastrophe threatens to upend the future for which schools are supposed to prepare students.

Lizzie Rothwell is an architect, parent, and organizer in Philadelphia. During the fracas around whether schools should open during the waves of COVID variants in early 2022, she got involved with a citizen science campaign that became popular across America. Parents worked with their children to put carbon dioxide monitors in kids' backpacks, measuring the airflow in classrooms. Low CO_2 levels mean fresh air turnover, indicating that the virus would be less likely to hang around.

Meanwhile, the Philadelphia chapter of the DSA had been engaged in the national fight for a Green New Deal for Public Schools, with a recent legislative push starting in 2021. A report put together by the Climate & Community Institute had proposed a spending program to build and staff green school buildings. The legislation was introduced by Congressman Jamaal Bowman during the Build Back Better budget reconciliation process in 2021.[7] I was involved with the research and organizing around this legislation, helping write certain sections of the report that led to it. I was also involved in Philly DSA's education justice committee.

I first met Rothwell while organizing for education justice in Philadelphia. We talked about her and her son Luke's work measuring carbon dioxide in the city's schools, and how we could work together. Then she and Luke were profiled in *The New York Times* along with parents in other cities.[8] As the piece was in production, we wanted to scale up the project by securing more monitors, to connect with parents and teachers around the district concerned about school facilities, and ultimately to include the tactic as part of our Green New Deal for Public Schools organizing. What better way to make the case for transformative green school modernization than by exposing the lack of airflow in classrooms?

We also wanted to use the tactic to push for short-term and medium-term demands being made in the city's left coalitions around school safety and funding: Parents pushing for outdoor lunches at schools and the progressive revenue-organizing group Tax the Rich PHL were pushing for a wealth tax at the city level that could get more funding for the district's capital program.[9]

The Safe Air campaign took off. Philly DSA used member funds to purchase five more monitors from Aranet, and we distributed these to parents in our organizing networks. DSA members created a website that crunched the data coming in from those monitors and presented the measurements for each school.

The Times article came out, and the campaign kept rolling. Aranet reached out to Rothwell and donated five more monitors, which we distributed to more parents. We also started reaching out to teachers organizing at the building level. DSA organizers, following the creative thinking about ventilation during the pandemic happening around the country, came up with a novel tactic: Fundraise more to build do-it-yourself air purifiers called Corsi-Rosenthal boxes. These boxes combine air filters with box fans in a cube design to turn over the air in a room with high efficacy, and at only $75 a box, were fairly affordable.[10]

At first, we built these DIY purifiers at events where socialists and community members came and helped out. Then the campaign shifted to organizing box-build events at schools themselves, gathering parents, students, and teachers to build the boxes together and then put them in classrooms throughout the building.[11] These events featured in-depth conversations about school finance and its impact on student and teacher health. After doing builds at several schools, the campaign mobilized the attendees to go to a school board meeting and demand the district provide better air filtration, as part of a larger educational campaign to inform the community about the Green New Deal for Public Schools. A vote on the demand didn't pass, but it was close, and the Safe Air campaign continues today, having built one hundred box filters at twelve schools in Philadelphia.[12]

The communist educational theorist Derek R. Ford has written that air is a social relation, bound up with the built environment around us and the structural injustices inherent in it: "The air envelopes us and binds us together; it is a necessary condition for being and relating. And yet it is difficult to grasp. It is often only when something is 'wrong' with the air that we take notice. The technologies of controlling the air's quality, temperature, humidity, and flow conspire in an effort to make the air unnoticeable. But these technologies themselves act in unforeseen ways on air, lives, bodies, and social relations."[13] Our organizing to measure CO_2 in Philadelphia school buildings made this plain, creating a fun and engaging way to call for transformative financial policies to handle Philadelphia's school buildings and crumbling buildings nationwide. Federal legislators, we said, could pass the Green New Deal for Public Schools Act. They could create a government-sponsored entity to intervene in municipal bond markets, or better yet a national investment authority for public infrastructure like school buildings.[14]

In this interregnum where the old is dying and the new struggles to be born, the Safe Air campaign points to a kind of generative socialist organizing. Working in the trenches, particularly connecting school ventilation to the wider class struggle, is the kind of slow, grinding, hyperlocal work that over time builds trust and capacity and contributes to maneuvers on key terrains.

As one example, after a Twitter thread about it went somewhat viral, a handful of local parent organizers, scientists, and students reached out to us to get involved in the campaign. Two teachers at another school got interested in measuring the CO_2 in classrooms with their students. Then Rothwell and I were interviewed on Philadelphia's WURD radio about what happened to the students and our organizing around it, where we connected these struggles to Paul Prescod's insurgent DSA-backed campaign for Pennsylvania state senate.[15] Amid and between electoral cycles, where socialists vie for footholds in state apparatuses, campaigns like the Safe Air campaign show us why we can't and shouldn't be disheartened, that something is indeed in the air.

Something unexpected happened in Pennsylvania politics. A leftist state senator got bipartisan support from archconservatives in one of the most ideologically divided states in the country. Though the breakthrough didn't happen in the arena of education policy, I think the story tells us what defenders of public education can and should do in the face of so much destructive rhetoric and policy coming from the right.

Indeed, construction is a perfect issue to outshine the right—and that's where the story from Pennsylvania comes in.

In July 2022, the Whole-Home Repairs Act passed in the commonwealth's General Assembly. The program, which received $125 million in state funding over the term of the 2022 state budget, provided public resources to rebuild and fix up housing throughout the state.[16] The politics of the act's passage were remarkable. The legislation came out of socialist state senator Nikil Saval's office. (Full disclosure: I helped write Saval's school-funding platform and voted for him.) But Democrats had only a tenuous hold on state power in Pennsylvania, so how did Saval and his team do it? They were able to garner support from several top-ranking Republicans by focusing on the crumbling housing infrastructure in their districts.

For example, GOP state senator David Argall represented State Senate District 29. Argall was the head of the powerful Government Committee and very conservative. Yet blight had been a key issue for him. "You're going to see blight in any town in Pennsylvania that has faced economic difficulty," he said. "It doesn't matter whether it's big or small. If the coal mine closed, if the steel mill closed, if the major, important employer left town, that town is going to have some challenges."[17] Saval and his team knew that home repairs would be a constructive issue that would resonate with people who aren't supposed to agree with him on anything else. So Argall, along with other influential Republicans, got behind it, and the policy passed. I think this same kind of constructive politics could work in public education.

Could we change the terrain of this fight over education by focusing on fixing up and rebuilding all kids' school buildings, across geographic, racial, economic, and cultural divides? In the same way that passing infrastructure legislation, industrial policy, and the climate agenda at the federal level gave Democrats something to fight for and fight on in the early 2020s, perhaps we can develop innovative yet concrete ways to shore up the popular cause of public education infrastructure.

The school-building blight is everywhere, including in Argall's district. Remember the teacher who could see the sky in her elementary school in Panther Valley? That was Argall's region. The wheelchair ramp at Panther Valley Elementary was so cracked it couldn't be used, but there wasn't enough money to buy concrete and repave it. Years after Pennsylvania's school-funding lawsuit was filed, all these things still needed to be fixed.[18]

What's the lesson here? In short, it's that the same constructive politics that passed the Whole-Home Repairs Act could work in public education. School buildings across the country need help, whether their districts are urban or rural or the voters in them are liberal or conservative. Building our schools back better represents a unifying and concrete battery of improvements that could undercut the acid of the right-wing's efforts to foment racial and gendered hate at the local, state, and federal levels.

School buildings sit at the nexus of every level of American government. We know that constructive politics can work at the local and state levels, as the political alignment behind the Whole-Home Repairs Act makes plain. And at the national level, there are several encouraging trends that make the issue look even better. Far from coincidentally, infrastructure was a cornerstone of the national Democratic strategy early in Joe Biden's presidency. From the bipartisan infrastructure bill to the Inflation Reduction Act, in the first half of Biden's term, Democrats created a solid footing and a proven legislative track record to back up their promises to improve our civic infrastructure.

★ ★ ★

Victoria Kaplan, a friend who's been doing work at the intersection of organizing, school finance, and climate change, sent me a recording of a panel that she'd organized with People's Action on green schools. It was awesome. One of the reasons it's so great is that it features organizers talking about the strategies, tactics, and tensions they're encountering as they work for a Green New Deal for Public Schools in the post–Inflation Reduction Act (IRA) era.

In St. Paul, Minnesota, a group called TakeAction Minnesota, along with the St. Paul federation of educators, led a Healthy Green Schools Campaign. They wanted to get Inflation Reduction Act demands into the teachers' contract negotiation process, a kind of bargaining-for-the-common-good approach, but that didn't work. The district did agree, however, to create a climate justice stakeholder work group, so their organizing continues there.[19]

Progressive Leadership Alliance of Nevada had an IRA campaign coordinator working for solarization of Clark County schools. The goal, they said, was to save money on utilities each year and put that money into maintenance as heat waves slam the region. These savings projections were compelling enough to the district officials in Clark County that they were open to making these changes, even though they didn't necessarily believe in climate change.[20]

In El Paso, Texas, there was a campaign called Escuelas Frescas through the Amanecer People's Project. They canvassed people in El Paso about issues with schools and it turns out many schools didn't have adequate HVAC. For a campaign on that issue, organizers talked to parents about these facilities issues when they picked up their kids from school. They call it a pickup lines tactic, which is smart. They got contact information from those conversations to do turnout for a school board meeting and demand IRA funding for fixes.[21]

ONE Northside in Chicago, Illinois, had a Green Schools for Chicago campaign to create decarbonization centers in city schools. They're pointing to $14 billion needed to rectify environmental injustices. They had mayoral support, a movable school board, and a big school board election coming that the left had a candidate in. Like organizers in St. Paul, this group worked with the Chicago Teachers Union to bargain for green school facilities updates using Inflation Reduction Act and Bipartisan Infrastructure bill money.[22]

In Milwaukee, Citizen Action Wisconsin had a campaign to secure funding for green facilities updates to specific schools. They had very specific numbers: $30 million in federal grants, a ten-year climate-mitigation plan with $20 million in rebate tax credits projected. They were also calling for a revolving green fund that reinvests savings into other planned projects. Their organizer said that they're "doing this because our schools are under attack," which is exactly the framing I think we should use.[23]

While some who follow climate finance politics in the United States said that the IRA was anti-populist, and I think that's largely right, we have here examples of movement groups navigating that law, which can ultimately benefit the working class. This tension does show up in some reflections the presenters mention that are worth considering.

UnDauntedK12, a nonprofit advocacy organization working to decarbonize school infrastructure, found more than four hundred public school projects across thirty-seven states that could benefit or were benefiting from Inflation Reduction Act funding programs. On their website, they featured a ribbon-cutting ceremony for Greenbriar County Schools in West Virginia, which opened the state's largest solar array in October 2024, along with a ground-source heat pump. The federal program provided $2 million for the project and the district will save more money in the long term for efficiencies, while putting less carbon into the atmosphere.[24] They pointed to $10 million for ground-source heat pumps in Loudoun County, Virginia, schools; money for a tornado-damaged elementary school in Upper Dublin, Pennsylvania; $3.8 million for a net-zero school in Menasha Joint School District in Wisconsin; and on and on.

Between the People's Action campaigns and UnDauntedK12's work tracking districts' usage of Inflation Reduction Act programs, we saw glimmers of that green dream, what I call in the conclusion a new political economy of public education, under the auspices of what's been called Bidenomics.[25] The elective pay tax credit program and green banks were challenges to the municipal bond market regime, cushioning the cost for districts and even changing the types of players in the drama of municipal finance. A report from Aspen Institute's education arm noted thirteen policies in the Inflation Reduction Act that school districts could benefit from, of which the elective pay investment tax credit and Greenhouse Gas Reduction Fund stood out for their novelty.[26]

The tax credit has been likened to a mail-in rebate for green investment and production; it provided public schools up to 60 percent reimbursement for qualifying projects. Due to its tax credit structure, the program could provide trillions in such reimbursements, while other IRA programs open to schools are more limited in amount. Likewise, the Greenhouse Gas Reduction Fund has been called the country's first green bank, with the potential to restructure credit flows for infrastructure projects and open up new avenues for financing.[27]

But like Italian theorist Antonio Gramsci said, having an optimism of the will should come with a pessimism of the intellect. Many were critical of the old structures out of which this new arrangement was born. Chief among them was economist Daniela Gabor, who argued that most of the Inflation Reduction Act (and other policies in Bidenomics like the CHIPS Act and the Bipartisan Infrastructure bill) were part of what she calls the Wall Street consensus because they merely de-risk green investment by private financiers, making green development more attractive to big investors.[28]

Rather than challenging big green finance with a big green state, the de-risking green state makes it easier for big finance to go green if it wants to. The same goes for fossil fuel production and consumption. There are no disincentives to petroleum corporations; in fact, fossil fuel production and consumption have increased since this supposed new green industrial policy. This all points to Brett Christophers's argument that private markets and commodification will never solve the problem of greenhouse gas emissions.[29]

As Gabor and colleagues have put it recently, there are carrots in these programs, but no sticks.[30] When we look at specific school projects, the reality is somewhere in between. Consider the case of Buckley Elementary School in Manchester, Connecticut, the state's first net-zero school.[31] While this school didn't receive Inflation Reduction Act money, a critical look at the political economy of the project reveals the complexity of the new green dream.

A predominantly white and high-income suburb of New Haven, Manchester hired CMTA, a company that specializes in net-zero renovations, to do the work on Buckley. This is the same company that UnDauntedK12 mentioned in the Greenbriar County Schools case. The project included solar arrays, weatherization, and geothermal heating and cooling. Manchester Schools' director of communication, Jim Farrell, documented the details of the Buckley net-zero project as it happened, along with other facilities projects in the district.[32] Farrell tells of Gene DeJoannis, a retired engineer and environmentalist who had been a central force advocating for net-zero emissions in the district's school buildings. DeJoannis stated the case very clearly: "Schools last a long time, so the extra care we take now will pay dividends for many years." Farrell reported that town officials have had to bump up costs by 5 percent, or $3.8 million, to reach net-zero targets.

Local taxpayers were responsible for $47 million of the total cost after state reimbursement and other factors. Part of that reimbursement came from the state's energy utility, and the Connecticut Office of School Construction Grant and Review process reimbursed the town for two-thirds of the cost of the project. I imagine the tax credit and other Inflation Reduction Act programs would support these reimbursements, offering financing for local and state programs so that other districts could follow suit.

But many of these reimbursements would flow to CMTA, part of the Legence network of "sustainable builders"—private construction and maintenance companies branded more green than not.[33] Legence is a company within Blackstone's portfolio, and if Manchester's Buckley project were an IRA project, CMTA-Legence-Blackstone could benefit from tax credit reimbursements.[34] There's Gabor's de-risking Wall Street consensus in action. If the green bank was involved, however, it could represent a challenge to that consensus by negotiating lower fees or interest rate structures for the school district.

Connecticut founded the county's first Green Bank in 2015, the institution was a small part of the Buckley project from what I could tell. Farrell mentions that "in yet another sustainability initiative, the town is working with partners including Connecticut Green Bank to install photovoltaic panels atop nine buildings (including seven schools) at no cost to the community, but bringing an estimated $3 million in energy savings over 20 years." Yet Manchester still had to engage with the municipal bond market to finance this project.

In 2016, a city referendum, a result of a local initiative called "School Modernization and Reinvestment Team Revisited" in 2012, led the city to sell $93 million in bonds. Manchester decided to borrow each year in $15 million increments for these and related municipal projects. Each time the city borrows from the municipal bond market it faces fees and interest. Manchester banks with FHN Financial Capital Markets and consults with Shipman & Goodwin as bond counsel, in addition to paying for credit ratings. Manchester and other municipalities would save millions if the national green bank capitalized Connecticut's historic green bank and got it more involved, which could secure lower fees and interest rates, but it's not clear if, when, or how such a collaboration might work.

Going back to the People's Action campaigns, you can see this complexity. There's an interesting moment when the El Paso organizer is talking in the video about financing, specifically how the group messaged the complex machinations of the funding available for green school infrastructure. They mention that, because the IRA works through rebates, the initial financing in El Paso will have to be through bonds. The organizer says this required building trust with parents, since it can mean increases in taxes that they'll have to pay, and ultimately more money to Wall Street.

Another wrinkle I noticed is when the Chicago organizer talked about how the state's green bank is controlled by the Illinois Finance Authority, which they say is governed by 40 percent corporate interests, while the rest are noncommunity NGOs and other government actors. This might be a hindrance since, even though it's a public investment body, it might not be serving the public's best interest—or at least not if the public is understood as the diverse working class—since it doesn't have representation in its leadership. But the organizer mentioned that the Coalition for Green Capital is proposing to route federal money from the IRA to another entity to get around the Illinois Finance Authority.

As always, one has to contend with the ruling class when fighting for diverse working-class goals like a Green New Deal for Public Schools, which takes up and takes on thoroughly ruling-class institutions like the municipal bond market and various carbon-emitting industries. These two wrinkles are examples of the possibilities and limitations of the IRA for school districts, viz. the ruling class and their institutions as obstacles. The IRA's tax credit policy is a rebate system that reimburses districts for infrastructure expenses, which relies on municipal bonding. Remember that the Green New Deal for Public Schools legislation introduced by Jamaal Bowman in 2022 provided more than $1 trillion in grants, disbursed through the Title IA system, which could have challenged this reliance. The IRA doesn't.

The green banking aspect of the IRA is one of the more powerful challenges to the municipal bond market in the legislation. Yet if the green banks that the Greenhouse Gas Reduction Fund capitalizes are captured by groups that don't represent diverse working-class interests, then this challenge to the bond market may not challenge the ruling class. And recently, the new Environmental Protection Agency under the second Trump administration is trying to claw back that green bank money through the courts.

In the debates around Bidenomics, there were two promising proposals—ultimately blocked—that had the potential to unlock a greater transformation in public infrastructure: a Green New Deal for Public Schools and a national investment authority. The Inflation Reduction Act programs could be considered vestiges of these more muscular approaches, and they are perhaps the best opportunity to clean and green public schools while taking on the municipal bond market regime. They offer a more expansive vision of green industrial policy for economic and social justice, with the potential to directly confront the challenges of a fragmented and segregated schooling system. And you know it's a good policy when conservatives start calling its proponents communist.

It sounded like a 1950s red scare moment, but it happened in November 2021. Republican Senator John Kennedy, in a southern twang, told a Biden administration nominee during her confirmation hearing, "I don't know whether to call you colleague or comrade."[35] He asked whether she'd formally left the Komsomol, a Soviet youth league. Kennedy was trying to delegitimize Saule Omarova, a candidate for the comptroller of the currency. Indeed, she was born in the Soviet Union and gave up her citizenship to that nonexistent country decades ago. She had since worked in conservative administrations. But Kennedy couldn't help grilling her on her membership in the Communist Party.

The absurdity of Kennedy's comments even had his own party members shaking their heads and apologizing on his behalf. But like so many references to the United States' Cold War history, this red-baiting resonated in an outsize way. For a brief moment, communism was viral in the news cycle (like that time Bernie Sanders said it was true and good that Fidel Castro increased his people's literacy rate exponentially after the Cuban Revolution—which, by the way, is right).[36]

And yet. Omarova had proposed some radical financial policies during her time in the academy after working for the Treasury Department under the second Bush administration. The research Omarova worked on at Cornell as a professor, and its implications for school finance—specifically, finding constructive alternatives to the toxic bond market—is really interesting. Capitalists in both political parties had good reason to attack her. She has created a framework for infrastructure investment policy that any practical-minded communist now might feel okay about.

Kennedy's off-the-wall comment spoke to the larger opposition from arch-capitalists in both parties to Omarova. The ultra-capitalist Pat Toomey, for instance, couldn't believe some of the things that Omarova was proposing, along with Thom Tillis and Tim Scott. Scott was scandalized that she proposed having people's bank accounts at the Federal Reserve, calling it "the people's ledger." (I mean, why shouldn't there be more democratic power in finance, in this case personal banking?)

When it came time to move her nomination forward, conservative Democrats told the Biden administration to drop her. She then backed out of her own accord. Omarova took to NPR and called out the politicians who abandoned her, saying that she was standing up to finance capitalists, specifically big banks, and they defeated her.[37] Her research does legitimately challenge existing capitalist finance, particularly in how the federal government invests in its infrastructure like school buildings.

In the hearing, Tillis brought up another one of Omarova's ideas that she's worked on recently: a national investment authority (NIA). According to a short memo she'd written on this proposal, the NIA

> would be a federal entity created by an Act of Congress. It would design, finance, and implement a national strategy of economic development with an emphasis on long-term sustainability and social inclusion. It would act as a direct financial market participant, channeling both public and private money into large-scale infrastructure projects that typically do not get funded in private capital markets. Such projects would include both physical infrastructure (such as energy, transport, broadband internet, water management) and critical social infrastructure (such as public education, affordable housing, and healthcare).[38]

How would the NIA do this? First, by creating a national investment bank (NIB):

> The NIB would be the NIA's lender arm. It would focus on credit-based infrastructure finance, along the lines of the established "government-sponsored enterprise" (GSE) model. It would support and amplify the flow of credit into infrastructure projects through a combination of direct federal grants, loans, guarantees, insurance, securitization, and secondary market-making. For example, the NIB would purchase and pool revenue bonds and project bonds issued by municipalities,

> public utilities, and other government instrumentalities, as well as qualifying bonds issued by private entities for the purposes of financing publicly beneficial infrastructure projects.

Basically, the NIB is a public buyer in the municipal bond market that would incentivize private capital to finance public infrastructure. Run by a board of five to seven people appointed for ten-year terms, this bank could finance big projects.

A corresponding national capital management corporation (nicknamed Nicky Mac) would "guarantee the return of the principal investment to passive investors in funds that prioritize commercially unprofitable projects like toll-free roads, adult education centers, or public parks." Omarova worked on this idea with Robert Hockett at Cornell, a Federal Reserve lawyer gone rogue who has supported all kinds of initiatives like this (he even came to the event I helped organize to demand using the Municipal Liquidity Facility to finance school building construction).[39]

The proposals for a national investment bank and authority don't sound that radical. But strip away the discourse about private investment, and so on, and you find a significant challenge to a powerful fraction of the ruling class. It would be something like a public option for public finance, much like a public option in health insurance markets where the federal government can buy down the cost of health care for its people. At my most optimistic, this kind of reform has the potential to break the first cracks in heavily commodified apparatuses, directing them toward more democratic and popular control. This vision of public finance for public infrastructure puts labor back in the financial driver's seat, at least one hopes.

The threat, of course, is that Gabor's critiques hold true for such an entity, and it just becomes another arm of imperial state capitalism and its ravages rather than challenging it. Hockett and

Omarova cite James Olson's history of the Reconstruction Finance Corporation, a public financing engine behind the New Deal as a central influence on their thinking. But Olson tells a slightly different story that shows a faith in capitalism at the heart of the NIA proposal.[40]

The title of the book is telling: *Saving Capitalism*. Olson's thesis is that the New Deal financing engine was a public alternative to private financing, yes. However, the institution itself was explicitly not socialist but rather state capitalist. In line with the left reading of the New Deal generally, he says the purpose of the Reconstruction Finance Corporation was to prevent socialism from happening. Hockett and Omarova aren't explicitly anti-socialist in their writing, but you can see state capitalism throughout. They're constantly appealing to private markets, bankers, and capitalists to go along with the proposal because it's ultimately good for them to have the government in charge of public infrastructure. It's more stable; it's more certain; it's not prone to violent crashes. They say their policy is business-friendly. But they also call it a paradigm shift, almost saying it would be revolutionary in its democratic status.

State capitalism is the political-economic framework for social democracy: Get the state in the financial driver's seat rather than private markets so that the private markets can work better to serve the working class. But private markets can't fully serve the working class because they're inherently exploitative. State capitalism isn't socialism, but rather when the state steps in for longer or shorter periods of time to make sure capitalism is covering its bases. Because if it leaves out portions of the population, then that population could get unruly and blame capitalism, which we surely can't have.

If Hockett and Omarova's vision is state capitalist, and state capitalism is anti-socialist, and the Inflation Reduction Act's strategy for school facilities financing is consistent with their vision, then that strategy is anti-socialist. How are we supposed to wage a campaign with working-class teachers, parents, and students where the demand is "get the school district to go into debt to private firms and then get the district to apply to the federal government to reimburse them!" Not an appealing prospect. The situation is clearly state capitalist: It gets the government involved in the private markets to shore up the hegemony of private firms as they serve public purposes.

In an episode of the best leftist political education program right now, *The Dig* podcast from those days in the early 2020s, host Dan Denvir asked left historian and economist Tim Barker what he thought about the IRA.[41] Barker distinguished public investment from what the progressive economist Paul Samuelson characterized as "the bribe to capital formation." He said the IRA and everything that came out of the Biden administration on infrastructure is a clear case of what Samuelson meant: bribing private firms to invest rather than the government building the decarbonized school, which would entail the government investing in schools itself.

Do policies like Omarova's proposed national infrastructure authority or Biden's legislation in the Inflation Reduction Act have to be state capitalist? Did the New Deal financing program have to be anti-socialist? What if these policies always operate on a unique and uneven terrain where, depending on how labor fights, we could get to a more socialist policy? What if they're the gateway to something non-reformist? The only thing we know for certain is that the future is uncertain. The categorization of a policy like the IRA as state capitalist, plain and simple, is way too reductive and deflating, particularly given the exciting organizing that's happening on the ground right now in the People's Action campaigns.

I don't think there are any ironclad a priori answers to this question because class struggle takes place in the din of history, a froth of forces where nothing is predetermined and the classes that get themselves together for themselves can make their own destinies.

I just don't know whether these proposals are opportunities for the working class to do that.

When you look at who hates these policies, it certainly seems that way. Politicians like Pat Toomey and the editorial board of *The Bond Buyer* all had a keen interest in things like a national infrastructure authority not existing.[42] They want to have control over making tax-free profits from municipal bonds. They want to be the ones who control the market for public credit. They make a lot of money doing this. Retired millionaires and billionaires, credit rating agencies, investment banks, corporate banks, bond insurance agencies, whole sectors of law firms, consultants, advisers—all these people make their parasitic living off privately controlled public finance. When school districts need money to fix up their buildings, they have to go to this bondholder class, an unelected group holding the keys to public education and leaving communities with very few if any mechanisms to decrease their power.

The NIA is publicly controlled public finance. School districts could go to the NIA instead of private bankers for resources. The bondholder class stands to lose their control if such an authority existed. This is the reason why Pat Toomey, who also opposed Omarova, killed off the Municipal Liquidity Facility. These kinds of proposals challenge the bondholder class. Getting democratic control of public finance would take power away from capital by taking up and taking on the predominant form of finance capital hegemonic today. The question is whether this can lead to the school finance we need. To do this, we will have to take up the existing regime from the inside to some degree, which will involve more creative finance, like looking at pensions, as I do in part 3.

To conclude this part on bonds, though, I want to end with a fascinating example of what this can look like—from the early 1900s.

A student in my history of school funding seminar gave a fantastic presentation about her school district a few years ago. In most of my classes, I ask students to look at their own districts to find interesting things. This particular student grew up in and then proceeded to work for the Tredyffrin/Easttown district, about half an hour west of Philadelphia. The story she found was remarkable in a number of ways. First, the school district was never formally segregated. It was integrated. Throughout the nineteenth and twentieth centuries, the district never systematically separated Black children and white children. When a racist superintendent tried to segregate it in the 1930s, people in the district organized, pulled their children out of school, and didn't relent until the policy was revoked. My student showed us a film that students from the district made doing oral history work with elders who'd been children during this fight in the 1930s.[43] Solidarity had built up over time.

Tredyffrin/Easttown High School, an integrated school, was the result of the first "jointure" of high schools in Pennsylvania. The role that bonds had in its construction points to a rare resource of possibility in an otherwise toxic financing regime.

High schools were required by the state in the late 1800s. Jointure meant letting families pay taxes across district lines so students could go to a high school in a neighboring district.

In 1907, there was an amendment to the 1895 jointure law that let districts issue bonds together and collectively assume the cost of constructing new high schools to fulfill the state's mandate.[44] Tredyffrin and Easttown were the first to take advantage of the amendment, issuing a bond for $40,000 that same year, 1907. According to local archives, the money was "divided as follows: Easttown $17,660, Tredyffrin $22,340."

It was therefore through bond issuance that the districts sealed and strengthened their collaboration. The historian Esther Cyna has written about the case of Durham, North Carolina's integration efforts, which offers a contrast. In Durham, the county and city districts, which had been segregated, wanted to merge, and advocates made this proposal by issuing a bond across district lines. The Durham issuance failed at least five times, starting in 1955, and didn't pass until 1991.[45] We read that essay in my history seminar and the student smartly contrasted this Durham history to Tredyffrin/Easttown, which actually passed a bond issuance to merge districts for their new high school almost ninety years earlier, in 1907. Each situation featured a Black/white divide. But in the Tredyffrin/Easttown case, people apparently couldn't wait to share finances to build a school for all their kids, whereas Durhamites were against it.

These stories make me think about the word "bond." The financial meaning of the word is very different from the social meaning. A financial bond is a loan between borrower and lender at a rate of interest, whereas a social bond is a sympathetic, solidaristic connection between people. The bond obligations rarely fulfill the obligations we have to one another. But in the Tredyffrin/Easttown case, the meanings converge. The financial bond happened, I imagine, because of the social bonds between the people of the two districts across differences. I'd also guess that this bond issuance strengthened the bonds between them.

In a socialist America, I'd want bonds between people rather than competitive, super-expropriative bonds. I'm wondering whether we could use this tactic today to pass the legislation we want and need. I know that there's a small chance right now of tax base sharing, Vermont's Act 60, or even the Green New Deal for Public Schools passing at the state or federal level. But if districts in regions all over the country agreed to issue bonds across district lines, distributing the principal and interest through a sharing scheme, we could create the basis to fuse constituencies in favor of more liberatory legislation from the ground up.

You'd have to organize across some of the thorniest constituencies out there: school district people, like business officials and superintendents; parents and retirees within the district boundaries; and unions representing firms and shops there. You'd have to get everyone to agree to a plan to issue this shared bond of solidarity. Then you'd have to pass bond issuance referendums in each district. But the issue of school facilities cuts across typically siloed ideological boundaries and creates possibilities—the possibility that we could have school bonds across race/class/regional lines rather than isolating, alienating, and super-expropriative school bonds on the municipal credit market.

Generally speaking, school buildings are a winning issue in the battle over public education. While the right foments regressive outbursts over critical race theory and queer representation in school materials, deconstructing public education piece by piece, the forces of genuine progress can rightly say they're committed to quality inclusive education—and safe, nonpolluting schools to deliver it. This sort of appeal redirects conversation across all the ideological divides that now convulse education politics and takes optimal advantage of significant financial policy now in place to back it up.

But given the prevailing terms of engagement in the school wars, we also must ensure that we double down on our efforts to protect and strengthen intersectional democracy. The only reason this right-wing reaction has galvanized at this moment is because of the progress we've made. It's a nonnegotiable demand to protect our people. But that means going on the offensive in addition to defending against the right-wing menace. So as the right seeks to tear down all sorts of protections and provisions for kids, why not build?

Part III

Contribution or Death: A Socialist Approach to Teacher Pensions

8
Solidarity or Markets

In France in 2023, centrist president Emmanuel Macron forced through a change to the French retirement age from sixty-two to sixty-four, relying on an archaic protocol in the French government that let him bypass votes in parliament. In response, the French public led an uprising involving mass strikes and disruptions to multiple industries and services.[1] The change was part of Macron's larger attempt to reform French pensions, which pay workers at their salary level after they retire until they die.

A pension is money you and your employer put away while you're working that you get when you get old and stop working. As Marxist economist Michael Roberts puts it, "Pensions are really deferred wages, deductions from income from work to pay for a decent income when people retire. After decades of work (and exploitation), workers . . . should be entitled to stop and enjoy the last decade or so of life without toil, without being in poverty. Literally, they will have earned it."[2]

The tension with pensions is that the ruling class doesn't want to pay for workers' retirements. It's too expensive, they say. The pensions are too big, they say. They're mismanaged, corrupt, inefficient, wasteful, and so forth. What they'd like to do is to make them smaller (by increasing retirement age, e.g.) or privatize them. So whenever you hear someone say, "Why don't the French people just retire a little later?" what they're really saying is "Why don't the French want to be exploited for longer?"

It can all seem a little far away and strange to us in the United States, particularly when France is more heavily unionized and has a much stronger tradition of striking, disruptions, and social upheaval in response to government incursions into the French quality of life. In the United States, pensions by sector or company are rare, and they are almost exclusively limited to the public sector after private equity raiders stole private pensions. We more commonly have Social Security, a federal pension that provides payments according to certain percentages of the amount you put in via withholdings, when you retire, and so on. Employees who don't work for public entities can also have privatized retirement plans like 401(k) or 403(b) (the nonprofit version), which are managed according to variable rates and come with fees from the private banks that manage them, a system of savings that retirement economists Teresa Ghilarducci and Tony James say needs saving.[3]

But what's happening in France isn't so far away from us in the United States, particularly in education. Teaching is one of the few professions, along with police, government workers, military, and the like, that still have pensions. And it seems like they're headed toward a similar kind of place to the French situation: a debt crisis, irate workers, and a chorus of scolds accusing them of being greedy and lazy.

Teacher pensions are caught in that education tug-of-war I described in the introduction. Privatizing public pensions is part of the right-wingers' pull, while moderates meekly look around, maybe disagreeing, maybe not. Meanwhile working-class communities suffer and the whole system gets dragged to the right. In the background, the context for this rightward pull is the evisceration of public policies.

Understanding pensions is essential for rounding out the picture of our current school finance regime and envisioning a socialist alternative. Pension funds are huge pools of capital that come with big costs to states and school districts. They've also been a big reason why people decide to become and continue working as teachers: You get more security for retirement. They're a material reality for school districts and come to bear on the life and death of our educators, including incentives to become and stay a teacher.

How do these huge pools of capital work?

Jean-Pierre Aubrey, writing for the Center on Retirement Research, found that funding teacher pensions is largely a state and local affair, and we don't know a whole lot about how that state-local dynamic happens.[4] As of 2023, the Public Plans Database reports that public pensions generally have about $5.5 trillion in assets, cover about 15 million retirees while 12.2 million active workers contribute to them, and pay out about $393 billion in benefits each year. Numbers specific to teacher pensions are hard to find.

There's no teacher pension policy on the federal level, unless you count Social Security. In about fifteen states, retired teachers weren't able to receive this benefit if they also received pensions until the Biden administration changed the policy in 2024.[5] Now all retired teachers who get public pensions can also get Social Security. Also, the federal government regulates how much pensions are supposed to save to maintain solvency.

When it comes to the state policies, they differ vastly. According to Aubrey, two-thirds of states provide explicit money for teacher pensions, fifteen of which pay the full cost of contributions on behalf of school districts. The other third of the states provide some funds, but in varying ways, and this multifarious funding has decreased over time.

In this chapter, I'll critique some voices that raise the alarm about pensions and seek to implement a more capitalist version of Macron's policy. These voices describe teacher pensions as in an impending crisis that threatens to take down the whole system, but, in fact, the system is more durable than some say. Since pensions are a significant benefit for teachers, consequential for district budgeting, and perpetually at the center of statewide budget debates; since they're one of the last vestiges of solidarity in public finance, and they're huge mountains of capital that make important investments across different markets (and thus could be leveraged for investments we want to see)—teacher pension policy is essential for making public schools as public as possible.

Part 3 is a socialist-forensic examination of teacher pension policy. In this first chapter, I'll introduce key terms, like defined benefit versus what capitalists deceptively call "defined contribution plans," and lay out generally how to understand teacher pensions ideologically by contrasting two frameworks for understanding them: market-orientation versus solidarity. In chapter 9, we'll see whether there's actually a problem with teacher pensions. In chapter 10, I'll contribute to the leftist debate about pension policy by proposing what I call green fiscal mutualism, using a historical precedent for leveraging the investment power of teacher pensions for public school infrastructure.

The post-pandemic period brought an explosion of school district budget crises. Through my newsletter and social media, I started getting requests from people around the country to look at their districts' money problems from a left perspective.[6] District leadership tended to take a particular line on these crises: The end of pandemic relief programs from the federal government and declining enrollments were their excuse to cut programs, fire teachers and staff, and close schools.[7] I found myself digging into various districts' financial statements, watching YouTube recordings of school board meetings, and reading local reporting to figure out what exactly was going on. Then I'd advise organizers. This helped movements on the ground to push back against reflexive austerity in response to alleged fiscal implosions, which felt like an echo of the post-2008 traumas of budget crises and closures.

Sometimes I found that the administration's characterization of the crises was far from reality. One telling request was from Ann Arbor, Michigan, where what looked like a crisis in enrollment and federal money drying up was actually about pensions.

Ann Arbor Public Schools was facing a budget shortfall of $25 million in 2024. If we consider some of the typical losses that districts were facing then (enrollment drops, federal fiscal cliff), Ann Arbor had some: $1.4 million in state funding decreased, for instance, and there was an additional $3.4 million decrease in "overall district revenues," which came, said reports, from an increase in hiring and a decrease in enrollment over the previous nine years. But $5 million was just a fifth of the $25 million problem. Why was the budget gap so big? One vague line from local reporting on the crisis caught my eye: "Several factors contributed to the budget shortage, including $14 million in state support from last year's budget that was misallocated to this year's."[8] Aha. Turns out $14 million came from a pension problem having nothing to do with enrollment or federal relief money. Here's what happened.

In March 2024, a financial consultant named Marios Demetriou gave a presentation to the Ann Arbor district's board members (called trustees).[9] It was the spiciest, most intense school finance meeting I'd seen in a long time. Right at the beginning of the meeting, Demetriou said the following, sounding simultaneously mealy-mouthed, confusing, and innocuous:

> We have—we had in the budget an item that happened last year, um, it was for the unfunded accrued liability

> for retirement and, um, we get that every year but also last year there was also one time that came in and then it was, with the unfunded accrued liability. . . . We get the money and then next payroll we send it back to the state on the revenue side. . . . This one time item that happened last year was still in the budget so we are removing it, it's not happening this year so we're removing it.

Most people in an audience of community members, and maybe even school board members, would probably just skip over that comment. Like, what? What's he talking about? Unfunded accrued liability? Happens every year? Let's dig into it.

The "unfunded accrued liability" for retirement has to do with pensions. Specifically, as the Michigan teacher pension defines it, this is "the difference between the [present value of the] *estimated cost of future benefits* and *the assets that have been set aside to pay for those benefits*."[10]

Pause here for a moment. Pensions provide defined benefits to retirees. A defined benefit is an amount of money that you'll get no matter what. If you have a defined benefit retirement policy, you'll receive a specific amount (usually a percentage of your salary at retirement) every year until you die. Employers and employees contribute to a collective fund that's managed by publicly elected or appointed officials whose job is to invest that money and pay out the benefits to which retirees are entitled.

A defined benefit is very different from what free marketeers call a defined contribution, where you're not guaranteed any amount on any basis. This "defined contribution plan" is just a savings account (lol). Those private equity raiders, the ones who ruined private pensions, came up with the term "defined contribution" in the 1970s to help steal corporate pension assets, making the plan seem like a robust substitute for defined benefits. The phrase "defined contribution" is pure capitalist propaganda. From here on out I'll use the term defined isolation plan instead. You'll see why.

With a defined isolation plan, like a 401(k) or 403(b), you're only guaranteed that your employer will contribute a certain amount to your retirement, along with whatever you decide to contribute. The account is managed by a private company, an investment outfit, that makes money from investing your retirement savings in the stock market and charges fees to do it. If the stock market tanks, you might lose your entire retirement, as many did in 2008. Pensions are more protected because the money is collectivized and the employer takes on some of the risk that individual employees could face as the economy churns. Even though pensions took a big hit in the crisis, pensioners still got a good amount of what they were promised.

As I was writing this book, I got a new job, and the example is instructive for illustrating this distinction between defined benefit and defined isolation. At my first university, which was public, I paid into a public pension that guaranteed me 80 percent of my final salary after I retired at sixty-five until I died. So no matter what, the Pennsylvania State Employees' Retirement System—managed by appointed public officials—would pay me around $100,000 every year after I retired. But my new job was with a private university, which has a 401(k) defined isolation plan. The university contributes 4 percent to my account every year, matching my own 4 percent contribution, but that account is managed by a private company investing it in whatever they thought would make them the most money. There's no guarantee for how much I might actually get when I'm too old to work. If capitalists tank the economy again, I might be up the river without a paddle.

Okay, back to Ann Arbor. Since the Michigan Employees' Retirement System has to pay out defined benefits to their retirees, they need income to build and maintain the fund. The pension gets that income through payments from employers, like the state and school districts, who set aside a certain amount to contribute to the fund, and also contributions from employees, withheld from salary. That's what a pension contribution is: the employer and employee adding money to the fund so teachers can live when they retire. In the case of teacher pensions, the employer is the state and school district, and these contributions come out of the school budget. You can maybe see the challenge: The pension needs enough money to pay out what it promised to its retirees, and the pension managers have to calculate what that amount is year to year, over very long periods of time. When pensions need more and more but states and districts can't pay enough, you get what's called a pension's unfunded liability.

But as Aubrey found, more than two-thirds of states have explicit laws for using state money to maintain these teacher pensions (this becomes important later for when neoliberals start characterizing pensions as being in a big crisis that threatens district budgets). Fifteen states make the full payment. And Michigan is one of those states. Michigan has a policy that makes payments directly to the school district according to what the pension managers think needs to be paid into the pension fund to make sure it has enough to pay out its defined benefits and try to meet that unfunded liability, which builds up over time. Nerds called actuaries move little beads around on their abacuses to calculate how much the pension is owed to maintain its fiscal strength. The actuaries report that need to the pension managers, who then tell the state and districts what amount of payroll should go toward keeping the pension healthy. But a lot of times, contributors to the fund can't pay what's needed, and this unfunded liability builds up over time. Thus we get the unfunded actuarial accrued liability.

Again, it's helpful to see the language as it's written to familiarize yourself with it. According to Michigan's Office of Retirement Services, the unfunded actuarial accrued liability is "the difference between the retirement system's assets and the pensions accrued (for past service) to current and future retirees."[11]

This complex payment was at the heart of Ann Arbor's budget crisis.

As I mentioned, Michigan does this interesting thing where instead of paying directly into the pension fund, they pay school districts and municipalities a certain amount of money to cover the cost of retirement benefits. Then, at the end of every year, the districts have to pay it back to the state. There's a cycle of giving and paying back to help districts cover the costs of putting money into the pension.[12] The policy is something like a parent giving their teenager an allowance so they have cash up front, and then taking it back later according to family expenditures for groceries, facilities, and so on, to teach the kid about money. This pedagogical goal is probably not the motivation behind Michigan's retirement contribution policy, but it does show districts how much the pensions need, exposing them viscerally to the amount of money it takes to maintain the pension. Again, the state gives the district a sort of allowance and the district has to pay this allowance back to the state at the end of the year. It's how Michigan manages the pension's unfunded liabilities, by giveth and taketh-ing away.[13]

So here's what happened in Ann Arbor. When putting together its yearly budget in 2023 for the following year, Ann Arbor budget officials forgot to put this allowance payment in both the revenue and expenditure sections, incurring a huge loss. It's like if the teenager didn't pay their parents back and the parents came around asking for the money, but the teenager had already gone out and bought a really expensive video game. In Ann Arbor's case, it put the district in a $14 million hole.

During the school board meeting in March 2024, one trustee caught what Demetriou had said about this mistake. The trustee rightly called the missing $14 million a "tremendous amount of money," summarizing the problem well and asking pointed questions as any good board member should:

Trustee 1: For this year's budget they put in the $14 million expecting us to get it [on the revenue side], which is a presumption, number one, but why wouldn't it also be in the expenditure side if it's always gone back?

Demetriou: I cannot answer the question why, I wasn't here.

Trustee 1: It's just an enormous amount given the numbers . . .

Demetriou: I'm trying to correct whatever is . . . um I'm trying to tell you the truth [about what] is happening but . . .

Trustee 2: So that $14 million was on one side, but not the other?

Demetriou: Correct.

Trustee 1: I'm right to assume it gave us a distorted view of what our budget and our fund balance was.[14]

So that's what happened: The budget office, in putting together their budget, forgot to list the $14 million in both the revenue (money coming in) and expenditure (money going out) columns. The budget officials only put the allowance in the revenue column, thereby assuming the district had $14 million more than it actually did. But how did it happen? That's a good story too and one that helps to show the din of struggle around school finance in a vivid way.

After chatting with someone from the district, I found out that Ann Arbor district officials made this budget boo-boo in a froth of controversy. The previous superintendent, Jeanice Swift, was forced out after a bitter period of tension with the district. This bitterness came to a head when a school bus aide attacked a student with autism.[15] The episode was apparently the last straw for many in the community who didn't like Swift's approach to special education. The school board was nothing if not embattled, with trustees resigning due to getting bullied, for example (which was a national trend at the time), and local disagreements about spending over the previous five years, not to mention the fires and furies around pandemic-related school closures.[16]

In the fray of that already difficult situation, after intense debate in the community, the board also passed a resolution to support a cease-fire during Israel's ongoing genocide in Gaza, an issue that made national headlines and brought lots of attention to Ann Arbor Schools.[17]

So the community was divided to say the least, and anger converged on Superintendent Swift. There was a movement to demand her immediate removal, which the teachers union opposed. Two trustees on the board, who also happened to make up the finance committee, were strong Swift supporters. And it was in this turmoil that district officials made the accrued liability mistake, on top of an already-worsening budget situation.

Eventually, Swift left, and interim superintendent Jazz Parks was brought in to lead the district. She called up Demetriou, who had been the district's finance leader until he retired in 2020, after the departure of the executive director, who had replaced yet another leader. There was a lot of turnover and Parks needed to right the ship, so she brought back Demetriou to sort things out (she called him a finance ninja, he just looked tired).

And, well, he sort of did sort things out. Demetriou discovered the huge pension-related shortfall when he looked through the books, leading Parks to alert the district to the financial crisis at hand. The district was working on it. But in the meantime, the schools had to lay off around sixty people from the district. Teacher pension policy was at the center of this crisis, but very few people knew it.

This Ann Arbor pension whoopsy-daisy is also instructive when we zoom out and look at the state policy landscape that brought the onetime payment into being, and the efforts to reform the pension at the state level. Even though I painted a somewhat negative picture around the Michigan give-then-take-away policy, it's actually kind of a good thing. Before 2012, Michigan districts were totally responsible for paying down the extent to which the pension wasn't funding itself according to contribution rate calculations.

But then in 2012, the state passed a cost-sharing policy by which the state would cover any unfunded liabilities over 20.96 percent above a district's payroll. That means the district doesn't have to pay for any unfunded liabilities above that threshold. This is where the debate has been on the teacher pension policies in Michigan: What should the threshold percentage be when it comes to state cost sharing? Two positions emerged in 2024, when Governor Gretchen Whitmer and the state legislature started discussing budget policies for the following year: the union position and the libertarian position.

The Michigan Education Association, the state's teachers union, agreed with the threshold policy since it lets districts off the hook and puts more onus on the state. This point of view is more collectivist since it pools the liability rather than individualizing it among the districts. According to the union, the state could clearly afford to continue collectivizing the pension accrued liability for school districts in their retirement payment plans. The union claimed the state had an extra $670 million in its coffers for public education and was on track to overfund its unfunded actuarial accrued liability for health care for retirees.[18]

On the other side were libertarians at the Reason Foundation claiming that the Michigan teacher pension had $29 billion in unfunded liability. Ever the promoters of individuals against government, they sought to protect taxpayers from having to pay one penny more in taxes to fund that unfunded liability.[19] They jumped into the debate advocating a much lower threshold for how much liability the state would cover.

This debate between the union and the libertarians mattered to the tune of millions of dollars for districts like Ann Arbor and around the state. If that threshold had been any lower, even by a tenth of a percentage point, Ann Arbor may have had to fire more people.

Leftists have to think about these policies! Getting into the difference between solidarity and market fundamentalism in pension policy is one way in.

In his book *Dismantling Solidarity*, sociologist Michael A. McCarthy reminds us that defined benefit public pensions are a kind of welfare program.[20] Others might go so far as to say it's a mutual-aid pact. In addition to fulfilling the rights that people have to live their lives, welfare takes care of people when they can't take care of themselves. Health care takes care of sick people. Education takes care of people who have to learn stuff that they don't know. Unemployment programs take care of people when they lose their jobs. Retirement programs take care of people when they get old.

The greatest welfare policies in American history were passed in the wake of the 1929 market crash and the Great Depression that ensued, usually called the New Deal. Social Security was the flagship program for old age. McCarthy looks back to the politics of Social Security to show that our approach to old age could have been a lot better, and that public sector pensions were actually a compromise.

Specifically, he looks at a piece of legislation called the Wagner-Murray-Dingell Bill from the 1940s. In addition to federalizing unemployment insurance, creating a national universal health care insurance system, and increasing disability insurance, it "extended old-age and survivors' insurance to practically all employed persons . . . offered benefits for permanent disability, liberalized benefits by increasing minimum payments, and raised the maximum by making eligibility less restrictive through a new formula for computing average earnings." It was a significant addition to and step up from Social Security.

The bill was called the American Beveridge plan, named after the British policy that created a more expansive welfare state there postwar. Wagner-Murray-Dingell was introduced in 1943, 1944, and 1946 but failed to pass Congress each time. We could have had a national insurance plan that covered everyone as they got to old age. Instead, we got sector-by-sector pensions.

It's worth following McCarthy's thinking about these different kinds of plans. For example, in his argument, he doesn't use the more common private/public distinction to talk about pensions. Instead, McCarthy helpfully assesses pension policies using a solidaristic or market-oriented spectrum. He cites a helpful phrase in defining what this means: "As programs in capitalist societies become more solidaristic, the costs of addressing social risks (such as illness, poverty, disability, and old age) are pooled across the population. In Peter Baldwin's phrase, 'the terms of misfortune's reapportionment' do not rest on the shoulders of individuals or families, but instead are mutually agreed on at the level of policy and set by the standards of the day."[21]

On the other hand, McCarthy says, you have markets, where the terms of misfortune's reapportionment rest on individual shoulders. As programs become more market-oriented, individuals increasingly confront the economic uncertainty of life alone, their needs met or unmet by their own private dealings. A greater reliance is put on their personal or familial savings or performance on the labor market.

So when we're thinking about teacher pensions, the question we have to ask ourselves when reading or listening or engaging in conversation about the topic is whether any given policy spreads the cost of social risk collectively or individually, whether the policy is a solidarity policy or a market policy. The more we reapportion misfortune on individual terms, the more we leave people out in the cold to fend for themselves. A market policy might be more "efficient" according to some metric based on dollars in, dollars out at a specific point in time—but is it solidaristic? Does the policy make us face the social risk of aging together or alone?

McCarthy is a leftist historical sociologist, and his goal in the book is to show that retirement policy in the United States after World War II was a process of dismantling solidarity, embodied in the shift from solidaristic defined benefit programs to market-oriented defined isolation programs, like the 401(k). He takes this to be a bad thing. Contrast his position to someone like Chad Aldeman, whose work is typical of the market-oriented project.

If you got interested in teacher pensions and wanted to know more about them, and you googled basic terms like teacher, pension, and the like, Chad Aldeman's blog at TeacherPensions and his writing on pensions for neoliberal outlets like the Bellwether foundation will inevitably come up. At first, his numerous blogs, reports, and articles, with their colorful and well-designed graphs and figures and tables, seem like a neutral intellectual project just trying to understand what the heck is happening with teacher pensions. But after you get a handle on the solidarity versus market-oriented distinction in retirement policy, and what defined benefit and defined isolation really mean, his blogs read like the writings of a soldier in the fight to dismantle solidarity. It's clear from the tone and claims, along with the material and institutions associated with his work, that the ideological project here is to restructure public educators' pensions to make them more market-oriented.

Reading Aldeman is a good case study of anti-solidarity. He argues that pensions are inefficient. He claims they worsen the lives of teachers and that they take resources from students. Oh, and they're even racist (he had a special George Floyd edition of his blog where he makes this argument). He makes these claims by calculating pension costs for school districts and comparing them to per-pupil costs and per-employee costs, tracking these costs by racial demographics and teacher turnover and declining student enrollments. He also tracks pension debt, which is when school districts owe back payments on their pension obligations.

In June 2023, in a post called "How Much Do School Districts Spend on Teacher Pensions?" Aldeman notes that pensions cost districts as much as they spend on tutoring, about $63 billion a year. In that blog post, he said districts spend $1,549 per student on teacher retirement costs on average. New York City apparently spends more than $4,700 per student on these costs. The implication is that districts can and should be spending this money on students rather than retirees.[22]

But pensions worsen the lives of teachers too, by preventing them from getting paid more, he says. In Chicago, for every $1,000 that goes to teacher salaries, the district pays $520 toward teacher pension costs. In New York City it's $340; $330 in Philadelphia. Finally, Aldeman includes a shocking statistic: that retirement costs for state and local educational agencies have risen 322 percent since 2004, outpacing health care and salary costs.

It's hard to come away from reading the blog thinking anything other than that teacher pensions are in a terrible crisis, and things should be changed quickly and dramatically, which is where one gets a whiff of the ideology. The change he recommends is moving toward a defined isolation model rather than defined benefit, or at least a hybrid model. Instead of using solidarity to provide defined amounts of income for teachers in their old age, we should use a market-oriented approach that leaves teachers out in the cold to handle the risk of aging alone as individuals facing the market.

Aldeman makes these claims by estimating pension costs for school districts—what districts spend on pensions—and comparing that to districts' per-pupil enrollments and costs and per-employee costs in terms of wages. I was curious about where all these numbers were coming from and how Aldeman got to them, so I read the methods section, which provides some . . . illuminating perspective. Kudos that he even included this section, as it undermined much of what he claims in the post. He admits that "the methodology I came up with here is certainly not perfect, and there are some sources of error that I'll discuss." While every quantitative study's methods are limited in myriad ways, and it's commendable that Aldeman recognizes his own, it's extra important to dig into his admissions here because his writing is so ubiquitous and what typically gets read, studied, and digested from this writing on teacher pensions are the top-line findings rather than the big conjectural leaps taken to get there.

Aldeman begins the methods section in the blog post by writing, "I set out to estimate how much school districts spend on teacher and other employee pension costs." Three things of note about this seemingly innocuous sentence. First, we know from Aubrey's work at the Public Plans Database that states make big contributions to teacher pension plans, as well as local school districts' contributions. Two-thirds of states make some explicit contribution, while the other third do what the researchers call implicit ones. Michigan's policy is just one example: the state pays the district money to contribute to the pension, which the district pays back up to a certain amount, to cover unfunded liabilities in the pension fund. So it's reasonable to ask what role state financing plays here, and whether Aldeman is really measuring how much money districts spend (more on this later). Is Ann Arbor's district expenditure really a simple district-level expenditure if it's getting that money from the state that it has to pay back specifically for that purpose?

Second, Aldeman includes "other employees" in his estimates. This means people like superintendents and other highly paid administrators who aren't teachers but are covered by teacher pensions. Should superintendent pension costs be lumped with teacher pension costs? This is a question I've come back to again and again while trying to understand teacher pensions. To what extent are the highly paid management positions responsible for increases in retirement cost? Even the disgraced superintendent who embezzled millions of dollars from his district in Long Island, the subject of the 2019 Hugh Jackman movie *Bad Education*, gets a pension of nearly $180,000 a year.

Third, it's a small thing, but Aldeman uses the word "estimate" with respect to his goals, viz, school district expenditures on retirement costs. Later in the methodology section, he says "the numbers here should be treated as *plausible estimates* rather than *precise budget amounts*" (my emphasis). What's the difference between a plausible estimate and a precise budget amount?

Basically, he's saying that the numbers he's coming up with can be used but aren't precisely what we'd find in budgets if we actually look at them (like Ann Arbor's, for instance). Spot some ideology here too. What counts as plausible? Who determines what's plausible and what's implausible? The ideology occurs in the passivity. The word "plausible" itself comes from the same etymological root as applause and plaudit, that is, what's worthy of applause. So who's clapping here and why?

If Aldeman has a market-oriented project, rather than a solidaristic one, then data supporting market-oriented conclusions will likely be more plausible, particularly in the absence of precision. In other words, these numbers *can be used* . . . if you're pushing a market project in pension policy. (He even says, "Anyone looking for a precise number for a given district should consult with the district finance office." Right, that is, anyone not doing a market project.) When it comes to the question about state contributions versus school districts, he says plainly that "I'm attributing all 'employer' contribution rates to a given school district, but in some places, the state pays some or all of the 'employer' contribution rate. In those cases, I'm attributing spending to a district that comes from the state, so the estimates here should be interpreted more as 'spending attributable to a district' rather than 'spending that directly comes out of a district's budget.'"[23]

Okay, so Aldeman doesn't know how much a state contributes to a pension for any given district he's talking about . . . in a post about district expenditure. When he says that New York City or Chicago or Philadelphia is "paying" a certain amount of money toward teacher retirement, he actually doesn't know if it's the district or New York State, Illinois, or Pennsylvania. That makes a big difference, because state funds work differently than local district funds. The money can't just go toward any old thing, like teacher salaries or curriculum or facilities. That's precisely the mistake that Ann Arbor made, at least in practice, when the district didn't declare the state's recurring payment as revenue and expenditure.

The turn of phrase "spending attributable to a district" is a wondrous sleight of hand consistent with his distinction between precision and plausibility. You can see the ideology still at work. Spending in this sense is "attributable"—that is, can be attributed, if you happen to agree with the ideology—to a district without really knowing whether or how we can attribute that spending to the district. It's plausible rather than precise. But plausible to whom?

Again, in the case of Ann Arbor, you could claim that $14 million was coming out of the district's budget and could have gone to tutoring, and the like. But actually the state was paying the district that amount specifically as an allowance for unfunded accrued actuarial liability. All the district had to do was pay the state back with the money the state gave it at the beginning of the year. It wasn't revenue for tutoring or anything else. The district literally can't do anything with that money except pay the state back for its accrued liability—which, by the way, was created in the first place because people who believe in markets so much tanked the economy in 2008 and sent public pensions spiraling with the market, and refused to be generous during what was supposed to be a period of recovery as neoliberal austerity ruled the day. Aldeman never mentions anything like that, of course.

When you break it all down, it's flabbergasting, particularly when you remember that what's at stake here is the amount of money that old teachers, who spent their lives educating kids, will get when they're too old to work. Aldeman's highly ideological research takes advantage of crises, like the one in Ann Arbor, to subtly advocate for less solidaristic pension policies. One imagines Aldeman would be on the Reason Foundation side of the debate about payment thresholds, for instance, rather than on the union side, fighting for markets rather than solidarity.

Now, with this distinction in hand, we have the tools to parse the debate about the alleged teacher pension crisis a little more intensively.

9

Is There Really a Teacher Pension Crisis?

A lot of people say that pensions are in crisis. But are they? How do we know what's really going on with teacher pensions?

Probably my favorite line of Marx is that between equal rights, force decides. He's talking about how workers own their labor and sell it on the market to capitalists who purchase it, but because each has an equal right as buyer and seller of that strange commodity, you get a class struggle. This struggle manifests everywhere in society since it's how we make our material lives. We could say too that where equal numbers exist, force decides. If you've got a dataset that you think is reasonable and you've got backing, then it's the force of class struggle that decides the truth of your claims rather than some other criterion. The same is true for teacher pension research.

In trying to understand whether or not there's a teacher pension crisis, I've developed a way of organizing the debate. Before we get into some forensics on this question, let me sketch those positions out first.

Keep in mind the key distinctions I made in chapter 8 between defined benefit and defined isolation, and that the former is more solidaristic than the latter, which is market oriented. Throughout the pension debates, I've noticed a difference between more solidaristic voices, who typically want to keep pensions healthy, and more market-oriented voices calling for a defined isolation rampage. The difference is between what I would call a contribution approach to teacher pensions and a cost approach to them.

The contribution approach focuses on the quantity, quality, and history of contribution rates to pensions (how much individuals, districts, and states put into the pension), and the context in which these pension contributions occur: how they're calculated, how they're collected, how they're invested.

By contrast, the cost approach focuses on the cost of those contributions in an expansive sense: how high they are, how much they "take" from other kinds of expenditures, and how unsustainable they might be for the pension in the long term. The two different approaches end up with different analyses and recommend different kinds of teacher pension policies. Cost-side people are usually ringing an alarm about the crisis in pensions: The costs are increasing so much that we have to do something drastic! Aah! Typically, for cost-siders, this means pushing defined isolation plans to replace defined benefit plans because they cost less.

Contribution-side people take a more measured tone and perspective in their approach. They tend not to advocate the dismantling of solidarity through defined isolation plans (or maybe any radical change), sticking with assessment of defined benefit plans to ensure their ongoing health and navigate the roadblocks they face. Notably, contribution-siders are less likely to cry crisis. They'll note the difficulties, challenges, and puzzles that teacher pensions present, but they rarely say there's a crisis that, oh my goodness, needs to change right now or else the world will end. This, I think, is because defined benefit plans are more solidaristic than defined isolation plans. In general, a contribution approach is more solidaristic than the cost approach.

Since these are different positions with a lot at stake (can public school teachers afford to get old?), people who take the cost perspective have a lot to answer for. They're advocating a radically anti-solidaristic policy that leaves elderly public educators, one of the few categories of workers who are currently guaranteed a more stable retirement, to face the social risk of aging alone. We can't let the cost-siders just say that pensions are in crisis or that of course we need defined isolation plans. We can say, no, we disagree! And there are good reasons for disagreement, as we saw in the last chapter—big holes in that market-oriented, anti-solidarity approach. Those holes, and other ways they appear in the teacher pension crisis debate, are what this chapter is about.

The cost-side researchers crying crisis are on the side of private retirement investment managers whose goal is to make as much money as possible for themselves rather than guarantee you a defined benefit. That research needs to be audited: They cut corners and make logical and empirical leaps to push market ideology. In general, by focusing on cost instead of contribution, they conveniently ignore many of the capitalist machinations that come to bear on why teacher pension contributions are the way they are. Which is a final point: It's important not to forget contribution when thinking about cost, because the ways that contribution rates get calculated are directly dependent on changing market conditions, investment decisions, and, well, capitalists, rather than greedy retiring teachers taking money away from students. I'll get to that in chapter 10. Let's start with some work from a contribution-sider, which provides a contrast to a cost-side study, showing the class struggle in teacher pensions pretty clearly.

Contribution-siders always mention context. As Andrew G. Biggs points out in a 2023 special issue of the research journal *Educational Researcher*, when it comes to the very data on which teacher pension research relies, "public-sector pensions are not covered by the Federal Employee Retirement Income Security Act of 1973, meaning that there is no centralized collection of public pension financial disclosures."[1] So, right from the start, if there's no central place to analyze public pension numbers, then you're going to have competing claims using competing datasets. It's also notable that there's no information on public pensions before 2001, so you can't do any long-term analysis that would show current trends as relatively normal or reasonable.

Biggs has been publishing on teacher pensions for the last twenty years. He's up front about where his numbers come from and their specific limitations. He gets his data from the Public Plans Database (PPD), a source I mentioned in chapter 8.[2] A quick look at the website shows that the "website is developed and maintained through a collaboration of the Government Finance Officers Association (GFOA), MissionSquare Research Institute, the National Association of State Retirement Administrators (NASRA), and the Center for Retirement Research at Boston College."

I mention this just to say that there are a number of different government and intellectual institutions that maintain these numbers, rather than a single foundation or author looking directly at the Bureau of Labor Statistics, for instance. Certainly there will be ideological interests at play in any research, but Biggs's numbers are coming from a pretty variegated set of institutions, which indicates to me that there isn't the same market fundamentalism at work in his analysis as in Aldeman's.

In his article about teacher pension solvency, Biggs tells us that his numbers come from thirty-one teacher pension plans in the PPD dataset, which itself has limitations. Due to the lack of centralized data reporting generally, not every plan has information for every year available. Another aspect of the PPD is that its figures are as reported by teacher pensions in actuarial valuations, comprehensive annual financial reports, and other filings. These figures are calculated using standards promulgated by the Governmental

Accounting Standards Board, which are themselves political, as pensions researcher Tom Sgouros points out.[3]

For example, to figure out whether a pension is doing well, we have to make assumptions about how much money the pension fund will be able to make in returns to its investments over long periods of time. But no one knows the future! So they have to guess using something called a discount rate, which takes into consideration how much assets will be worth in the future. They call that the present value of future pension benefits because that's what managers and researchers think, in the present, that the pension will be able to pay out, in the future.

Basically, calculating what the pension will be worth is kind of an interstellar brain twister. You have to make all kinds of assumptions about what today's money will be worth when teachers retire in the future. (Yes, I'm referring to the movie *Interstellar* there; time travel is sort of important when it comes to pensions.) Here's how it works. The government standards board allows the present value of future pension benefit liabilities to be calculated using a discount rate equal to the expected return on the pension's investments. A higher discount rate means you assume the fund will earn more in the future, meaning you need to put less in now; a lower discount rate means you assume less growth for the fund and need to put more in now to cover future costs. Until about ten years ago, this discount rate was in the range of 7–8%. Then political pressure from conservatives pushed it down to 6-7.5% over the last decade (even though the historic averages of many big funds has actually been over 8%, which shows you how ideological this technical stuff is). Other figures, such as annual required contribution rates and funded ratios, are based on these present assumptions about future values too, which end up being really important for how we understand the health of teacher pensions.

So this all means that, going back to the contribution versus cost distinction, when we dig into teacher pension costs, there can be even more ambiguity in the reported numbers we use when we think about them. Who is making these interstellar calculations, and how?

For instance, Biggs tells us that the Bureau of Economic Analysis's National Income and Product Accounts and the Federal Reserve's financial accounts of the United States "publish pension liability figures that are calculated by using a corporate bond yield as the discount rate." Is a corporate bond rate, which might be lower than would make sense for teacher pensions, an appropriate discount rate when thinking about teacher pension contribution costs? Or should we assume 7–8 percent, which, according to Biggs, is higher than some analysts think is appropriate?

This question about how big the assumed rate of return, that is, the discount rate, should be when we think about teacher pensions will become key to the socialist approach to teacher pensions in chapter 10. For now, think about the fluctuation in inflation over the last couple of years, how we're in a new regime of rates after a couple of decades of frankly wild quantitative easing that funded the ruling class's recovery (which was a non-recovery for the rest of us) after 2008. Wouldn't all that impact our understanding of what pensions have for future retirees, and thus what school districts and states owe? How does market-oriented or solidarity ideology influence the actuarial decisions here? And then how does that shape the pension debate itself? It's up to the researchers and analysts behind the datasets, and the decisions they make about the numbers we read in reporting and research about the pensions themselves.

It's an epistemological problem in teacher pension policy, which quickly becomes a political one. How can we know the truth about teacher pensions? To what extent should bond yields, average risky assessments over time, or regimes of interest rates determine teacher pension contributions? It's not clear. Between equal numbers, force decides: If the analysts are pegging things to investments or risk or rates or the Fed, and thus have an interest in those kinds of entities, they'll make that calculation.

Also, I mentioned that Biggs is studying teacher pension *solvency*—whether pensions have enough money to cover their obligations—and thus the difference between assumed rates of return, for instance, bears on the problem of what we should establish as the contribution rates that school districts and states should be making to pensions so they remain solvent. This is a very different question than the one that Chad Aldeman was asking about what districts and states are spending on those contributions. But as we'll see, that number is also debatable.

To sum up the lesson of this little introduction to Biggs's contribution-side article: You have to look at where people get their numbers and how they calculate those numbers to see how people claim to know what they know about teacher pensions, and who benefits from their conclusions. Biggs is very clear about that context, like how interstellar certain assumptions can be. That awareness, and what I'd call sympathy for the solidaristic teacher retirement policy, infuses his analysis of teacher pension solvency when we contrast it with other cost-side analyses. Like, for instance, how he finds that teacher pensions are solvent.

Notably, in the beginning of Biggs's article, he says that state and local contributions to public retirement and savings between 1998 and 2018 increased only .9 percent. He doesn't break that out into teacher retirement plans, but he's using his Public Plans dataset to talk about the increase in cost. He claims that, "by 2019, the median teacher pension plan had assets equal to 11.4 years of benefit payments. While this is a near-halving of the assets-to-benefits ratio since 2001, the median teacher retirement plan could nevertheless make full payments for approximately a decade without any contributions from either employers or employees."

Oh! So is there a pension crisis? Biggs thinks the more optimistic view is that most teacher pensions have sufficient investment reserves that the worst-case scenario—insolvency of the plans—is highly unlikely in the near term and, for most pensions, unlikely even beyond that. Thus, for most teacher pension plans, fears of imminent insolvency are very likely overblown. Again, you can sense the solidaristic ideology in his approach. When we look at the context around contribution, attending to the health of teacher pensions, which we want to keep around, we find that they're solvent.

Contrast this approach to that of Jess Gartner, Jason Becker, and Anthony Randazzo at Allovue—a school finance consulting firm—who posted an analysis looking at the coming pension debt crisis for teachers.[4]

These authors say that pension debt happens when districts owe the pension funds certain contributions but can't keep up with the payments. The Allovue authors argue, for instance, that the public education system will be on the hook for around $600 billion in pension debt by 2030. Retirement systems for teachers are assuming their payroll grows at 2.9 percent over the next decade, and whether using that rate or a more conservative 2 percent payroll growth level, projected pension debt payments between 2020 and 2030 are between $605 billion and $635 billion. This amounts to a $600 billion budget cut to school districts in the next seven years, something Equable, a research outlet looking at pensions, has called "hidden cuts" to school funding.[5]

Pitting pension costs against school funding costs is a deft move, which is something that Aldeman did in that post I examined in chapter 8. Like Aldeman, the Allovue authors focus on cost, and the ideology comes out when they recommend changes to how pensions are managed (in a pretty saucy way, which I respect). Rather than any political-economic context, the authors point to the mismanagement of pensions as the problem. They say that unfunded pensions crush district budgets and that having "candid conversations" around pension reform can sound "anti-teacher." Indeed, talking about messing with pensions arouses the same vital energies that shut down France in 2023. They reply, "*You know what's anti-teacher?* Keeping teacher salaries flat for decades, maintaining a system that benefits the few at the expense of many, and risking the very solvency of public education—that is anti-teacher. The trend of pension debt as an increasing proportion of public school spending is not fiscally sustainable. We need to cut through the moralizing and have some hard conversations."[6]

Saucy, right? And they're not entirely wrong: We should have some hard conversations. But those hard conversations should be ideologically informed by solidarity, not market orientation and isolation. We can take issue with their framing of these issues too.

They ideologize pension debt in a very anti-district way. What if pension debt isn't when school districts owe a pension money, but rather when things turn out worse than the pension fund's actuaries think? Is it school districts' job to manage the pension? No, it's the managers! But the Allovue authors frame pension debt like school districts are at fault when things turn out badly for the fund, which isn't right. They do the same thing when they characterize unfunded liability as a district budget cut. That's just not how pension finance works.

You don't have to finance a retirement program at 100% for it to cover its obligations. The situation depends on larger demographic conditions. Social Security was 11% funded for 70 years and it was fine, for example. The baby boom made this problematic, sure, but it's all relative. If a state's economy grows at 3% but you're missing 2% of pension payments, it doesn't really matter. Also, along with everything else, the way we break down and think about pension costs, specifically unfunded liabilities, really matters. For example, amortization payments are different than normal costs, and unfunded liabilities are mostly amortization payments, which we can control (particularly if everything evens out at the end of the year). Flattening over these distinctions is anti-solidaristic.

The issue isn't necessarily black and white, and the Allovue article is a good case. This comes out in their recommendations. They recommend (1) more transparency and dialogue about pensions, (2) using state general fund dollars for pension debt payments rather than district dollars, (3) adopting more realistic assumptions for investment to make returns, and (4) getting more creative with how pensions work for teachers, like what South Dakota and Colorado do (which is what's called adaptable pension design) or the hybrid plans in Michigan, Oregon, and South Carolina, where teachers can choose a defined isolation plan.

The first two recommendations make sense, but, like we saw before, what makes an assumed rate of return "realistic"? Who gets to decide what counts as reality in that case? And, yes, there you have it, the recommendation of defined isolation plans in the fourth point.

We don't hear about the context around contribution calculations. According to Biggs in a blog post he wrote for the Brookings Institution, there's a big problem with federal regulations' expectations for contributions and overreliance on equity investments. "In 2001, the median teacher retirement system was 96 percent funded, buoyed by the tech bubble in the stock market. But in 2001 the tech bubble melted down, and then in 2008 the housing market melted down and triggered the Great Recession. By 2019, the median teacher pension was only 70 percent funded." Richard Johnson and Erald Kolasi, writing for the Urban Institute, say teacher pensions got caught in the wave of austerity-think after the 2008 financial crisis and have had a rough go since then:

> Most states provide less generous pensions to teachers hired in 2018 than to teachers hired in 2008. Over the past decade, 43 states raised the contributions that teachers must make to their retirement plan or cut the retirement benefits they will receive. Nearly one-half of state teacher plans raised the age at which teachers can begin collecting their pension, and nearly one-

> third reduced the share of salary that a pension replaces. Among plans that made these changes between 2008 and 2018, the average retirement age increased almost five years and the average replacement rate fell nearly 6 percentage points.[7]

So, is the problem that there's a ton of pension debt, necessitating defined isolation plans? Or is the problem a less generous, more market-oriented regime of thinking that's dominated teacher pension policy for the last few decades? Is there even a problem at all when we look at the numbers? Again, Biggs's conclusion is that teacher pensions are solvent but should be careful about their investments.

My contention in this last part of the book is that there's less of a problem than people like Allovue think, and while there is, in fact, a problem with teacher pensions, that problem is more about the anti-solidaristic policy paradigm used to manage them. You know what's anti-teacher? Anti-solidaristic, neglectful retirement policies that force elderly public educators into facing the social risk of aging on their own, forcing people who are in their old age to gamble on the stock market and giving them no recourse if they lose everything in a crash.

I want to do a few more forensic analyses along these lines. One of them comes from a place called Equable.

The Equable Institute published a report called *America's Hidden Education Funding Cuts*.[8] Just pause for a second here: Equable is such a nice-sounding name. It's very smooth and uses a popular concept in social justice discourse, equity, in its brand. Its website is colorful and well designed, just as inviting as the name. Further, the report itself is smartly framed as examining cuts to public education, a popular rallying cry from teachers unions and movements. No one wants funding cuts, right? And these are hidden cuts—spooky!

In this report, the Equable authors make a stunning claim: that teacher retirement costs for employers (what employers put into the pension funds for teacher retirement) have increased 322 percent since 2004. It's stunning because that's a huge increase. You rarely see numbers like that in research. Aldeman would pick this funding number up in his blog too, making a lot of hay out of just how costly teacher pensions have become. Three hundred twenty-two percent is astronomical. The Equable authors include horrifying graphs with lines going up and up. Similar to Aldeman's logic in the post I examined in chapter 8, the Equable authors call these increases "hidden education funding cuts" because the money that districts and states spend on retirement contributions has become so high, they have to cut spending on other items.

The *Hidden Cuts* report makes clear that its authors are measuring K–12 spending at both the state and district levels in terms of "actual state retirement plan contributions as a share of total K–12 spending." Specifically, they're talking about the change in the percentage of growth of retirement as a share of total spending. Here the wheels should screech to a halt on Equable's smooth operation.

The National Association of State Retirement Administrators (NASRA) called bullshit almost immediately after this Equable report was published, but their critique never got the same media attention as the original report. Authors writing for NASRA found that the authors of the Equable report:

> Overstates the percentage of education spending consumed by teacher pension contributions by drastically understating total public education expenditures; Makes tenuous claims that increasing teacher pension contributions are impairing states' ability to deliver a quality public education by crowding out other education funding priorities; Excludes longer-term context of spending on pension costs; Omits necessary contextual information on factors driving differences in pension cost levels.[9]

These critics of Equable come to similar conclusions that I've articulated in response to Aldeman and Allovue. They're picking up on how tricksy the Equable report's claims are. And I have questions too. Does "change in percentage of growth in retirement as a share of spending" mean we're calculating the difference in contributions to retirement plans from year to year versus the difference in total K–12 spending from year to year? For instance, if in year X this retirement cost was 1 percent of total spending, and the next year it was 1.2 percent, then the growth was 20 percent?

And when it comes to total K–12 funding, is that total K–12 spending per state? Per district? Federally? And is "actual state retirement plan contribution" different from normal cost, and how is that related to the different discount rates that pension policies use to calculate the contribution rates? And why is the 322 percent a combined number of "state and local" contributions, while the graph itself is titled "actual state retirement plan contributions"? Wouldn't it be actual state and local plan contributions? I'm with the NASRA report: this doesn't make sense.

Zooming out, it's also hard to square the 322 percent figure with Biggs's finding about solvency. How could the increase in average state and local contribution to retirement across occupations and industries be .9 percent while when it comes to teacher retirement costs it's 322 percent? It doesn't add up. If teacher retirement costs really rose that much, wouldn't that .9 percent figure be much bigger, given that teachers make up a pretty big population of state and local employees in the country?

The Equable authors say this huge increase is because of pension debt too, but is pension debt even a real problem if the pensions are solvent? Maybe it's just because Equable authors and their venue, which aligns with Aldeman, are so focused on cost? When I looked at some Bureau of Labor Statistics numbers from the time the report was published, tracing a data source that the Equable report cited, I saw that the cost of defined isolation plans was ten times less expensive than that of the defined benefit plans. Defined isolation plans are a capitalist's plan: They serve big banks, private companies, and go-go investing rather than pooling risk and creating solidarity. If your ideological project is to reduce government spending no matter what, even if it means having less solidarity with elderly teachers when they retire, then finding ways to make numbers add up to the astronomical 322 percent makes sense.

The Equable authors note in the report that "data collected for this report came from a wide range of sources, including the Census Bureau, state and local retirement systems, and the National Association of State Budget Officers (NASBO)." Like Biggs, they say that "both the NASBO and Census data have strengths and weaknesses which are summarized in this report and detailed in the complete methodology." In ProPublica's nonprofit tracker, according to Equable's 2021 tax forms, it got the majority of its revenue ($806,418) from private sources, receiving only about $80,000 from government grants. Since 2018 the institute has gotten about $8 million total—Equable's donations are hurting! The institute calls itself bipartisan, which reads neoliberal to me. It doesn't list a board. It doesn't disclose donors. Compare that to the PPD, which has been around for decades and works more from professional actuarial data, and the contrast begins to come into focus.

The Equable authors' argument, and their 322 percent number, is more market oriented: To what extent are school districts taking money away from students and teachers by having to pay pension costs? The question about retirement costs is ideologically configured to undermine the stability of the defined benefit, while the question about solvency is ideologically configured to assess the stability of it.

They're interested in showing that districts are spending way too much on defined benefit retirement plans. They find a way to show this using the percentage growth numbers, blurring the edges around the state/local shares. Biggs, in contrast, is curious about whether teacher pensions are solvent, whether they can meet their obligations generally speaking, not finding more ways to show how expensive they are. These datasets answer different questions, and the researchers are asking different questions, with different ideologies.

The more solidaristic approach is Biggs's: To what extent can and will teacher pensions, using defined benefit structures, meet their obligations? Will the pensions run out of money? He concludes that no, cries of crisis are overblown; these teacher pensions can meet their obligations for at least a decade even if you cut off funding today. He shows that public pension costs have increased only .9 percent in nearly the same time frame that the Equable report shows them increasing 322 percent. While teacher pensions certainly have issues, there's no need to cry crisis—unless you want to dismantle solidarity.

One more forensic look into research on the teacher pension crisis shows us how anti-solidaristic ideology can work in this space, this time with some alliteration.

Robert M. Costrell's "The Three R's of Teacher Pension Funding: Redistribution, Return, and Risk" was published in a special issue of *Educational Researcher* alongside Biggs's piece.[10] Costrell's approach in the article is to use California's teacher pension, CalSTRS, as a case study for specific cost imbalances in teacher pensions generally. (He admits that CalSTRS isn't representative—indeed, it's one of the biggest in the world, not just the country—but he uses his calculations to generate projections anyway.) His goal is to present the "gap between benefits and contributions in a simple integrated framework," considering how

1. employer contributions to pensions redistribute money intergenerationally because they're made on behalf of early career teachers and "help fund the benefits of those who stay longer";
2. "much of contributions for future teachers go towards

unfunded benefits for today's teachers" because of "over-optimistic assumptions of the expected return on investments"; and

3. risky investment decisions create "costs that are off-the-books."

Thus his catchy redistribution-return-risk framing as the three R's of teacher pension funding.

Using this framework is a good way to talk about cost problems, he says. In California, he finds that the "full cost of a career teacher's annual accumulation of benefits can be as high as 46.6 percent of earnings, nearly triple the corresponding contributions of 17.5 percent." That means the pension needs to pay out triple the amount of what comes in from contributions. Here we see another tripling number, sort of like the Equable report's 322 percent. Costrell even has his own calculation of this cost increase from a paper he published in 2015, that "employer contributions now account nationally for about $1,600 per pupil," up from $500 (inflation adjusted) from 2001, another tripling. So how did Costrell get to 46.6 percent? And what's the ideology involved? I'll take each R in turn and give a mathematico-ideological retort to each.

Just to begin with, I have a retort to Costrell's claim that the problem is 46.6 percent big. In general, Costrell's goal is to show that "newly earned benefits continue to cost more than the contributions designated to fund them." Basically, there's a gap between what's coming in and what's supposed to go out. Costs are higher than revenue. The CalSTRS contribution rate is 17.6 percent of teachers' earnings (that's the pension's revenue) but it turns out, he says, that it actually pays out 46.6 percent of earnings, leading to a big funding gap.

The way he gets to his magic 46.6 percent is by adding up all the costs of redistribution, return, and risk: The full cost for sixty-five-year-old retirees is 46.6 percent of their career earnings;

17.5 percent is funded by uniform contributions, another 3.8 percent is *redistributed* from contributions for others, 6.2 percent is the deferred cost if the long-run *returns* come in at 1 percent below assumed, and the extra cost of the *risk* borne to guarantee their pension is 19.1 percent of their earnings. It's all so bad! The pension costs so much more than it takes in from contributions! Panic! But wait—let's look at each number and the responses we gave to each premise. We can and should be pretty suspicious here.

There's a sleight of hand in Costrell using the 46.6 percent number, in that it seems like the gap between contributions and payouts is close to 50 percent. But it's not. The contribution rate for the pension fund is already 17.5 percent. So the problem isn't really 46.6 percent big; it's actually 29.1 percent big, because Costrell is saying that he found 29.1 percent more costs. So let's break down where that 29.1 percent of other problems is coming from in the three R's.

Costrell's first premise is that younger teachers' money is being redistributed to older teachers. He says, "An individual who leaves at age 45, with benefits that cost only 8% of earnings, is effectively seeing almost 10 percentage points worth of contributions redistributed to fund the benefits of others. Conversely, the benefits for an individual existing at age 65, which cost 21.3% of earnings, are effectively being funded by contributions for others of almost 4% of earning, on top of the contributions made by or for herself."

Some noticings about this point. First, notice the word "effectively." I think Costrell has to qualify the relationship between contributions by younger teachers and annuity to older teachers like this because it's not causally or maybe even factually true in an obvious way. If you took out that qualifier "effectively," you'd see that he couldn't argue that the benefits from younger teachers are actually going to older teachers. Of course, we can see this amount, the difference between contribution and benefit, that he's calculated as that intergenerational redistribution if we trust him. But why should we? It's a lot like Aldeman's saying that pension costs are "attributable" to districts, without being able to so attribute them.

For instance, by Costrell's logic, it could be that the number of people who live until they're 100 and collect their pensions are effectively getting a redistribution from the people who die when they're 65 and don't collect anything. Maybe that's what's happening! Second, even if we grant that this amount, this difference between contribution and benefit, is effectively redistributed from old to young, isn't that how we'd want a solidarity policy to work? He's literally just describing intergenerational solidarity. Some people give up some of their benefits to others so the latter can live well later too. The givers understand that they'll be taken care of also, and understand that, okay, if they leave early they won't be able to take advantage of the program.

The next big premise in Costrell's argument is about how bad current assumptions about return are. Costrell says that the ways the California teacher pension's managers think about how much the pension fund will make from its investments are too optimistic, which, if true, creates pension debt because it will end up needing more than it can provide.

Pensions typically assume 7–8 percent returns on investment, but Costrell says that CalSTRS got only 5.8 percent between 2001 and 2019. Let's grant him that the primary source documents actually say this (which they might not!). If we use a 6 percent return, he says, the numbers don't look good. Costrell says, "The benefits of those retiring at age 65 would cost 27.5 percent of earnings over their careers, of which 17.5 percent is covered by current contributions." Thus, currently earned benefits are not being fully funded.

The point about return here is a central node, maybe the point of tension, between the cost side and the contribution side. You can't talk about return assumptions without talking about the political-economic contexts in which these assumptions occur, which ultimately configure pension costs. Costrell is no exception. And the weakness of the cost-side perspective shows when he talks about that very context in the 2001–2019 period: "Long after the bull market of the 1990s had passed, most plans continued to assume their investments would earn 8 percent or more annually. Clearly, this became untenable following the crash of 2008."

Two things here. Costrell's adverbs are good signs of the ideology in his account. Notice how he says "clearly," as a kind of throat clearing, or nervous grinning shrug, to make way for a noticeably passive construction to talk about investment return assumptions. These assumptions, which were normal actuarial assumptions, "became untenable" following the crash of 2008.

I had to laugh. It's as if the assumptions are things by themselves, existing in a void-like vacuum, and change magically, on their own, rather than existing as thoughts in people's heads in a society with a history. It's not like pension return assumptions just "became untenable" suddenly, shockingly, without cause. No, actually, capitalists and lawmakers were stupid and tanked the economy.

So yeah, pension assumptions about the returns they can get had to change. And during the supposed recovery, neoliberals kept up their bad economic policies rather than being even the slightest bit generous, particularly in the public sphere, and public pensions suffered. To blame a public pension for this situation is abhorrent. Calling these assumptions "overly optimistic" is like saying that a murder victim was "overly optimistic" in assuming their murderer wouldn't murder them.

So, I retort: The 6.2 percent part of the 29.1 percent—(which is questionable math)—the problem of lower returns than pensions assumed, which Costrell is holding against the pension in terms of return—this dip happened because Wall Street freaks ruined the economy in 2008.

We should blame capital! Public pensions are just trying to take care of public servants when they become too old to work. These pension managers made certain assumptions that served them well historically before capitalists tanked the world, and they kept up with those assumptions because they didn't really have any other option when those capitalists' lawmakers decided to keep pushing their neoliberal austerity regimes despite the crisis. Claiming this returns issue as a cost problem is gross.

Finally, for the last R, Costrell talks about the way this return can vary by the riskiness of pension investments, not just assumptions about returns. When you don't invest in risky assets, you stand to lose money because you're not making as much as you might be able to. Because pensions don't do enough risky investing, they stand to lose money. They pay a risk premium. "Thus, the full cost of risk-free benefits is much higher than that calculated by public pension plans."

Private defined benefit pension plans have to report this risk premium in the form of a discount rate, which is "equal to the low-risk return on high-grade corporate bonds, regardless of the plan's actual portfolio." But public pensions don't have to do this. So Costrell says there are "hidden costs." Costrell assumes a 4 percent discount rate "which is about the return on high-grade corporate bonds used to evaluate the cost of private sector defined benefit plans" and finds that "the full cost of CalSTRS is 38.8%," which, apparently, is what happens when you consider "the cost of overestimating the long-run return on risky assets . . . and other tangible and intangible costs of risk."

This is a lot of leaps. First and most importantly, it's not reasonable for public pensions to be held to the same standards as private pensions. Shouldn't public pensions be in a different category? They don't have to worry about getting liquidated. Their approach to risk is paradigmatically different than the private sector. Second, it's all speculative thinking here, speculations upon speculations, and Costrell cites the "principles" involved in risk assessment, while wildly abstracting to get these numbers. He doesn't know the actual composition of CalSTRS's portfolio. He doesn't know the actual risks involved (which is also kind of a problem with the Governmental Accounting Standards Board, since it doesn't talk much about investment risk, but that's another can of worms). He just applies the numbers "in principle" and gets this massive conclusion that, conveniently, fits his argument. This is how he gets the 19.1 percent part of the 29.1 percent here, the lion's share of his finding.

So, I retort: The 19.1 percent part of the 29.1 percent—the risk premium costs pensions incur when they don't invest in the most lucrative investments—is wild speculation (Costrell says nothing about the actual portfolio) and a category mistake (that public pensions should be treated the same as private ones).

Every number comes from somewhere; every number is ideological; Costrell's argument is seriously flawed. So we have to ask again, is there a pension problem? Biggs has already said, in the same special issue, that, yes, while costs have gone up, the pensions themselves aren't at risk of insolvency. So the pensions are fine. They can pay out their annuities. Biggs even includes CalSTRS in his dataset—and he looks at thirty-one pensions, not just one, like Costrell. So what's going on here?

Costrell shows his anti-solidarity colors. When it comes to defined isolation plans, he says, "There are no hidden costs to be paid later. There are no hidden subsidies from some employees to help cover the retirement costs of other employees." Then he really shows the anti-solidaristic ideology of this stance: "Each employee has his or her own retirement. The ultimate retirement benefit is uncertain, depending on the choice of investments and the return, but the cost is not."

Here's the market ideology in plain sight. He's saying that our teacher pension policy should follow this imperative: What old people who can't work might get from their retirement savings might be uncertain, depending on what they end up with—but, hey, at least the cost is certain! The solidarity is severely lacking. He gets it exactly backward. We should want to be as certain as possible about what our old teachers who can't work will get as they age, not how much trying to take care of them will cost us now. What's the purpose of public programs costing anything to begin with? To provide things for people! Not to not spend! The pyrotechnics involved in Costrell's talking about this cost problem are staggering: These cost-side people go to all kinds of great lengths to prove their point.

Anti-solidarity people like Costrell, the Equable report's authors, and Aldeman (and the Allovue authors, kind of) will find all sorts of weird ways to cry crisis and new and creative approaches to talking about the cost of public pensions, whereas someone like Biggs—and others, we'll see in chapter 10—will have more solidarity.

10
Green Fiscal Mutualism

You can learn a lot when leftists disagree in public. The disagreement I'm interested in here is one about what to do with public pensions.

The cover story for the January 2018 issue of *In These Times* was "Wall Street Isn't the Answer to the Pension Crisis. Expanding Social Security Is," by Doug Henwood and Liza Featherstone, heavy hitters on the left.[1] Henwood even went on C-SPAN to talk about the article.[2] Then pensions researcher Max Sawicky responded to Henwood and Featherstone in the magazine, saying no, there's no pension crisis, and that Henwood and Featherstone's recommendations were misguided.[3] Henwood responded, saying yes, there is a crisis.[4] Sawicky responded again, in a fourth piece for *Jacobin*, saying no, again, there is no pension crisis.[5] Literally, the "noes" and "yeses" were in the headlines.

This debate wasn't specifically about teacher pensions, but it's helpful for understanding what a socialist approach to teacher pensions might be and what, if anything, we should propose to change about public teachers' retirement policy from a left perspective.

Weirdly, Henwood and Featherstone agree with the cost-siders that there's a pension crisis. But they have a totally different ideological project. They're not market-oriented. Far from it. They want retirement funds out of markets entirely (pension funds are 67% of private equity's capital![6]). They'd rather get rid of pensions whole hog in favor of a more robust social security system at the federal level, like the Wagner-Murray-Dingell Bill Michael McCarthy talked about in *Dismantling Solidarity*.

They make their left-wing cost-side argument by focusing on the unsustainability of pension needs. Whereas Chad Aldeman gets his data from the Bureau of Labor Statistics and Equable, Costrell gets his data from the CalSTRS pension, and Biggs gets his data from the Public Plans Database, Henwood and Featherstone get their numbers from the Federal Reserve.

They write that state governments have promised $5.9 trillion to present and future retirees. Unfortunately, the pensions don't have anywhere near that kind of money, either on hand or in the foreseeable future. Crisis-driven cuts have only made the situation worse. The Fed has calculated that, all told, the nation's pension accounts are $1.7 trillion in the hole. Others put the shortfall at closer to $4 trillion.

Henwood and Featherstone have their own scary graph to illustrate what they call "the gap," showing the hole pensions need to fill. Like the 322 percent graph from Equable, it looks bad. But let's think about it for a second. In terms of having enough money right now, Biggs, in his study of thirty-one teacher pensions, has already told us that teacher pensions are not at risk of insolvency. The claim that Henwood and Featherstone are making, though, is that pensions generally don't have enough money to pay out their retirees' annuities over the next few decades, which, despite pensions' current solvency, remains an open question.

Why is it an open question? In Henwood's C-SPAN interview, he talked a lot about investments, Wall Street, bonds, and the performance of the stock market. It turns out that your position on whether pensions are in crisis depends on how you think about Wall Street investment performance over the long term.

Pensions pay out annuities to current retirees right now in the present, but the funds have to do this for future retirees too. The pensions are managed by investment experts who buy and sell stocks and bonds using the pension's money. Their goal is to bring in returns that will keep the fund in good shape over time so that the pension can keep its promise to every future retiree.

To manage the pension, these experts have to read a lot of tea leaves. Will pension investments make good returns? How will the stock and bond markets perform? To research the pension and assess whether it can keep its promise, you have to argue for your interpretation of those tea leaves. When we ask whether the pension won't be able to pay these benefits at some point in the future, whether distant or near, we have to make some assumptions about how much pensions can make on their investments in stocks, bonds, and so forth.

No one knows the future. The leaves can tell many stories. But we can make assumptions about the future to do our best when we plan. Are public pensions' assumptions about future returns bad or good? If you think they're bad, then you think that pensions are in crisis. If you think they're good, then you think pensions are fine. That's where Henwood and Featherstone and Sawicky disagree.

Henwood and Featherstone cite a Stanford economist who found that public pensions assumed a 7.6 percent return on their investments. Henwood and Featherstone call that assumption "recklessly optimistic" given poor market performance before and after the 2008 financial crisis. They recommend that pensions should assume the return that a standard Treasury bond gets, which is maybe more appropriate for a public pension fund than a corporate bond, but also much more conservative. Those bonds get around 2.5 percent (this was in 2018, before the Fed increased rates!). When you assume that pensions will get a 2.5 percent return, the cost crisis becomes extremely alarming, just as it did in Costrell's view: The pensions won't be able to pay out their annuities if that's what they're going to make from the market.

In chapter 9, I discussed how Costrell made a similar case, showing that CalSTRS had only a 5.8 percent return on its investments between 2001 and 2019. While Henwood and Featherstone think anything above 7 percent is recklessly optimistic given the stock market performance, they also mention that while 2.5 percent might be too pessimistic, it's a better way to think about the whole situation given how bonkers the market is.

This is basically where Sawicky hits Henwood and Featherstone. He says there's no reason to assume market conditions will be that bad. He also says that if you look at public pensions from the Government Accountability Office lens (rather than the Fed, PPD, Bureau of Labor Statistics, etc.), there's no reason to panic—indeed, there's no crisis with pensions if you don't make these assumptions. They're not insolvent. There's no risk of them losing money.

Sawicky also disagrees with the politics of Henwood and Featherstone's argument. He doesn't like the left being in league with neoliberals and right-wingers bent on destroying unions and privatizing pensions. He also doesn't think a big, public social security program is a feasible policy to propose. Bernie Sanders's electrifying campaign was only two years old when Henwood and Featherstone were writing; they may have gotten caught up in the excitement, and Sawicky is skeptical. Why put the pension programs we have, some of the last bastions of solidarity in retirement policy, on the chopping block in favor of a pie-in-the-sky proposal? Sawicky recommends supporting pensions as they are, protecting them from right-wing attacks, and making them serve the working class better than they do.

Rather than a cost or contribution line of demarcation in this debate, it's more about whether you're a two or a seven—that is, whether you think it's better to assume a 2 percent market return or a 7 percent market return. Henwood and Featherstone are two-ers and Sawicky is a sevener. I think Sawicky has a point here: Henwood and Featherstone's approach is some eleven-dimensional chess where they use right-wing talking points to advocate a left-wing project. Why not lead with the left-wing project? Why even mess with the right-wing talking points? Doesn't that cede the right crucial ground?

What does this debate tell us about the socialist approach to teacher pension policy?

Let's think about the ideology here. Henwood and Featherstone are socialists. They don't trust capitalism to provide a stable, generous, humane, or moral mode of distribution for the social risk of aging. They're ultimately making the case for a big, public social security program at the federal level that would supplant the pensions that exist now. This perspective comes through when they tell some wild stories about how pension investments actually undermine workers' rights and lives. Here's one of them.

> Kohlberg Kravis Roberts was a private equity firm that bought the grocery chain Safeway in the 1990s. They cut 63,000 working class jobs when they closed stores and restructured the company so it was profitable. They made \$7.2 billion on their \$129 million investment. Where'd they get that money? Partly from investments made by Oregon, Washington State, and Michigan public pensions. The public pensions put in money and got back good returns. They made some money for their retirees' annuities, but that money came from the pillaging of grocery store workers.

Stories like this abound. The political economy of Henwood and Featherstone's market assumptions is important to think about. Shouldn't socialists want old-age policy out of the market? We shouldn't take from some workers to give to others, they say. When they cite right-wing economists on the pension crisis, they're doing this to advance a larger socialist project, which turns the market ideology behind those claims on its head.

But Sawicky is also advancing a socialist project by being more realistic, and he's got a point. He takes on the political economy of these market assumptions by suggesting that pensions are invested in all kinds of things, and these terrible stories could be found in any instance of investment. Why hurt workers by telling these stories and putting their pensions at risk? (I made a similar point when writing about Costrell's argument about risk: Since we don't dig into all the actual pension investments, we have to make assumptions about the portfolios, and we imagine them with ideology.)

But neither side of this debate looks at where this problem actually comes from: discounting.

Recall that discounting is the process by which pension managers make assumptions about the present value of the pension fund based on speculations about future returns on pension fund investments. In a previous chapter, I referred to the film *Interstellar* as an allegory. I was thinking specifically about the part where a couple of astronauts go down from a spaceship onto a planet whose gravity is such that time passes very differently for their colleagues left on the spaceship. For every minute they're on the planet, a year passes for the astronaut back on board the ship. They went down and did what they had to do in what felt to them like a few minutes, but by the time they got back to the ship their comrade had waited twenty-three years for them to return. (Also, as Liliana Doganova says in her amazing book about discounting, from which I learned all this, Kim Stanley Robinson's *The Ministry for the Future* is based on this kind of insight.[7])

You have to operate in that temporally projected mode of thinking when it comes to discount rates, which, for pensions, are calculated using something called an "assumed rate of return." Equable helpfully defines the process this way:

> Assumed rate of return is the single most important assumption that pension systems make to ensure they have enough funding to pay benefits promised. To determine the amount of required contributions, a pension fund and its actuaries make educated guesses about how much they think they can earn by investing those contributions. That educated guess is called the assumed rate of return [which is a kind of discount rate]. The higher the assumed rate of return, the fewer contributions teachers and their employers have to make. The lower it is, the higher contributions need to be in order to pay for the benefits promised.[8]

I like this definition. First, because it makes the explicit connection between the discount rate (how much pension managers expect the contributions to grow in the future) and the contribution cost (how much should be put in right now). The cost of pensions is not an immutable thing that just exists out there in nature. We change it based on speculation. The definition further underscores this speculative contingency with its language of the "educated guess." Not only can you mess with discount rates; the people who set these rates are just guessing! Finally, the definition makes plain that these educated guesses are typically made from a distinct perspective: that of the investor. Even though teacher pensions serve educators, it's not the educator's perspective with which such decisions are made. It's a kind of mythical "investor" who's only interested in the highest possible returns.

Liliana Doganova's book *Discounting the Future: The Ascendancy of a Political Technology* brilliantly unpacks the history, sociology, economics, and politics of discounting, which, it turns out, is at the heart of financial capitalism (not just teacher pensions). A couple of insights from her book guide my thinking about the socialist approach to teacher pensions, my own contribution to the Henwood and Featherstone-Sawicky debate, and become important for the end of this book.

Doganova says that the famed twentieth-century economist Irving Fisher articulated the basic concept of discounting as a definition of value in the early 1900s, though its history is actually rooted in the early political economy of tree farming. She traces discounting's history in capitalism as one way to understand what people mean when they talk about financialization, or the process of an economy becoming dominated by financial investments rather than traditionally productive activities like manufacturing. When discounting, as valuing over time, became all about returns to the investor—and the investor only, rather than the public—that's what she calls financialization.

Two vignettes from *Discounting the Future* are really helpful for articulating the importance of discounting for a socialist perspective on school finance and pensions in the era of climate change.

In the 2000s, Nicholas Stern, an economist at the London School of Economics, was tasked by the British government with writing a report about the economic impacts of climate change. In 2006, he published his report, which has become known as *The Stern Review*. In it, he concluded that the costs of not acting to reduce climate change were equivalent to losing 5 percent of global gross domestic product each year, whereas acting in a drastic way involved only a 1 percent reduction. It caused a huge stir.

Doganova says that the trick that allowed this conclusion "lay in a redefinition of the discount rate," given that in climate change, "we are not in a situation in which one individual is deciding whether she should consume now or save for later. We are in a situation in which current generations are deciding to consume now and thereby depriving not themselves, but future generations, of the possibility to consume later, the 'later' of current generations being actually the 'now' of future generations."[9] Stern presumed that "future generations deserve the same ethical attention as the current generation," which means, economically, in terms of discounting, that the discount rate used to value assets in the future should be very low, approaching zero. Stern argued that, to properly account for climate catastrophe in economics, there "should be a fundamental change in discounting to allow for reaching the conclusion that it is worth acting now to save the future." The future, in this sense, should not be discounted (that is, valued less than the present). "Climate action," writes Doganova, "is thus justified. More than that, it becomes urgent."

While *The Stern Review* created a big kerfuffle in economics, it's important to note here because it shows how the discount rate is ethical, political, and subject to change based on our ideology. In education, we tend to value future generations quite highly. It's the whole purpose of educating. If that's true, then when it comes to school finance, we should reflect it in our discount rates for teacher pension funds and all kinds of school finance policies. This is one way a teacher's perspective might differ from an investor's.

Or maybe, from a socialist perspective, we don't want to use discounting at all. In the 1970s, when socialist Salvadore Allende came to power in Chile, one thing that his administration did was nationalize the copper mines, one of the biggest sources of income for the country's economy. But what does "nationalize" mean exactly? The state took over control of the mines from private companies, expropriating the value of the mines. And how did the state calculate the value of the mines, to figure out what, if anything, it owed the companies? The state intentionally didn't use discounting,—it didn't talk about future productivity at all. The socialists rejected this whole concept. Instead, the state talked about past productivity, valuing the mines according to what they produced for the Chilean people in the past rather than speculating about what they'd be worth in the future. When Allende's economists were done with their calculations, they argued that the companies actually owed the government money!

Again, what's important in this example for our present purposes is to see how the valuation of something like a copper mine or a teacher pension fund can be creatively done in line with our ideological tendencies. We don't have to just accept the financial practices that are used today; we can be creative about how we value pension funds and use those funds toward purposes we deem necessary. Like, for instance, making sure there's a thriving environment for students to live in rather than a dystopia.

In general, I think the two-versus-seven debate misses an opportunity to think more creatively about pensions, investment, and the climate crisis. While there is certainly an important debate to be had about what rates we should use when thinking about and managing pensions, I also think we should be talking more about where contribution money comes from and goes; that is, we should have a debate about ideological and philosophical approaches to managing pension investments, not getting lost in either-or framings that stipulate the assumed-rate-of-return should be 2 percent or 7 percent. We should be philosophical, ethical, and broadly intentional about what the discount rate should be when pension managers make decisions.

One philosophical-ideological approach to teacher pensions that I think socialists should get behind is green fiscal mutualism.

I get the term "fiscal mutualism" from Michael Glass and Sean Vanatta's research on the history of teacher pensions in New York State. Between 1947 and 1962, the New York State teacher pension actually held upwards of 10 percent of its fund in school bonds. That's right, the teacher pension was invested in the districts' infrastructure, using that huge pool of capital toward the very facilities where the teachers were working and students were learning.

Glass and Vanatta call that period one of fiscal mutualism, when the public pension was invested in public infrastructure, like school districts. Rather than focusing exclusively on investor returns, the pension was focused on supporting the public infrastructure its members used throughout their careers. But that approach would change as the teacher pension changed its thinking about investment. Whereas before the 1970s, it invested in public infrastructure, by 1972, the pension held nearly 80 percent in private securities and few if any school bonds.[10] What if we revamped fiscal mutualism for the time of climate change, hewing our teacher pension discount rates according to educators' values rather than investors'?

Here's one way I think this could work. If there were sympathetic minds in the federal government (a big if!), the Treasury could bundle school bonds into a financial instrument and sell that security to teacher pensions through a renewed Build America Bonds program. The program could stipulate that, if pensions buy a certain amount of the new bonds, a baseline for coverage of pension returns would kick in. Let's say it's 6.8 percent, which is on the low side of what all the actuaries use. If the teacher pension invests 45 percent of its portfolio in school bonds and makes only a 5 percent return in a given year, then the federal government would cover any costs incurred by the lost 1.8 percent. The pension would get even more money if the school bonds are green bonds or the bond revenues go toward green infrastructure. In this case, the pension could also set its discount rate in a way that prioritizes lower contributions.

Basically, to use a term that's in vogue right now in political economy and finance studies, this policy proposal *de-risks* public teacher pensions' investment in green public school infrastructure, simultaneously creating a safety net for pensions interested in doing fiscal mutualism. There's even a way to do this green fiscal mutualism that doesn't rely on a friendly federal government. States have a multitude of financial authorities that issue bonds, as well as an increasing number of green banks. Unions and community organizers could organize campaigns that pressure state governments to de-risk teacher pension investment in green school bonds through borrowing authorities and green banks.

In this green fiscal mutualism approach to teacher pensions, the money that teachers, states, and districts contribute to retirement funds thus gets used to generate revenue for the infrastructure those teachers work in as they educate students. If things go pear-shaped with the school bonds for whatever reason (which is actually rare), the state or federal government steps in and does damage control, making sure the pension costs don't go through the roof in the process. Meanwhile, school buildings put less carbon in the atmosphere and reduce the likelihood that its students won't have a world to live in. This approach has a number of benefits.

The first problem green fiscal mutualism would address is teacher pension contribution increases given volatile market outcomes. Whether we think the market will perform well or poorly, it's certainly true that poor performance leaves teacher pensions on the hook for high contributions. School bonds are an historically safe investment. The second problem it addresses is the ongoing crisis in public school infrastructure. We have a country full of toxic schools, at least half of them in need of significant repair. These schools are underwritten by toxic finance policy: As I've written about throughout this book, districts borrow more than half a trillion dollars on Wall Street. There's no federal policy for this school buildings problem, which, I think, demands a federal solution and, barring that, new solutions at the state level.

By de-risking teacher pension investment in green school bonds we can shore up any potential crises in teacher pensions (such as they might be) and actively do something about the ongoing school infrastructure crisis in hard-hit areas, while continuing to encourage green infrastructure that won't poison the planet our students are supposed to grow up and live in.

A good case study for all this—both the need for green fiscal mutualism and how it could work—comes from Chicago Public Schools. I'll end the chapter with it.

In late 2024, there was a budget crisis in the city to the tune of nearly $1 billion. A lot of that crisis had to do with the schools' budget. According to the mayor's office, the crisis in money for schools was created in large part by a rogue $175 million pension contribution payment. "The $222.9 million year-end projected budget deficit is driven by a decline in specific revenue streams, including . . . the City not receiving the budgeted $175 million reimbursement for pension contributions for Chicago Public Schools (CPS) non-teacher staff."[11] How did this $175 million gap open up? Some intricate city pension policy changes. Former mayor Lori Lightfoot had shifted the responsibility for that non-teacher staff pension payment locally. The pension is called the Municipal Employees' Annuity and Benefit Fund of Chicago (MEABF) and covers paraprofessionals, clerks, and school assistants. Mayor Brandon Johnson wants the district to pay it too.

It turns out pension contribution payments—including this pension payment that added a lot of pressure to the crisis—didn't just fall out of the proverbial coconut tree. They exist in the context of all that's around them. In other words, they're calculated by people using protocols that are highly speculative, contested, and contestable. Looking at the MEABF's assumed rate of return is a good example of what I've been talking about in this chapter, but also how there's room to maneuver and politicize teacher pension policy when fighting to make education as public as possible.

Let's rewind. In 2023, private consultants recommended a 7 percent discount rate for the MEABF.[12] Fast-forwarding to 2024, we can see how that rate is partly behind the district's $175 million problem. A slightly different rate, even by fractions of a percentage point, buttressed by de-risked pension investment from the teacher pension, could reduce the weight of this contribution responsibility.

Why not get people talking about this, raise awareness that Wall Street thinking gets us to this place, not working-class thinking?

For instance, if one were to organize around this issue of the pension's assumed rate of return, a short-term demand would be to ask the MEABF managers to change the discount rate calculation to reflect educators' values and lower the $175 million contribution payment. That might mean increasing the discount rate above 7 percent. Just like Stern's creative use of the discount rate, the reasoning here is that students' families need housing now, for example, and we live in a time of great uncertainty. If there were a de-risking policy in place at the state level, there'd be increased confidence in this move. There's no need to use Wall Street thinking to needlessly put ourselves into an austerity crisis. We can use the discount rate to push for our values.

In the medium term, with an increase in the MEABF discount rate, Chicago Public Schools could adopt a green fiscal mutualism that serves people before profiteers. The city and its leadership might demand that one of the state's central financial entities, Illinois Finance Authority, de-risk MEABF investment in the school district itself, focusing on green infrastructure projects for schools. Rather than continuing to go into further debt, the Chicago school community could use the pension fund to support the schools and vice versa rather than treating them as isolated pools of capital that have to be managed by investor-type thinking. This mindset prioritizes myopic fiduciary duty, a one-dimensional strategy that only values dollar returns using past trends in a social and political and ethical vacuum. In my scheme, if MEABF returns come in below a certain threshold after investing in Chicago Public Schools bonds, the state finance authority can fill in the gap, prioritizing the needs of Chicago's people. And if there were ever a friendly federal government open to these sorts of ideas, we could further capitalize state green banks for this explicit purpose, or even start the National Investment Authority to create new products that would de-risk the pensions further.

These kinds of policies can go hand in hand with the policies I've discussed throughout the book, which I'll sum up in the conclusion under the banner of green fiscal mutualism. For now, here's one last way to think about teacher pensions: organizing.

My old neighbor in Philadelphia was a longtime labor organizer. Her husband was a teacher and unionist also. One afternoon, we were talking about the state of things in the labor movement—specifically, left-wing caucuses organizing to mobilize big teacher unions. Then she said something that stuck with me. The older teachers in these huge unions, she said, always vote in elections, and they tend to vote with the older leaders because they've known them for a long time. But there's something possibly more powerful than their sense of familiarity with existing leadership: their pensions.

If you spend your career in a public service profession, or any profession with a pension, you start to really appreciate that pension. As a fixed benefit, a big portion of whatever salary you finish your career at is yours to take home until you die. So if anyone messes with your pension, like they did in France in 2023, you pay attention because that's your livelihood as you age and can't work to earn.

So my neighbor wagered that if the relatively younger left-wing caucuses in the union could come to understand the ins and outs of their unions' pension policies, and then propose ways to improve those policies or at least show that existing leadership isn't doing as much as it could for pensions, then that might sway the older voters in an election. Fighting on pensions is smart and could also result in big wins.

Conclusion

A Plan for Public Education

There are thirteen thousand school districts in the United States and many of them were struggling when I sat down to write the conclusion to this book.

The world after the pandemic had settled into its chaotic normal: once-in-a-hundred-year weather events every month, a school shooting every week, and Donald Trump winning a second presidency. Hope was in short supply. The ideological struggles in U.S. school districts over the previous five years had been intense. Groups like Moms for Liberty, the right-wing backlash to the George Floyd rebellions in the midst of the pandemic, launched well-funded and sort of well-organized attacks on what they called "critical race theory" and "gender ideology." This racist, patriarchal, transphobic ideological formation, underwritten by privatization advocates, has brought these energies to school board meetings and school board elections and produced gobs of posts, reports, and screeds as part of a right-wing incursion into the schools, and then infected the federal government, sending everyone reeling.

Underneath the more bombastic and headline-grabbing froth there was a deeper tendency: the line that racial capital and its representatives took on the school budget in that moment, which put profit and its racial tendencies before public education. Sometimes the rationales for cuts and privatization sounded reasonable when announced and reported to school communities: enrollment decline, expiration of federal COVID relief money, falling space utilization. They had numbers that looked, and actually were, unto themselves, not untrue. But these numbers were deployed in the context of a larger web of political-economic structural forces. What kept me up at night was that very few people, including school board members, students, superintendents, labor leaders, teachers, parents, and so on, understood the public finance policies through which those forces work on school districts and communities. Yet racial capitalists have time and resources to study these, take advantage of them, and outmaneuver communities.

Meanwhile, local journalists, hollowed out by the decline of community newspapers, became basically stenographers for capital, rarely raking any muck on the capitalists at all, just taking school leadership at its word. In places where intellectuals with a national focus wouldn't think to think about, communities went without the critical analysis they needed to fight back. Diverse working-class school districts were left high and dry as the forces of racial capital worked against them, closing schools and worse.

Every day I got a new message from someone in some district asking me to look into their budget crisis. By June 2025, the list was more than 150 districts long.

Two things had happened to me that got the word out about my socialist approach to school finance. First, Jennifer Berkshire and Jack Schneider had me on their podcast, *Have You Heard*. It's one of the few education podcasts that takes an unabashedly pro-public stance and does great interviews across the spectrum of teachers, students, parents, academics, organizers, and community members who focus their energies on holding that rope in the tug-of-war against privatization. The podcast featured me and my story in a way I wasn't exactly anticipating, but I was happy with how it came out—and apparently others were too. I heard from a mom in Ohio, a superintendent in Wisconsin, a school board leader in Chicago, a teacher in southern California, a videographer in Connecticut, and a nonprofit leader in Florida—all of them wanting to talk to a socialist about school finance.

Meanwhile, as Twitter died a slow and painful death over the pandemic, I got into TikTok as a way of getting information out there. I found an audience after I began taking requests to look into school district budget crises. My videos were about a minute long and focused on a detail from a district's crisis I thought was particularly interesting or telling. Each video inspired comments from others and more requests.

One commenter on TikTok asked me to look at the situation in the Newberg, Oregon, school district. A brief look at Newberg gives us an example of the kind of local struggles that socialists can and should get involved with, particularly as we get the steady flow of repulsive dispatches from the Trump administration.

In 2024, Newberg's district, Newberg-Dundee School District, announced a nearly $4 million budget deficit. It came down to some misunderstanding of how to estimate state grants, but those mistakes were made in the din of the current milieu. In 2021, the new right-wing wave of culture war descended on Newberg-Dundee.[1] A right-wing school board got elected.[2] This new leadership prioritized banning LGBTQ+ and Black Lives Matter flags in classrooms and talking a big game about banning books, but, it turns out, they didn't quite understand how these kinds of policies work.[3] A county judge overturned the ban first. Then the sitting superintendent, Joe Morelock, refused to enforce the ban. The new board, dissatisfied, fired that superintendent and appointed a right-wing superintendent, which began an administrative churn, including "significant turnover among administrators, including its directors of finance and communications as well as the director and coordinator director of special programs."[4]

The people of Newberg didn't appreciate their new school leaders either, so they voted out the right-wingers in 2023. But when the new, more progressive leadership team (called the Yamhill Group) came into their positions, they found the money was in disarray.[5] There was a $4 million hole for the school year. Even more troubling was a looming $11 million deficit for the following year, which threatened to reduce the school year by ten days and imperil new science and health curricula that were set to be implemented. The whole situation prompted student walkouts in the spring of 2023.[6]

The culture war has costs, like when the right-wing budget office forgets to estimate supplemental expenditures correctly while district leadership focuses on banning books. Researchers John Rogers, Rachel White, Robert Shand, and Joseph Kahne found in 2024 that right-wing culture wars cost public school districts upwards of $3.2 billion, like when school board members have to pay for legal teams to handle expensive court cases brought by plaintiffs funded by right-wing think tanks and billionaires, or the costs of increasing security at school board meetings when there are bomb threats and other calls to violence against district leaders.[7] The Newberg-Dundee case is just one among many in the larger tug-of-war happening throughout America's schools right now where the left faces profound fiscal challenges in the wake of the right's ruination of education. When left-wing candidates run for and win office, they face extremely complex budgetary problems as they try to pick up the pieces and uphold and even strengthen public education.

Here's where I want to contribute with this book: Rather than fighting to protect public education from the scary momentum the right-wing always seems to generate and waiting for moderates to get their shit together and push back (which they don't actually want to do), the left should get wonky to figure out how to make education as public as possible. This means finding more money for education, of course, but that money should not just be funneled into public education as it is. Instead, new resources should be marshaled as part of a larger project that goes on offense rather than playing defense. As the right tries to make public education as private as possible, and the center remains squishy, the left should go on offense when it comes to policy, and make education as public as possible.

As I looked at district budget crises all over the country, from Chicago to Newberg-Dundee to Philadelphia to Carmel Clay to Panther Valley, I realized that these crises are nothing new. They may have new details, but school districts have existed for generations in this country, and they're subject to similar cycles of fiscal crisis. Even if socialists win elections—for mayor or city council or Congress or President—they come up against the hard-to-understand, decentralized patchwork of the American racial capitalist school finance regime, a teeming scene of property taxes, mill rates, assessments, state funding formulas, reimbursement programs, municipal bonding, and pension policies. These things are stubborn, esoteric, and immensely powerful. But they're not set in stone.

I've called this school finance regime a weak link in the chain of American racial capitalism because when you mess with it, the rest of the chain starts to shake. People have deep spiritual and material investments in the schools in their communities. That's why the right-wing uses education as a terrain to fight and push their agenda.

Instead of getting dragged into that tug-of-war, we should change the whole game and try to transform the policy regimes that put public education in peril. We should advance an agenda for a truly public education for all: not subject to the tyrannies of the local property tax, the instability of state funding structures, and the hands-off neglect of the federal government.

We need public education that's not bought and sold as investment commodities for retired millionaires on Wall Street, subjecting school districts to racist interest rates, fees, and credit ratings on the municipal bond market. We need public education that doesn't give ground to free market fanatics who want to ditch defined benefit retirement programs in favor of anti-solidaristic defined isolation plans, leaving retired educators vulnerable to the rapacious vicissitudes of market crises and pushing new teachers away from the profession.

In this book, I've described this wretched system's status quo and proposed policies that could make public education as public as possible. Here's a summary of some of those policies, which I think could be combined in any number of ways, based on a green fiscal mutualism for the diverse working class:

1. Incentivize and implement regional fiscal disparities programs in every metro region of the country, with taxbase and debt sharing between municipalities to fight the tyranny of the local property tax, compressing inequalities by race and class. Twin Cities schools have been doing this since the 1970s, and it works!
2. Incentivize and implement state funding programs that create a high floor for mill rates (the number of dollars taxed for every thousand dollars of assessed value) and reasonable ceilings for per-pupil expenditures in every school district, calculating adequate per-pupil expenditures according to weighted assessments of district needs and redistributing the remaining funds from districts with high property values to districts with low property values. Vermont schools did this in 1998 and it was extremely effective.
3. We have to make the federal Department of Education strong, smart, and for the people. Instead of calling for increasing appropriations for Title I funding at the federal level, and instead of making existing categorical grants into block grants and zeroing them out, we should be calling for exponentially higher minimum allocations to districts through the Elementary and Secondary Education Act. Rather than tripling or quadrupling Title I, we should call

for a $5,000 per-pupil minimum from the program and talk about what's needed from appropriations and authorizations to get that done.

4. There should be a federal value-added tax that provides funding for public education around the country. This is what Richard Nixon wanted to do in 1971 before the Supreme Court decided that because the word "education" doesn't appear in the Constitution, the federal government has no obligation to pay for it.
5. Replace the municipal market for school bonds with a national investment authority that pools the flow of public infrastructure revenue to decrease states' and localities' exposure to the cruelty of capital. Saule Omarova has been calling for this program and it'll be great!
6. All these policies could be put under the banner of a Green New Deal for Public Schools, but specifically greening this approach would require something like Jamaal Bowman's federal legislation going by that name, which has been reintroduced by Ed Markey in the Senate and so far has received more signatories in Congress than any other Green New Deal legislation, providing trillions of dollars for physical and social educational infrastructure. We need that.
7. Enact a decentralized green fiscal mutualism by restarting the Build America Bonds program to de-risk teacher pension investment in green school bonds. Use state-level financial authorities and existing green bank programs to compensate for any losses in return incurred by teacher pension investment in green school bonds. This will shore up retired teachers' wages when they get too old to work and decarbonize school buildings, making the present and future more stable and safe for students. In the short term, whoever is in charge of the federal government, no matter whether the Inflation Reduction Act is cancelled, unions

and local organizing groups should draft plans and campaign for green fiscal mutualism at the state and local level, getting state financing authorities (particularly green banks) to de-risk teacher pension fund investment in green school bonds in districts around the state. You can start doing this right now.

We know these things can happen. The pandemic was a portal for American education finance, and in terms of positive things coming out of it, we actually saw the emergence, however briefly, of an entirely different financial regime for the funding of public education on both the fiscal and monetary side. On the fiscal side, we saw the federal government spend billions on education relief, monies with which districts could hire, build, and do their work. The relief packages were a view into what federal spending could be, what the federal government could do all the time, rather than the paltry and confused 8 percent of total public education funding historically or the theocratic capitalist slash and burn ripping through the Department of Education right now.

But maybe more exciting, and just as obscure, was the Federal Reserve's pandemic response program called the Municipal Liquidity Facility, which I talked about in part 2. This was a special vehicle created by the Fed that had the power to loan directly to local governments on whatever terms the Fed determined. The stated reason the Fed created the facility was, having learned from the 2008 financial crisis, its leaders realized they needed to create backstops (or safety nets) during the pandemic crisis to prevent all the capitalists from pulling their money out of markets due to fear of losing it in a crash. They basically said, "Hey, you don't have to worry about losing your money because we're here now to make sure the market doesn't crash. We the government can be a lender of last resort." One of those markets is the municipal bond market, where public school districts get money for all kinds of things, both operating and capital costs. And it worked: The markets didn't crash.

But the fact that this facility was created, that it was deemed legal and then implemented at all, was a portal to a new political economy of public education. This facility showed us that the federal government, with its bank and currency, can actually provide direct loans to local and state governments on whatever terms it decides, due to the Federal Reserve's independence.

The Fed could give long-term zero-interest loans, due according to whatever time period parties come up with. A lot of modern monetary theorists peed their pants with excitement at the sense of possibility the Municipal Liquidity Facility opened. Why? Because public school districts along with other state and local governments have to sell themselves as investment products on Wall Street and get private credit with high interest rates and fees for all kinds of reasons, eating into their budgets to the tune of 8–10 percent every year.

The Municipal Liquidity Facility showed us it doesn't have to be that way. And in the debates following the creation and implementation of this program, we saw a new horizon open up: The Build Back Better legislation emerged in Congress when the Democrats had a trifecta in 2021, part of which was Bowman's massive and amazing Green New Deal for Public Schools. Bowman's legislation, reintroduced later on by Senator Ed Markey of Massachusetts, didn't make it into Build Back Better, and Build Back Better didn't make it into the budget reconciliation. But the Green New Deal for Public Schools, influenced by the pandemic portal and the Municipal Liquidity Facility, influenced others—and we ended up getting the Inflation Reduction Act (IRA) and the bipartisan infrastructure bill. The former had elements of that transformative political economy of public education in its elective pay tax credit and Greenhouse Gas Reduction Fund, as well as other reimbursement programs for decarbonizing infrastructure that school districts can take advantage of. The people who put those kinds of programs together are still out there and I'm pretty sure they want to go further than the half measures moderates permitted in 2022.

As of this writing, we still have vestiges of those programs, which are sometimes called Bidenomics.[8] These specific programs were critiqued on the left for being not populist enough, too technocratic, and mere de-risking, and for being part of a larger imperial military project, a new Great Power politic, rather than some kind of post-neoliberal generosity.[9] While these critiques are valid, we shouldn't essentialize these policies into anything too simple. They're made of multitudes, development is always uneven, and I think they contain within them the seeds of a new paradigm for school finance.[10]

I also think the pandemic portal opened up space for this new political economy of public education because we see actual changes: According to UnDauntedK12's Inflation Reduction Act tracker, there were hundreds of public schools starting to take advantage of the IRA programs and decarbonize their schools.[11] Electric buses replacing gas engines, electric heat pumps replacing boilers, old light bulbs replaced with high-efficiency LED lights, ground-source heating, solar arrays—public school districts are getting reimbursements for all these projects, which come along with updates to aging and crumbling infrastructure and provide longer-term savings due to higher efficiency of energy usage. It's a kind of small green fiscal mutualism, using the Internal Revenue Service and Department of Energy to help school districts and states make their buildings safer, better, and less expensive to maintain—all while creating the conditions to challenge the hegemony of the traditional bond market.

Even if the second Trump administration gets rid of these programs (which help a lot of red states), these state and local levels are spaces of possibility for the left as we organize. School finance is a galvanizing issue that people across the diverse working class care about. People care about their kids. They care about how high taxes are. They care about how much they pay in rent and how much property is worth in their municipalities. They care about climate catastrophe and whether the air in their kids' schools is cool enough to concentrate. School boards are still democratically elected across the country, and while these elections have been politicized by the right wing, they often don't know how to handle the various aspects of school finance realities competently, much less transformatively. If anything, they create fear and loathing and push people further away from the schools. We can draw folks in with radical financial policies that take up and take on racialized private property by building up diverse working-class communities at the infrastructural level, and make education as public as possible.

Acknowledgments

There are many people and groups to thank for bringing this book into being.

Thanks to Eleni Schirmer for generously telling Ishan Desai-Gellar that maybe I'd have something of interest for The New Press. Thanks to Ishan, who worked with me on my proposal to hone it and get it through for acceptance, and continued to be a studious and careful editor during the early process of getting the manuscript ready. Beth Zasloff was a fastidious and sharp editor of the manuscript, bringing out ideas and sculpting it with great care, and Tom Sgouros provided essential feedback and suggestions to the section on pensions (as well as a deep read at the end), along with logistical work and notes from Mia Fullerton. Thanks to Marc Favreau and the rest of the team at The New Press as well.

The book wouldn't exist without the amazing group of readers who subscribe to my weekly newsletter, *Schooling in Socialist America*. Your comments, questions, and encouragement over the years directed my interest and kept me focused on the balance of forces. Ryan Phleger and Alan Gao were particularly keen readers.

As always, Jason Wozniak and Dana Morrison were comrades in writing and thinking and organizing, and thanks to the Debt Collective and Democratic Socialists of America for being an organizing home as the book took clearer shape.

In the earlier stages of my work on the book, the Safe Air Campaign of the Philadelphia Democratic Socialists of America (DSA), part of the Education Justice Committee, was a constant source of energy and inspiration. It was Hannah Halliday who first suggested that perhaps a good campaign would be to build Corsi-Rosenthal boxes with school communities, and Greg Windle, whose dogged organizing and incisive reporting so informed my thinking about Philly, gave form and longevity to the campaign, while Lizzie Rothwell's indefatigable citizen science in air-quality measurement and activism enlivened the work. (And thanks to the DSA's national Green New Deal Commission, particularly Nafis Hasan and Matt Haugen, for support.)

Keeanga Yamahtta-Taylor, years ago, mentioned to me that we need a good Marxist take on school finance, which nudged me toward this focus. She connected me with Mike Glass, whose work has been crucial for my own. Mike commented on early drafts of this manuscript, as well as following my newsletter from the beginning. Likewise, Esther Cyna's incisive thinking has influenced me greatly, and her invitations to lecture as well as co-author on these subjects have helped me articulate some of the core premises of the book. Jeff Vincent has also been generous and helpful in sharing resources and networks and providing feedback. Claire Cahen, Kelly Goodman, Dan Cohen, Marc Joffe, Matthew Gardner Kelly, Dwight Berg, Dan Urevick-Ackelsberg, and Tom Sgouros provided helpful dialogue throughout, specifically when it came to my thinking about school bonds. Thanks also to Gaby Betancourt and Saqib Bhatti for thoughts on pensions.

Mark Lieberman was an early supporter of this project, and his reporting and comments have been helpful. It was his interest in my initial proposal that public education should be as public as possible that lent legitimacy and authority to the choice of title.

Nikil Saval let me work on his 2020 campaign's school funding platform, giving me a big confidence boost. Daniel Aldana Cohen, ever the connector, introduced me to Raj Sicora in Jamaal Bowman's office, starting a fruitful dialogue, as well as the great folks at the Climate & Community Institute, like Batul Hassan, from whom I've learned a ton about climate politics. Cohen, along with Akira Drake Rodriguez (whom I met through Howard Ryan's Who Rules Philly? group and has been a great thought partner too on school infrastructure in Philly and beyond), generously invited me to work on the Green New Deal for Public Schools report and legislation.

Others have also supported me and influenced my thinking on school, politics, infrastructure, and finance policy in racial capitalism, including Elaine Simon, George Donnelly, Malcolm Harris, Astra Taylor, Scott Ferguson, Robert Hockett, Yitzhak Feygin, Camika Royal, Ee-Seul Yoon, Max Sawicky, Sara Ross, Marialena Dawn Rivera, Louise Seamster, Doug Henwood, Nathan Tankus, Amanda Kass, Sebastian Anti, and Ben Brumley—the last two especially helped with my forays into quantitative methods, Sebastian trying to teach me the statistical calculation program R and Ben patiently listening to me fumble through statistics.

When Jennifer Berkshire invited me to appear on *Have You Heard*, my ideas and approach found a big new audience, connecting me to a whole network of public education organizers around the country; a special thanks to her.

Beki McElvain and Matt Clifford commented on early drafts of chapters too.

My parents, Ted and Ronni Backer, have been keen readers and generous supporters.

The Urban Climate Finance Network welcomed an education researcher in their midst for their first workshop in 2022, from whom I was able to learn a ton.

West Chester University granted me a sabbatical to work on the project, during which I wrote the first draft of the manuscript in the wonderful home of Tim and Caroline outside Paris, creating great writing conditions. I wrote a lot of the book in the beautiful home of Greg and Ginger in Bed-Stuy Brooklyn, accompanied by Oliver the rabbit. During that time in Brooklyn, and after we moved here permanently, the Comrades with Kids working group of NYC-DSA has been a nourishing community and audience to test out ideas; thanks especially to Jonathan Greenberg and Phoebe Gilpin for being research and organizing partners in the NYC school finance terrain.

The early drafts of this book were written during a time when Twitter was a pretty good place to be, and I connected and learned from many of the people I've mentioned here and so many others on that iteration of the platform. I got so much from reading others' thoughts, reading reactions to my thoughts, sharing others' thinking and having mine shared, and it was several Twitter threads of mine, and the reaction to them, that formed a sort of core for the book's vision and audience. I mourn the space that Twitter was and hope another iteration or platform might recapture that milieu.

The Build tendency of the national DSA was the first to publish some of my writings on finance on its website, for which I'm grateful, and *Dissent*, *Phenomenal World*, *The American Prospect*, *African American Policy Forum*, the Verso blog, and *In These Times* published essays on these topics later from which some material herein was taken.

Finally, my partner, Shelly, and daughter, Thisbe, and our dog, Sappho, are constant sources of love and joy and dialogue. Without them, none of this work could happen.

Notes

Introduction: Under the Tug-of-War

1. On extravagance and austerity in neoliberalism, see Melinda Cooper, *Counterrevolution: Extravagance and Austerity in Public Finance* (Princeton University Press, 2024). On the "war" in education: Jennifer Berkshire and Jack Schneider, *Education Wars: A Citizen's Guide and Defense Manual* (The New Press, 2024); Josh Cowen, *The Privateers: How Billionaires Created a Culture War and Sold School Vouchers* (Harvard Education Press, 2024); Megan Erickson, *Class War: The Privatization of Childhood* (Verso, 2015); Dana Goldstein, *The Teacher Wars: A History of America's Most Embattled Profession* (Anchor, 2015).

2. David I. Backer, "The Problem of Educational Power," *Philosophy of Education* 80, no. 4 (2025); "K12 Climate Action Plan," This Is Planet Ed, https://www.thisisplaneted.org/img/K12-ClimateActionPlan-Complete-Screen.pdf.

3. Michael A. McCarthy, *The Master's Tools: How Finance Wrecked Democracy (and a Radical Plan to Rebuild It)* (Verso, 2025).

4. C. Kirabo Jackson and Claire L. Mackevicius, "What Impacts Can We Expect from School Spending Policy? Evidence from Evaluations in the United States," *American Economic Journal: Applied Economics* 16, no. 1 (2024): 412–446; Bruce D. Baker, *Educational Inequality and School Finance: Why Money Matters for America's Students* (Harvard Education Press, 2021).

5. See Cowen, *The Privateers.*

6. Check out "Resisting Debt, Funding Justice," special issue, *Rethinking Schools* 37, no. 4 (2023), for trenchant analysis of all this, particularly

Eleni Schirmer, "School Debt: The Great Unequalizer," https://rethinkingschools.org/articles/school-debt-the-great-unequalizer.

7. Baker, *Educational Inequality*; Leslie S. Kaplan and William A. Owings, *Critical Resource Theory: A Conceptual Lens for Identifying, Diagnosing, and Addressing Inequities in School Funding* (Routledge, 2022); Jeff Swensson, Lynn Lehman, and John Ellis, *The Thief in the Classroom: How School Funding Is Misdirected, Disconnected, and Ideologically Aligned* (Rowman & Littlefield, 2021); Eric Blanc, *Red State Revolt: The Teachers' Strike Wave and Working-Class Politics* (Verso, 2019); Jack Schneider and Jennifer Berkshire, *A Wolf at the Schoolhouse Door: The Dismantling of Public Education and the Future of School* (The New Press, 2020).

8. School finance can also be very law heavy, with many academic accounts focusing—for good reason—on the national and state school funding lawsuits that have done so much to secure more (though not necessarily enough) money for public education. In this book, I focus more on grassroots organizing than the machinations of courts and lawsuits, though, as in the civil rights movement, these intersect quite often, and you have to talk about laws and how they work to talk about school finance.

9. Modern monetary theory (MMT) argues, among other things, that taxes don't pay for public programs because governments issue their own currencies and have their own banks and reserves, and that money is a public good. While MMT doesn't feature explicitly in this book, the book should be read as an attempt to make sense of school finance after learning about it and being formed partially by it. I did a lot of the thinking behind what's written here after the Federal Reserve created the Municipal Liquidity Facility to address the economic crisis created by the pandemic in 2020. In a way, I identify with how Martijn Konings put it in the introduction to a special issue on MMT and the current political-economic scene in the academic journal *Boundary 2*: "MMT might be likened to a subject of psychoanalysis that, upon realizing that the world holds no deep secret, declares itself cured—but, when venturing back out, finds that its relationship to that world has undergone little practical change. It still has to do the work of deconstructing, transforming, or otherwise navigating the actual web of fictions, promises, lies, and obfuscations that it has built." While not dealing directly with MMT, this book tries to

do some deconstruction, transformation, and "otherwise navigation" for school finance in the United States inspired by insights from MMT. Martijn Konings, "The Modern Money Tangle: An Introduction," in "The Gordian Knot of Finance," ed. Martijn Konings, special issue, *Boundary 2* 6, no. 1 (2024), https://www.boundary2.org/2024/12/martijn-konings-the-modern-money-tangle-an-introduction.

10. Derrick A. Bell Jr., "Brown v. Board of Education and the Interest-Convergence Dilemma," *Harvard Law Review* (1980): 518–533; Preston C. Green III, Bruce D. Baker, and Joseph O. Oluwole, "School Finance, Race, and Reparations," *Washington and Lee Journal of Civil Rights and Social Justice* 27 (2020): 483.

Chapter 1: Public Schools and Private Property

1. Marguerite Roza, "What Goes Wrong When Some School Board Members Don't Understand District Finances?," *Forbes*, July 28, 2022, https://www.forbes.com/sites/margueriteroza/2022/07/28/what-goes-wrong-when-some-school-board-members-dont-understand-district-finances/?sh=4603c2002e8d, 2022.

2. "About Us," Edunomics Lab, https://edunomicslab.org/about-us.

3. "Cash-Strapped Richmond Schools Ask IBM to Forgive Debt," Fox Reno, June 20, 2007, https://archive.today/20070519065650/http://www.foxreno.com/news/13539925/detail.html.

4. Patrick Hoge, "Hunger Strike for School Funding," SF Gate, May 11, 2004, https://www.sfgate.com/education/article/OAKLAND-Hunger-strike-for-school-funding-2780337.php.

5. Daniel Bacher, "Fasters Win Historic Victory in Struggle for Educational Equality," Dissident Voice, June 11, 2004, https://dissidentvoice.org/June04/Bacher0611.htm.

6. "'Richmond Unified School District' Finally Paid in Full," ABC7, June 1, 2012, https://abc7news.com/archive/8685984.

7. Shomik Mukarjee, "State Report Warns West Contra Costa Unified Faces Insolvency," *Mercury News*, May 29, 2021, https://www

.mercurynews.com/2021/05/29/state-report-warns-west-contra-costa-unified-faces-insolvency.

8. Esther Cyna, "Schooling the Kleptocracy: Racism and School Finance in Rural North Carolina, 1900–2018," *Journal of American History* 108, no. 4 (2022): 745–766.

9. D. I. Backer and E. Cyna, "Critical School Finance," *Journal of Educational Administration and History* (2024): 1–21.

10. Michael A. McCarthy and Mathieu Hikaru Desan, "The Problem of Class Abstractionism," *Sociological Theory* 41, no. 1 (2023): 3–26; and David I. Backer, "The Uses and Abuses of Class Separatism," Verso blog, January 10, 2019, https://www.versobooks.com/blogs/news/4201-uses-and-abuses-of-class-separatism.

11. Jessica Gerrard, Arathi Sriprakash, and Sophie Rudolph, "Education and Racial Capitalism," *Race Ethnicity and Education* 25, no. 3 (2022): 425–442.

12. Zeus Leonardo, "The Race for Class: Reflections on a Critical Race-class Theory of Education," *Educational Studies* 48, no. 5 (2012): 427–449.

13. Claudia Jones, "An End to the Neglect of the Problems of the Negro Woman!" *Political Affairs*, June 1949.

14. Charisse Burden-Stelly, "Modern U.S. Racial Capitalism," *Monthly Review* (2020), https://monthlyreview.org/2020/07/01/modern-u-s-racial-capitalism.

15. Nancy Fraser, "Expropriation and Exploitation in Racialized Capitalism: A Reply to Michael Dawson," *Critical Historical Studies* 3, no. 1 (2016): 163–178.

16. Benjamin Ward, "The Firm in Illyria: Market Syndicalism," in *The Economics of Co-Determination*, ed. D.F. Heathfield, 1–25 (Palgrave Macmillan, 1958).

17. Johanna Bockman, *Markets in the Name of Socialism: The Left-Wing Origins of Neoliberalism* (Stanford University Press, 2020).

18. Michael Parenti, *To Kill a Nation: The Attack on Yugoslavia* (Verso, 2000).

19. Harold J. Noah and Joel D. Sherman, *Educational Financing and Policy Goals for Primary Schools: General Report* (OECD, Centre for Research and Education, 1979).

20. Jelena Raković, Tom O'Donoghue, and Simon Clarke, *Leaders and Leadership in Serbian Primary Schools: Perspectives Across Two Worlds* (Springer, 2018).

21. See C. Kirabo Jackson and Claire L. Mackevicius, "What Impacts Can We Expect from School Spending Policy? Evidence from Evaluations in the United States," *American Economic Journal: Applied Economics* 16, no. 1 (2024): 412–446; Bruce D. Baker, *Educational Inequality and School Finance: Why Money Matters for America's Students* (Harvard Education Press, 2021).

Chapter 2: The Tyranny of the Local Property Tax

1. Tracy L. Steffes, "Assessment Matters: The Rise and Fall of the Illinois Resource Equalizer Formula," *History of Education Quarterly* 60, no. 1 (2020): 24–57.

2. David I. Backer, "Cooperation Analysis of Tax-Base Sharing in the Twin Cities: School Districts, Human Resources, and Structural Justice," *Journal of Education Human Resources* 41, no. 1 (2023): 14–35.

3. Daphne A. Kenyon, Bethany P. Paquin, and Andrew Reschovsky, *Rethinking the Property Tax–School Funding Dilemma* (Lincoln Land Institute, November 2022), https://www.lincolninst.edu/publications/policy-focus-reports/rethinking-property-tax-school-funding-dilemma.

4. Billy D. Walker, "The Local Property Tax for Public Schools: Some Historical Perspectives," *Journal of Education Finance* 9, no. 3 (1984): 265–288.

5. Robin L. Einhorn, *American Taxation, American Slavery* (University of Chicago Press, 2019); Camille Walsh, *Racial Taxation: Schools, Segregation, and Taxpayer Citizenship, 1869–1973* (University of North Carolina Press, 2018); Andrew W. Kahrl, *The Black Tax: 150 Years of Theft, Exploitation, and Dispossession in America* (University of Chicago Press, 2024); Michael

Glass, *Cracked Foundations: Debt and Inequality in Postwar Suburbia* (University of Pennsylvania Press, 2025).

6. See the chapter "Founding the Public School," in W.E.B. Du Bois, *Black Reconstruction in America: Toward a History of the Part Which Black Folk Played in the Attempt to Reconstruct Democracy in America, 1860–1880* (Routledge, 2017).

7. Matthew Gardner Kelly, "'Theoretically All Children Are Equal. Practically This Can Never Be So': The History of the District Property Tax in California and the Choice of Inequality," *Teachers College Record* 122, no. 2 (2020): 6; Matthew Gardner Kelly, *Dividing the Public: School Finance and the Creation of Structural Inequity* (Cornell University Press, 2024).

8. David Backer, "School Funding Inequality in Pennsylvania: A Base-Superstructure Analysis," *Pennsylvania Educational Leadership Journal* (2020).

9. David M.P. Freund, *Colored Property: State Policy and White Racial Politics in Suburban America* (University of Chicago Press, 2019).

10. Freund, *Colored Property.*

11. Philip Tegeler and Michael Hilton, *Disrupting the Reciprocal Relationship Between Housing and School Segregation* (Poverty & Race Research Action Council, 2017).

12. Kevin Carey, "No More School Districts!," *Democracy: A Journal of Ideas* 55 (2020), https://democracyjournal.org/magazine/55/no-more-school-districts.

13. Zahava Stadler and Jordan Abbott, "Crossing the Line: Segregation and Resource Inequality between America's School Districts. Education Policy," *New America* (2024).

14. Owen Daugherty, "Story of Mother Sentenced to Jail for Enrolling Child in Wrong School," *The Hill*, January 24, 2019. https://thehill.com/blogs/blog-briefing-room/news/434051-story-of-mother-sentenced-to-jail-for-enrolling-child-in.

15. Kathy Boccella, "Some See Racial Overtones in Upper Darby Superintendent Flap." *The Philadelphia Inquirer*, August 4, 2016. https://www.inquirer.com/philly/education/20160805_Some_see_racial_overtones_in_Upper_Darby_superintendent_flap.html.

16. Another way I've thought about this situation is by correlating school district property values with mill rates in a region of districts. When you divide these two numbers you get a ratio that shows who's paying the most in taxes in a way that considers the intensity of tax rates. When the districts are ordered from the lowest ratio to the highest ratio, the districts with the lowest property values have to tax at the highest rates to get relatively lower amounts for their schools. You can see that even though districts are in a regional community together, the districts are siloed and isolated from one another in a competitive way. When I teach students about school finance, I ask them whether it's fair that neighbors should have access to such different resources.

17. David Backer and Benjamin Brumley, "Measuring Cooperation in School Finance: The Gini Coefficient vs. the Coefficient of Variation," unpublished manuscript.

18. Backer, "Cooperation Analysis."

19. David I. Backer, "Socialist Grading," *Teaching Economic Inequality and Capitalism in Contemporary America* (2018): 103–109.

20. Backer, "Cooperation Analysis"; Paul Gilje, *How Could You Do This?: 50 Years of Property-Tax-Base Sharing in Minnesota* (Center for Policy Design Press, 2021).

21. Jared Swanson and Steve Hinze, *Minnesota's Fiscal Disparities Programs* (Research Department, Minnesota House of Representatives, 2020).

22. Swanson and Hinze, *Minnesota's Fiscal Disparities Programs.*

Chapter 3: Unstable State Structures

1. Fund Our Schools PA, "Students vs. Pennsylvania Department of Education." https://www.fundourschoolspa.org/students-vs-pennsylvania-department-of-education.

2. Public Interest Law Center, "Recapping Week One of the PA School Funding Trial." https://pubintlaw.org/cases-and-projects/recapping-week-one-of-the-pa-school-funding-trial.

3. See Preston C. Green III, Bruce D. Baker, and Joseph O. Oluwole, "School Finance, Race, and Reparations," *Washington and Lee Journal of*

Civil Rights and Social Justice 27 (2020): 483; https://www.ecs.org/wp-content/uploads/2016-Constitutional-obligations-for-public-education-1.pdf.

4. Pennsylvania Department of Education, "School Construction and Facilities (PlanCon)." https://www.pa.gov/agencies/education/programs-and-services/schools/school-construction-improvements-reconfigurations/school-construction-and-facilities-plancon.html.

5. Pennsylvania Office of the Budget, "Budget." https://www.pa.gov/agencies/budget.html.

6. Pennsylvania House Appropriations Committee, *PlanCon: A Guide to the Pennsylvania School Construction Program*. October 19, 2016. https://www.houseappropriations.com/files/Documents/PlanCon_BP_101916.pdf.

7. Pennsylvania State Board of Education, "Report of the Public School Building Construction and Reconstruction Advisory Committee." Pennsylvania General Assembly, May 23, 2018. https://pasenategop.com/plancon/wp-content/uploads/sites/81/2018/05/final-report-052318.pdf.

8. Carly Sitrin, "Push for Pennsylvania Vouchers, Backed by Governor, Could Upend Philadelphia Public Schools," *Chalkbeat Philadelphia*, June 27, 2023. https://www.chalkbeat.org/philadelphia/2023/6/27/23775306/pennsylvania-philadelphia-school-private-families-low-achieving-schools-funding-scholarships-budget/.

9. Chris Lehmann, "Josh Shapiro Is a Bad VP Pick Any Way You Look at It," *The Nation*, July 29, 2024. https://www.thenation.com/article/politics/josh-shapiro-vp-kamala-harris-wrong/.

10. Carly Sitrin, "Governor Signs Pennsylvania Budget but Vetoes Statewide School Voucher Proposal." *Chalkbeat Philadelphia*, August 3, 2023. https://www.chalkbeat.org/philadelphia/2023/8/3/23819164/governor-shapiro-pennsylvania-signs-budget-vetoes-school-voucher-program-republicans-democrats/.

11. Marialena Rivera, *What About the Schools? Factors Contributing to Expanded State Investment in School Facilities* (Intercultural Development Research Association, 2017).

12. Carmel Deca, "Take a Tour of the School Where Champions Are Made!!" February 8, 2023, TikTok, 1:47, https://www.tiktok.com/@carmeldeca/video/7197937009938156842.

13. Cheryl V. Jackson, "Carmel High School Seems to Have It All, Including Viral TikTok Videos," *Indianapolis Star*, February 13, 2023. https://www.indystar.com/story/news/local/hamilton-county/carmel/2023/02/13/carmel-high-school-students-tiktok-videos-natatorium-stadium-auditorium-studios-auto-shop/69899563007/

14. Krystal Thompson, "Carmel High School Tour Underscores the Haves and Have-Nots in America's Schools," *NBC News*, February 28, 2023. https://www.nbcnews.com/news/nbcblk/carmel-high-school-tour-underscores-haves-nots-americas-schools-rcna72028.

15. "Carmel Clay Schools, Indiana," National Center for Education Statistics. https://nces.ed.gov/Programs/Edge/ACSDashboard/1801200.

16. *Indiana's Education Funding, Explained. House Republican Fiscal Policy Department.* 2022. https://cdn.ymaws.com/www.indiana-asbo.org/resource/collection/13F09444-C611-4280-AAB9-5D2BA0559AA0/Indiana_Education_Funding_Explained__October_2.pdf.

17. School Finance Indicators Database https://www.schoolfinancedata.org/

18. State School Finance Profile 2019–20 School Year, *School Finance Data,* December 2022. https://www.schoolfinancedata.org/wp-content/uploads/2022/12/profiles20_IN.pdf.

19. David I. Backer and Camika Royal, "Toxic Finance: Underinvestment in Philadelphia's School Buildings, 1993–2021," *Journal of Educational Administration and History* 57, no. 1 (2025): 74–91.

20. Municipal Securities Rulemaking Board, *Municipal Market Data: 2021.* https://emma.msrb.org/P11636230-P11260317-P11685906.pdf.

21. Marialena Dawn Rivera, "Inequity and Privatization in School District Facilities Financing: A Mixed Methods Study" (PhD diss., University of California, Berkeley, 2016).

22. Jason Wozniak and Frances Negron-Muntaner, "Debt and Instructional Harm," *South Atlantic Quarterly* (forthcoming).

23. A state legislator introduced a bill in early 2025 that would dissolve public schools in districts where 51 percent of students in that district attend private or charter schools. This was the ultimate goal of charters and vouchers, though I wonder what the people of Carmel Clay would say about dissolving the beautiful schools they built by gaming the system rigged for them. See https://www.forbes.com/sites/petergreene/2025/01/07/indiana-considers-dissolving-public-schools.

24. Randy Arrington, "'Crumbling Schools' Tour Visits Page County," *Page Valley News*, July 14, 2021. https://pagevalleynews.com/crumbling-schools-tour-visits-page-county/.

25. Markus Schmidt, "House Panel Moves to End Tax Breaks for Confederate-Affiliated Groups," *Virginia Mercury*, January 20, 2025. https://virginiamercury.com/briefs/house-panel-moves-to-end-tax-breaks-for-confederate-affiliated-groups/.

26. "Crumbling Schools Tour. Virginia | Summer 2021." 2021. Flyer. *The Coalition of Small and Rural Schools of Virginia*, July, 2021. https://drive.google.com/file/d/133rtHeKKGP5aCflbgF6PkUtyuUYqEt7m/view.

27. Gordon C. Morse, "Virginia Must Repair Its Crumbling Public School Buildings," *The Virginian-Pilot*, June 26, 2021. https://www.pilotonline.com/2021/06/26/opinion-virginia-must-repair-its-crumbling-public-school-buildings/.

28. Virginia General Assembly, 2021, *Needs and Conditions of Virginia School Buildings*. https://studiesvirginiageneralassembly.s3.amazonaws.com/meeting_docs/documents/000/000/979/original/Needs_and_Conditions_of_Virginia_School_Buildings_6.3.21.pdf?1622733329.

29. Virginia Public School Authority, "Virginia Public School Authority." https://trs.virginia.gov/Boards-Authorities/Virginia-Public-School-Authority.

30. Jesse Higgins, "Virginia Just Made Its Biggest Investment in School Buildings in Over a Decade. Now It Has to Decide How to Dole Out the Money," *Charlottesville Tomorrow*, June 3, 2022. https://www.cvilletomorrow.org/virginia-just-made-its-biggest-investment-in-school-buildings-in-over-a-decade-now-it-has-to-decide-how-to-dole-out-the-money/.

31. Byrd Pinkerton, Jillian Weinberger, Sarah Kliff, and Amy Drozdowska, "Lawsuits and Slashed Tires: Vermont's School Funding Battle," *Vox*, November 26, 2018. https://www.vox.com/2018/11/23/18069882/vermont-education-school-funding-act-60-68-brigham-lawsuit.

32. Boris Kachka, "Call of the Wild," *New York Magazine*, October 8, 2009. https://nymag.com/arts/books/profiles/59881/.

33. *In re: Brigham v. State of Vermont*, 1997, Vermont Supreme Court. https://law.justia.com/cases/vermont/supreme-court/1997/96-502op.html.

34. Jack Hoffman, "Brigham Decision: Shared Responsibility for Funding Education," VTDigger, February 21, 2022. https://vtdigger.org/2022/02/21/brigham-decision-shared-responsibility-for-funding-education/.

35. Jane Fowler Morse, *A Level Playing Field: School Finance in the Northeast* (SUNY Press, 2007), chap. 3, "Sharing in Vermont."

36. See Morse, *A Level Playing Field*, 76.

37. Tufts University, "The Center for the Study of Race and Democracy." https://cspa.tufts.edu/node/406; https://www.cnbc.com/2022/11/10/what-the-millionaire-tax-in-massachusetts-means-for-the-wealthy.html.

38. Day Pitney LLP, "Massachusetts Voters Approve Millionaires' Tax," November 11, 2022. https://www.daypitney.com/insights/publications/2022/11/11-ma-voters-approve-millionaires-tax.; https://www.bostonglobe.com/2022/12/24/sports/millionaires-tax-red-sox-agents.

39. University of Massachusetts Amherst, "Labor Center." https://www.umass.edu/labor.

40. Kate Dore, "Critics Call State's Switch to Flat Income Tax a Boon for the Wealthy," *CNBC*, April 28, 2022. https://www.cnbc.com/2022/04/28/critics-call-states-switch-to-flat-income-tax-a-boon-for-the-wealthy.html.

41. Elinor Haider, "How Pennsylvania's Uniformity Clause Affects Property and Wage Taxes in Philadelphia," The Pew Charitable Trusts, March 9, 2022. https://www.pewtrusts.org/en/research-and-analysis/fact

-sheets/2022/03/how-pennsylvanias-uniformity-clause-affects-property-and-wage-taxes-in-philadelphia.

42. Educators for a Democratic Union. https://educatorsforademocraticunion.org

43. Mara Sapon-Shevin and Sue Novinger Robb, "How the edTPA Disrupts Relationships," *Rethinking Schools*, 2017. https://rethinkingschools.org/articles/how-the-edtpa-disrupts-relationships.

44. Winerip, Michael. "Move to Outsource Teacher Licensing Process Draws Protest," *The New York Times*, May 6, 2012. https://www.nytimes.com/2012/05/07/education/new-procedure-for-teaching-license-draws-protest.html.

45. Sarah Jaffe, "Barbara Madeloni and the Massachusetts Teachers Association," *In These Times*, May 13, 2014. https://inthesetimes.com/article/barbara-madeloni-massachusetts-teachers-association.

46. Yes on Question 2. https://www.yesonquestion2ma.com.

47. Nik DeCosta-Klipa, "Massachusetts Millionaires Tax Ballot Question for 2022." Boston.com, May 5, 2021. https://www.boston.com/news/politics/2021/05/05/massachusetts-millionaires-tax-ballot-question-2022.

48. "In a Stinging Rebuke, Ballot Question on 'Millionaires Tax' Is Rejected," *The Boston Globe*, June 18, 2018. https://www.bostonglobe.com/metro/2018/06/18/sjc-ruling-millionaires-tax-coming-Monday/unxBjYa0JGHKfMKUBzsMjO/story.html.

49. Ballotpedia, "Massachusetts Question 1, Tax on Income Above $1 Million for Education and Transportation Amendment (2022)." https://ballotpedia.org/Massachusetts_Question_1,_Tax_on_Income_Above_$1_Million_for_Education_and_Transportation_Amendment_(2022).

Chapter 4: One-dering About the Federal Government

1. A fun tidbit is that Trump's threat to get rid of the Department of Education originated with Reagan, who threatened it to juice up his voting base when he ran against Jimmy Carter—whose administration had

created the department in the first place. Conservatives have been making this threat since then.

2. C.C. Carson, R.M. Huelskamp, and T.D. Woodall, "Perspectives on Education in America: An Annotated Briefing, April 1992," *Journal of Educational Research* 86, no. 5 (1993): 259–310, http://www.jstor.org/stable/27541876.

3. Samuel E. Abrams, *Education and the Commercial Mindset* (Harvard University Press, 2016).

4. Gerald Bracey, "Righting Wrongs," *Huffington Post*, December 3, 2007, https://www.huffpost.com/entry/righting-wrongs_b_75189.

5. "Title I—Improving the Academic Achievement of the Disadvantaged," U.S. Department of Education. https://www.ed.gov/sites/ed/files/policy/elsec/leg/essa/legislation/title-i.pdf.

6. "Title I of ESEA: Targeting Funds to High-Poverty Schools and Districts," Alliance for Excellent Education. https://all4ed.org/publication/title-i-of-esea-targeting-funds-to-high-poverty-schools-and-districts/.

7. "Title I: A Brief Overview," National Center for Education Statistics, 2019. https://nces.ed.gov/pubs2019/titleI/summary.asp.

8. *Public Education Funding Inequity in an Era of Increasing Concentration of Poverty and Resegregation. U.S. Commission on Civil Rights*, January 10, 2018. https://www.usccr.gov/files/pubs/2018/2018-01-10-Education-Inequity.pdf.

9. Rather than simply abolishing Title I, which would take legislation, it may be possible for the second Trump administration to make the categorical grants—calculated using the formulas—into block grants, which conservatives have wanted for a long time. The Heritage Foundation's Project 2025 document, for instance, calls for making ESEA grants into block grants and to zero them out eventually, leaving all school funding to states and localities (which is already sort of how it is but would remove a key, if small, source of revenue for diverse working-class schools).

10. William Sonnenberg, "Allocating Grants for Title I," U.S. Department of Education, Institute for Education Sciences, January 2016. https://nces.ed.gov/surveys/AnnualReports/pdf.

11. Sharon Stein, *The Culture of Policy* (Teachers College Press, 2004); see chapters 2 and 3 for a fantastic reconstruction of the discourse used by policymakers in debating the Title 1 formulas.

12. "History of the ESEA Title I-A Formulas," Congressional Research Service, 2017.

13. "History of the ESEA Title I-A Formulas."

14. Timothy J. Conlan, "The Politics of Federal Block Grants: From Nixon to Reagan," *Political Science Quarterly* 99, no. 2 (1984): 247–270.

15. "School District Refuses CEO's Offer to Settle Lunch Debt After Threatening Parents," *ABC News*, July 24, 2019. https://abcnews.go.com/US/pennsylvania-school-district-refuses-ceos-offer-settle-lunch/story.

16. "What Is Lunch Shaming?" *American University School of Education*, June 30, 2020. https://soeonline.american.edu/blog/what-is-lunch-shaming/.

17. Adrian Horton, "'Lunch Shaming': School District Changes Policy for Students Who Owe Meal Debts," *The Guardian*, May 10, 2019. https://www.theguardian.com/us-news/2019/may/09/lunch-shaming-school-district-changes-policy-for-students-who-owe-meal-debts.

18. Kate Beem, "Hot Potato in the School Cafeteria: More Districts Outsource Their Food Services, but Some Raise Questions About Personnel Relations and Savings," *School Administrator* 61, no. 8 (2004): 34.

19. Jennifer E. Gaddis, "The Big Business of School Meals," *Kappan*, September 21, 2020. https://kappanonline.org/big-business-school-meals-food-service-gaddis.

20. "Community Eligibility Provision (CEP)," U.S. Department of Agriculture, Food and Nutrition Service. https://www.fns.usda.gov/cn/cep.

21. "School Nutrition Association." https://schoolnutrition.org.

22. "Unpaid Meal Charges," U.S. Department of Agriculture, Food and Nutrition Service. https://www.fns.usda.gov/cn/unpaid-meal-charges.

23. Ilana L. Linder, "Hangry for School Lunch Guidance," *Journal of Law & Education* 48 (2019): 215.

24. Anique Aburaad, "Opposing Viewpoints: There's No Such Thing as a Free Lunch," *Children's Legal Rights Journal* 40 (2020): 70.

25. "USDA Issues Pandemic Flexibilities for Schools and Day Care Facilities through June 2022 to Support Safe Reopening and Healthy, Nutritious Meals," U.S. Department of Agriculture, April 20, 2021. https://www.usda.gov/about-usda/news/press-releases/2021/04/20/usda-issues-pandemic-flexibilities-schools-and-day-care-facilities-through-june-2022-support-safe.

26. Ayelet Sheffey, "Bernie Sanders and Ilhan Omar Push for Free Lunch to Combat Hunger," *Business Insider*, May 10, 2021. https://www.businessinsider.com/universal-school-meals-bernie-sanders-ilhan-omar-free-lunch-hunger-2021-5.

27. Russell Falcon, "This Texas Bill Would Cancel Student Lunch Debt," *CW33*, April 29, 2021. https://cw33.com/news/texas-politics/this-texas-bill-would-cancel-student-lunch-debt/; https://www.inforum.com/news/north-dakota/north-dakota-lawmakers-pass-free-school-lunch-funding-after-all.

28. Melissa Duvelsdorf, Elizabeth Lester-Abdalla, and Nick Marcil, "How School Lunch Debt Creates Shame and Inequality—and Our Fight to Abolish It." *Rethinking Schools*, 2023. https://rethinkingschools.org/articles/how-school-lunch-debt-creates-shame-and-inequality-and-our-fight-to-abolish-it/.

29. EmilyAnn Jackman, "Pa. School District Cancels Over $20,000 of Student Lunch Debt," *PennLive*, September 1, 2022. https://www.pennlive.com/news/2022/09/pa-school-district-cancels-over-20000-of-student-lunch-debt.html.

30. George Allen, Paul Goldman, and Mark J. Rozell, "The Trump Hotel: An Unlikely Model for Modernizing Schools," *Politico*, March 7, 2017. https://www.politico.com/agenda/story/2017/03/trump-hotel-model-modernize-schools-000343/

31. David Dayen, "Bipartisan Senate Infrastructure Plan Is a Stalking Horse for Privatization," *The American Prospect,* June 21, 2021. https://prospect.org/politics/bipartisan-senate-infrastructure-plan-privatization-asset-recycling/.

32. Kyle Glazier, "Senate Passes Bipartisan Infrastructure Bill Expanding PABs," *The Bond Buyer,* August 10, 2021. https://www.bondbuyer.com/news/senate-passes-bipartisan-infrastructure-bill-expanding-pabs.

33. Jacob Baumgart, "PGCPS Will Build 6 New Schools With $900M of Private Money," *Patch*, October 23, 2020. https://patch.com/maryland/bowie/pgcps-will-build-6-new-schools-900m-private-money.

34. Erin Richards, "Revised GOP Plan for MPS Also Addresses Empty Buildings," *Milwaukee Journal Sentinel*, May 19, 2015. https://archive.jsonline.com/news/education/mps-resolution-gives-driver-autonomy-on-struggling-schools-b99503310z1-304282751.html.

35. CJ Szafir and Libby Sobic, "The Never-Ending Story of Milwaukee's Vacant School Buildings," Wisconsin Institute for Law and Liberty, March 2017. https://will-law.org/wp-content/uploads/2021/01/Final.pdf; https://will-law.org/wp-content/uploads/2020/12/empty-handed-report-with-appendix-.pdf.

36. See Preston C. Green III, Bruce D. Baker, and Joseph O. Oluwole, "School Finance, Race, and Reparations," *Washington and Lee Journal of Civil Rights and Social Justice* 27 (2020): 483, for a detailed and inclusive history.

37. Mark Brilliant, "From Integrating Students to Redistributing Dollars: The Eclipse of School Desegregation by School Finance Equalization in 1970s California," *California Legal History* 7 (2012): 229.

38. Richard W. Lindholm, "The Value Added Tax: A Short Review of the Literature," *Journal of Economic Literature* 8, no. 4 (1970): 1178–1189.

39. Archived at https://digital.library.unt.edu/ark:/67531/metadc1129.

40. Liam Ebrill, Michael Keen, Jean-Paul Bodin, and Victoria Summers, "The Allure of the Value-Added Tax," *Finance & Development,* June 2002. https://www.imf.org/external/pubs/ft/fandd/2002/06/ebrill.htm.

41. Monoka Venters, Meghan V. Hauptli, and Lora Cohen-Vogel, "Federal Solutions to School Fiscal Crises: Lessons from Nixon's Failed National Sales Tax for Education," *Educational Policy* 26, no. 1 (2012): 35–57.

Chapter 5: Toxic Finance

1. Eleni Schirmer, "School Debt: The Great Unequalizer," *Rethinking Schools* 37, no. 4 (2023), https://rethinkingschools.org/articles/school-debt-the-great-unequalizer/ (accessed April 2025); and Eleni Schirmer, "We're Burying Our Kids in Debt (Just Not the Way You Think)," *The New York Times*, August 27, 2021, https://www.nytimes.com/2021/08/27/opinion/school-debt-economy.html (accessed April 2025).

2. See Marialena Dawn Rivera, *Inequity and Privatization in School District Facilities Financing: A Mixed Methods Study* (University of California, Berkeley, 2016).

3. https://school-infrastructure.org/

4. Eric J. Brunner, David Schwegman, and Jeffrey M. Vincent, "How Much Does Public School Facility Funding Depend on Property Wealth?," *Education Finance and Policy* 18, no. 1 (2023): 25–51.

5. Casey Dougal, Pengjie Gao, William J. Mayew, and Christopher A. Parsons, "What's in a (School) Name? Racial Discrimination in Higher Education Bond Markets," *Journal of Financial Economics* 134, no. 3 (2019): 570–590.

6. David I. Backer, Eleni Schirmer, and Sebastian Anti, "In the Interest of Race: Discrimination, Interest Rates, and the School Bond Market," *Inquiry: Critical Thinking Across the Disciplines* (2025), www.pdcnet.org/collection/fshow?id=inquiryct_2025_0999_5_13_22&pdfname=inquiryct_2025_0999_5_13_22.pdf&file_type=pdf.

7. Nicole M. Boyson and Weiling Liu, "Public Bond Issuance and Education Inequality" (Northeastern University D'Amore-McKim School of Business Research Paper 4099121, May 2, 2022), http://dx.doi.org/10.2139/ssrn.4099121.

8. Dougal et al., "What's in a (School) Name?"

9. Ashleigh Eldemire, Kimberly Luchtenberg, and Matthew Wynter, "Black Tax: Evidence of Racial Discrimination in Municipal Borrowing Costs" (Hutchins Center Working Papers, 2022).

10. Destin Jenkins, *The Bonds of Inequality: Debt and the Making of the American City* (University of Chicago Press, 2021).

11. Alberta Sbragia, *The Municipal Money Chase: The Politics of Local Government Finance* (Routledge, 1983); Alberta Sbragia, *Debt Wish: Entrepreneurial Cities, US Federalism, and Economic Development* (University of Pittsburgh Press, 1996).

12. See Tom Sgouros, "Predatory Public Finance," *Journal of Law in Society* 17 (2015): 91. As Tom clarified in his helpful comments on the book, in this article, he thinks the specific practices he analyzes in this essay are predatory in particular.

13. David I. Backer and Camika Royal, "Toxic Finance: Underinvestment in Philadelphia's School Buildings, 1993–2021," *Journal of Educational Administration and History*, no. 1 (2025): 74–91.

14. Marc Joffe, *Doubly Bound: The Costs of Issuing Municipal Bonds* (Haas Institute, 2016).

15. Amanda Kass, Martin J. Luby, and Rachel Weber, "Taking a Risk: Explaining the Use of Complex Debt Finance by the Chicago Public Schools," *Urban Affairs Review* 55, no. 4 (2019): 1035–1069.

16. Jim Lebenthal and Bernice Kanner, *Confessions of a Municipal Bond Salesman* (John Wiley & Sons, 2006).

17. Jim Lebenthal, "Lebenthal Infrastructure ABCs," October 29, 2013, YouTube, 0:1:24, https://youtu.be/KyAnX3b64k4.

18. Megan McArdle, "The Vigilante," *The Atlantic*, June 2011. https://www.theatlantic.com/magazine/archive/2011/06/the-vigilante/308503/.

19. Freda Anderson, "Teaching Debt Pollution in Schools," Rethinking Schools, 2023, https://rethinkingschools.org/articles/teaching-debt-pollution-in-schools.

20. Robin Wigglesworth, "Happy 400th Birthday to the World's Oldest Bond," https://www.ft.com/content/5122706e-39ca-4bbc-95cc-373188a9b1c9.

21. Seán W. McCarthy, "Voters Know Bonds Are Key to Transformative Infrastructure," *National League of Cities*, December 19, 2022. https://www.nlc.org/article/2022/12/19/voters-know-bonds-are-key-to-transformative-infrastructure.

22. Securities Industry and Financial Markets Association (SIFMA), *Quarterly Report: US Fixed Income, 1Q24*. April 2024. https://www.sifma.org/wp-content/uploads/2024/01/SIFMA-Research-Quarterly-Fixed-Income-IT-1Q24.pdf.

23. Ellwood Patterson Cubberley, *Public Education in the United States: A Study and Interpretation of American Educational History; an Introductory Textbook Dealing with the Larger Problems of Present-Day Education in the Light of Their Historical Development* (Houghton Mifflin, 1919).

24. Brian Tallerico, "Billions Recap: Season 2, Episode 7." *Vulture*, April 2, 2017. https://www.vulture.com/2017/04/billions-recap-season-2-episode-7.html.

25. Joffe, *Doubly Bound: The Costs of Issuing Municipal Bonds*, 14.

26. Harold Brubaker, "Students Protest Education Inequity in March from Lower Merion to Philly's Overbrook High School," *The Philadelphia Inquirer*, August 30, 2020. https://www.inquirer.com/news/lower-merion-overbrook-protest-inequity-schools-i-will-breathe-20200830.html.

27. Maddie Hanna, "Lower Merion School District Says a Ventilation Flaw Could Have Fueled a COVID-19 Outbreak in Second Grade Classroom," *The Philadelphia Inquirer*, April 26, 2021. https://www.inquirer.com/education/lower-merion-school-district-penn-valley-covid-outbreak-hvac-20210426.html.

28. Laura Jimenez, "The Case for Federal Funding for School Infrastructure," Center for American Progress, February 12, 2019. https://www.americanprogress.org/article/case-federal-funding-school-infrastructure/.

29. U.S. Department of Education, "U.S. Department of Education Announces Distribution of All American Rescue Plan ESSER Funds and Approval of All 52 State Education Agency Plans," January 18, 2022. https://www.ed.gov/about/news/press-release/us-department-of-education-announces-distribution-of-all-american-rescue.

30. Bella DiMarco and Phyllis W. Jordan, "Covid-Aid Spending Trends by City, Suburban, Rural School Districts," *Future Ed*, June 20, 2022. https://www.future-ed.org/covid-aid-spending-trends-by-city-suburban-rural-school-districts/

31. "Letter to Miguel Cardona Requesting Support for School Facilities," *The School Superintendents Association*, January 21, 2022. https://www

.aasa.org/docs/default-source/advocacy/cardona-school-facilities-letter-request-jan-2022.pdf?sfvrsn=44bcb738_3.

32. Mary Childs, *The Bond King* (Macmillan, 2022).

33. Childs, *The Bond King.*

34. Childs, *The Bond King.*

35. Joffe, *Doubly Bound: The Costs of Issuing Municipal Bonds*; Marc Joffe, *Doubly Bound: The Cost of Credit Ratings* (Haas Institute, 2017).

36. While the municipal bond market is bad, it could get worse. As I was finishing the edits to this book, the Republicans took control of all three branches of the federal government. One of the budget reconciliation bills that was on the table suggested removing the tax-exempt status of municipal bonds, a policy associated with the federal income tax (something right-wing billionaires have wanted to get rid of for more than a hundred years), which would put school districts and governments in more direct contact with banks and investors, probably getting taken for even more money.

37. Advait Arun, "Overreading into Underwriting," Center for Public Enterprise, March 14, 2024, https://publicenterprise.org/overreading-into-underwriting.

38. Joffe, *Doubly Bound: The Cost of Credit Ratings.*

39. Tom Sgouros, "Predatory Public Finance," *Journal of Law in Society* 17 (2015): 91.

40. Logan Stefanich, "Parents File Lawsuit Against Alpine School District Over Potential Closure of 5 Elementary Schools," KSL.com, May 8, 2023. https://www.ksl.com/article/50639975/parents-file-lawsuit-against-alpine-school-district-over-potential-closure-of-5-elementary-schools.

41. Carleton R. Holt, *School Bond Success: A Strategy for Building America's Schools* (Rowman & Littlefield, 2017).

42. Ballotpedia, "Approval Rates of Local School Bond and Tax Elections." https://ballotpedia.org/Approval_rates_of_local_school_bond_and_tax_elections.

43. Becca Savransky, "Collapsing Roofs, Broken Toilets, Flooded Classrooms: Inside the Worst-Funded Schools in the Nation," ProPublica,

April 13, 2023. https://www.propublica.org/article/idaho-deteriorating-schools-repair-bonds.

44. Bill Poehler, "Gervais School Board Says Bond Passage Is Key to District's Survival," *Statesman Journal*, April 8, 2024. https://www.statesmanjournal.com/story/news/politics/elections/2024/04/08/gervais-school-board-says-bond-passage-is-key-to-districts-survival/73044141007.

45. "Copperhead Consulting and Paul Dorr," October 1, 2015, YouTube, 7:46, https://youtu.be/945AMsa6Zq8.

46. Alex Baumhardt, "Enemy of Public Schools: How One Man Has Spent 25 Years Thwarting Bond Money for Rural Districts," *APM Reports*, August 29, 2019. https://www.apmreports.org/episode/2019/08/29/paul-dorr-tactics-to-defeat-school-referendums.

47. https://youtu.be/04raq8aSXUM; Paul M. Secunda, "The Story of Pickering v. Bd. of Education: Unconstitutional Conditions and Public Employment," in *First Amendment Law Stories*, ed. Richard W. Garnett and Andrew Koppelman, 10–35 (Foundation Press, 2010).

48. *Pickering v. Board of Education*, 391 U.S. at 568 (1968).

49. Josh Mound, "Stirrings of Revolt: Regressive Levies, the Pocketbook Squeeze, and the 1960s Roots of the 1970s Tax Revolt," *Journal of Policy History* 32, no. 2 (2020): 105–150.

50. David Wildstein, "Majority of Special School Election Ballot Questions Fail," *New Jersey Globe*, September 17, 2024. https://newjerseyglobe.com/education/majority-of-special-school-election-ballot-questions-fail/; https://www.kaaltv.com/news/school-referendums-pass-and-fail-across-the-area.

Chapter 6: Nightmare Ouroboros

1. Tom Hals, "Bank of America Affirms Gun Pledge, Hints at Remington Loan Exit," Reuters, May 10, 2018. https://www.reuters.com/article/us-bofaml-remington/bank-of-america-affirms-gun-pledge-hints-at-remington-loan-exit-idUSKBN1IB2MX/; https://www.bizjournals

.com/columbus/morning_call/2016/06/morning-roundup-jpmorgan-ceo-decries-orlando.html.

2. Is Your Bank Loaded? https://isyourbankloaded.org

3. Amanda Albright and Danielle Moran, "Jefferies Emerges as Muni Market Winner of Texas Gun Law Shakeup," *Bloomberg*, December 22, 2021. https://www.bloomberg.com/news/articles/2021-12-22/jefferies-emerges-as-muni-market-winner-of-texas-gun-law-shakeup.

4. Stephen Gandel, "The Texas Law That Has Banks Saying They Don't 'Discriminate' Against Guns," *The New York Times*, May 28, 2022. https://www.nytimes.com/2022/05/28/business/dealbook/texas-banks-gun-law.html.

5. Jolie McCullough and Kate McGee, "Texas Already 'Hardened' Schools. It Didn't Save Uvalde," *The Texas Tribune*, May 26, 2022. https://www.texastribune.org/2022/05/26/texas-uvalde-shooting-harden-schools/.

6. Emily Rizzo, "Central Bucks School Board Passes Library Book Policy; Community Members Say It's a New Kind of Book Ban," *WHYY*, July 27, 2022. https://whyy.org/articles/central-bucks-schools-book-ban-policy/.

7. Emily Rizzo, "Pennridge Proposed Policy on Student Expression Goes 'Way Further Than Anything I Have Ever Seen,' ACLU Lawyer Says," *WHYY*, July 29, 2022. https://whyy.org/articles/pennridge-policy-student-expression-aclu/.

8. Municipal Securities Rulemaking Board, "Central Bucks School District," Electronic Municipal Market Access (EMMA). https://emma.msrb.org/P21443081-P21120316-P21531716.pdf..

9. Municipal Securities Rulemaking Board, "Pennridge School District," Electronic Municipal Market Access (EMMA). https://emma.msrb.org/P21539414-P21189940-P21608306.pdf.

10. Ivana Nedyalkova, "The City of Tomorrow: Exploring Politics and Dissent in Tech-Driven Urban Development" (master's thesis, McGill University, 2021).

11. "Berkeley Working to Finalize First-Ever Blockchain Microbond Issuance," Debtwire. https://info.debtwire.com/berkeley-working-finalize-first-ever-blockchain-microbond-issuance.

12. NEAR Protocol, "Berkeley's Future Blockchain Microbonds," May 14, 2021, YouTube, 39:16, https://www.youtube.com/watch?v=E_eWI3AGM-s.

13. Anna Armstrong, "Berkeley to Adopt Blockchain Technology for Microbond Financing Program," *The Daily Californian*, December 30, 2021. https://www.dailycal.org/archives/berkeley-to-adopt-blockchain-technology-for-microbond-financing-program/article_1f1de622-1d7c-5176-890c-0f2d7d70ee66.html.

14. Gordon Feller, "The Case for Microbonds," *City Journal,* June 8, 2020. https://www.city-journal.org/article/the-case-for-microbonds.

15. Paula Moore, "City's First Minibond Issue Pays Off," *Denver Business Journal*, October 15, 2000. https://www.bizjournals.com/denver/stories/2000/10/16/story1.html; https://www.denvergov.org/Government/Agencies-Departments-Offices/Agencies-Departments-Offices-Directory/Department-of-Finance/Our-Divisions/Cash-and-Capital-Funding/Investor-Information/Mini-Bonds.

16. Anna Armstrong, "Berkeley's Decision to Incorporate Blockchain into Microbond Financing Program Sparks Controversy," *The Daily Californian*, January 5 2022. https://www.dailycal.org/archives/berkeleys-decision-to-incorporate-blockchain-into-microbond-financing-program-sparks-controversy/article_05e3017e-38c3-5aa1-8187-5cd1faf6a2f3.html.

17. Robin Scher, "Crypto's Heavy Carbon Footprint," *CounterPunch*, January 13, 2022. https://www.counterpunch.org/2022/01/13/cryptos-heavy-carbon-footprint.

18. Todd L. Ely and Christine R. Martell, "Costs of Raising (Social) Capital Through Mini-Bonds," *Municipal Finance Journal* 37, no. 3 (2016).

19. David Golumbia, "Cryptocurrency Is Garbage. So Is Blockchain," Virginia Commonwealth University, June 16, 2020, http://dx.doi.org/10.2139/ssrn.3628519.

20. Sean Stein Smith, "Crypto Bonds Are Coming – What Potential Investors Should Consider," *Forbes*, December 13, 2021. https://www.forbes.com/sites/seansteinsmith/2021/12/13/crypto-bonds-are-coming--what-potential-investors-should-consider/.

21. Sebastian Sinclair, "France Trials CBDC, Blockchain for Government Bond Deals," *Coindesk*, May 11, 2023 https://www.coindesk.com/markets/2021/10/19/france-trials-cbdc-blockchain-for-government-bond-deals-report.

22. Smith, "Crypto Bonds Are Coming – What Potential Investors Should Consider."

23. Lang Yang, "School District Borrowing and Capital Spending: The Effectiveness of State Credit Enhancement," *Education Finance and Policy* 19, no. 4 (2024): 634–664.

24. Sean Kozlik, "Our Summary on PA's State Aid Intercept Program for School Districts," *Pennsylvania State Aid Intercept Program*, September 9, 2015 https://www.linkedin.com/pulse/our-summary-pas-state-aid-intercept-program-school-districts-kozlik/.

25. Paul Burton, "Debt Gone Awry at a Pennsylvania School District," *Bond Buyer*, May 25, 2016. https://www.bondbuyer.com/news/debt-gone-awry-at-a-pennsylvania-school-districtt.

26. Municipal Securities Rulemaking Board, "Penn Hills School District." Electronic Municipal Market Access (EMMA). https://emma.msrb.org/EP333571-EP38266-EP660292.pdf.

27. Nasiha Salwati and David Wessel, "What Are Build America Bonds or Direct-Pay Municipal Bonds?," *Brookings Institution*, July 7, 2022. https://www.brookings.edu/articles/what-are-build-america-bonds-or-direct-pay-municipal-bonds/.

28. Rebecca Martin, "Muni Investors Stage Rare Effort to Challenge $1 Billion Deal," *Bloomberg*, March 7, 2024. https://www.bloomberg.com/news/articles/2024-03-07/muni-investors-stage-rare-effort-to-challenge-1-billion-deal.

Chapter 7: Constructive Politics

1. Board of Governors of the Federal Reserve System, "Section 13: Emergency Economic Stabilization Act of 2008," https://www.federalreserve.gov/aboutthefed/section13.htm.

2. Andrew Haughwout, Benjamin Hyman, and Or Shachar, "The Municipal Liquidity Facility," *Economic Policy Review* 28, no. 1 (2022): 35–57.

3. Sean Fulmer, "Disagreements Over the Municipal Liquidity Facility Erupt," *Yale School of Management*, October 21, 2020. https://som.yale.edu/blog/disagreements-over-the-municipal-liquidity-facility-erupt.

4. Oscar Perry Abello, "How to Cancel Wall Street," *Next City*, October 15, 2020. https://nextcity.org/urbanist-news/how-to-cancel-wall-street.

5. Indeed, BLM activists were targeting the Fed in that moment along these lines, with which economic geographers Martine August, Dan Cohen, Martin Danyluk, Amanda Kass, C.S. Ponder, and Emily Rosenman open their fascinating article about reimagining geographies of public finance: "On 4 July 2020, hundreds of people participating in a Black Lives Matter (BLM) protest staged a die-in in front of the Federal Reserve Bank of Minneapolis. In online footage of the event, the camera focused on a massive banner reading 'Sovereignty,' as an organizer on a bullhorn described how central bank money 'has caused the shedding of blood.' Moments later, the entire crowd lay down in the middle of one of Minneapolis's largest thoroughfares, protesting the social violence brought on not only by anti-Black police brutality but also by the state's (in)actions during the COVID-19 pandemic. With the protest, organizers cast into sharp relief the connection between public finance, state violence, and racial capitalism, politicizing central bank actions and their uneven distributional impacts." Martine August, Dan Cohen, Martin Danyluk, Amanda Kass, C.S. Ponder, and Emily Rosenman, "Reimagining Geographies of Public Finance," *Progress in Human Geography* 46, no. 2 (2022): 527–548.

6. David I. Backer and Akira Drake Rodriguez, "Movements at the Fiscal/Monetary Crossroads: Financing a Green New Deal for Schools in Philadelphia," *Journal of Urban Affairs* (2024): 1–15.

7. Climate and Community Project. Green New Deal for K-12 Public Schools. https://climateandcommunity.org/research/gnd-for-k-12-public-schools

8. Emily Anthes, "The Hot New Back-to-School Accessory? An Air Quality Monitor," *The New York Times*, October 10, 2021. https://www.nytimes.com/2021/10/10/health/coronavirus-ventilation-carbon-dioxide.html.

9. Erin Arvedlund, "A Philly Wealth Tax Could Raise More Than $200 Million, Sponsors Say. But Critics Call It a Disaster," *The Philadelphia Inquirer*, April 1, 2022. https://www.inquirer.com/business/wealth-tax-philadelphia-city-council-stocks-bonds-20220401.html.

10. Fallon Roth, "Philly DSA Is Helping Parents Build DIY Classroom Air Filters Amid School Asbestos Closures," *Billy Penn at WHYY*, April 25, 2023. https://billypenn.com/2023/04/25/philadelphia-school-asbestos-air-filters-corsi-rosenthal.

11. Kristen A. Graham, "These Parents Are Making DIY Air Purifiers for Philly Schools. They Want One in Every City Classroom," *Philadelphia Inquirer*, September 22, 2022. https://www.inquirer.com/news/corsi-rosenthal-boxes-diy-air-quality-purifiers-philadelphia-schools-20220922.html.

12. Kristen A. Graham, "Philly Schools Need Air Conditioning. But Ventilation Is Also Lacking. These Groups Want A Change," *Philadelphia Inquirer*, May 22, 2024. https://www.inquirer.com/news/corsi-rosenthal-boxes-diy-air-quality-purifiers-philadelphia-schools-20220922.html; https://storymaps.arcgis.com/stories/3cf392b11af54ba386f732a1f02934e4.

13. Derek R. Ford, "The Pneumatic Common: Learning in, with and from the Air," *Educational Philosophy and Theory* 47, no. 13–14 (2015): 1405–1418.

14. Yakov Feygin and Pooja Reddy, "Building Our Municipalities Markets Better: The Case for a GSE for Municipal Finance," Berggruen

Institute, September 22, 2021. https://berggruen.org/news/building-our-municipalities-markets-better-the-case-for-a-gse-for-municipal-finance; https://berggruen.org/news/the-national-investment-authority-a-blueprint.

15. David Backer and Lizzie Rothwell, "ECOWurd," May 13, 2022, Soundcloud, 18:30, https://soundcloud.com/onwurd/ecowurd-51322-david-backer-and-lizzie-rothwell?utm_source=clipboard&utm_medium=text&utm_campaign=social_sharing.

16. Rachel Cohen, "How to Fight the Affordable Housing and Climate Crises at Once," *Vox*, April 17, 2022. https://www.vox.com/23025378/energy-efficiency-utilities-repairs.

17. Katie Meyer, "GOP Legislators Are Backing Philly Dems' Housing Bill. Why? Blight Is a Statewide Issue," *WHYY*, March 22, 2022. https://whyy.org/articles/gop-legislators-are-backing-philly-dems-housing-bill-why-blight-is-a-statewide-issue.

18. Mallory Falk "'It's Like We're Giving Permission for These Kids to Struggle': Inside a Rural School District Suing Pa. for More Equitable Funding," *WHYY*, December 13, 2021. https://whyy.org/articles/its-like-were-giving-permission-for-these-kids-to-struggle-inside-a-rural-school-district-suing-pa-for-more-equitable-funding/.

19. "Healthy Green Schools," TakeAction Minnesota. https://takeactionminnesota.org/healthy-green-schools.

20. "Environmental Justice," Plan Nevada. https://planevada.org/environmental-justice/.

21. Drew Pittock, "Escuelas Frescas Campaign Aims to Cool Down EPISD Schools with New AC Systems," KFOX14, July 15, 2024. https://kfoxtv.com/news/local/amanecer-peoples-project-el-paso-independent-school-district-texas-low-income-neighborhoods-inflation-reduction-act-joe-biden.

22. "Chicago Needs Green Schools!," ONE Northside, August 7, 2024. https://www.onenorthside.org/2024/08/go-for-green-schools.

23. "Climate Justice," Citizen Action of Wisconsin. https://www.citizenactionwi.org/climate-justice.

24. "Elective Pay Database." Undaunted K12. https://www.undauntedk12.org/elective-pay-database.

25. Andrew Yamakawa Elrod, "What Was Bidenomics?," *Phenomenal World*, September 26, 2024. https://www.phenomenalworld.org/analysis/what-was-bidenomics/

26. *K12 Education and Climate Provisions in the Inflation Reduction Act. Planet Ed*, 2022. https://www.thisisplaneted.org/img/K12-InflationReductionAct-Final-Screen.pdf..

27. "National Clean Investment Fund," U.S. Environmental Protection Agency, 2024. https://www.epa.gov/greenhouse-gas-reduction-fund/national-clean-investment-fund.

28. Daniela Gabor, "The Wall Street Consensus," *Development and Change* 52, no. 3 (2021): 429–459.

29. Brett Christophers, *The Price Is Wrong: Why Capitalism Won't Save the Planet* (Verso, 2024).

30. Katie Kedward, Daniela Gabor, and Josh Ryan-Collins, "Carrots With(out) Sticks: Credit Policy and the Limits of Green Central Banking," *Review of International Political Economy* (2024): 1–25.

31. Brianna Smith, "Buckley Elementary School Attains First Net Zero Energy Verification," *Better Manchester*, January 31, 2024. https://bettermanchester.com/2024/01/buckley-elementary-school-attains-first-net-zero-energy-verification/.

32. Jim Farrell, "Manchester Energy Efficiency Project: Starting a Savings Account," *Manchester Public Schools*, June 2021. https://www.mpspride.org/district-information/manchester-energy-efficiency-project.

33. "We Are Legence," Legence. https://www.wearelegence.com.

34. "From Therma Holdings to Legence," Blackstone. https://www.blackstone.com/insights/article/from-therma-holdings-to-legence/.

35. The Hill, "Corp Dems TANKED Biden's Top Bank Reg Pick When No One Was Looking, But He Can Push Back," November 29, 2021, YouTube, 11:20, https://www.youtube.com/watch?v=zoxhUMTtl7s.

36. Aaron Blake, "Bernie Sanders Greets His New Front-Runner Status with Greatest Hit: Praising Fidel Castro," *The Washington Post*, February 24, 2020, https://www.washingtonpost.com/politics/2020/02/24

/bernie-sanders-greets-his-new-front-runner-status-with-greatest-hit-praising-fidel-castro/; Martin Carnoy and Jeffery Marshall, "Cuba's Academic Performance in Comparative Perspective," *Comparative Education Review* 49, no. 2 (2005): 230–261.

37. David Gura, "Saule Omarova Gets Candid: Banks Sank Her Nomination to Become a Key Regulator," NPR, December 13, 2021. https://www.npr.org/2021/12/13/1063767973/saule-omarova-gets-candid-banks-sank-her-nomination-to-head-occ.

38. Saule T. Omarova, "A National Investment Authority: Financing America's Future," The Justice Collaborative Institute, July 2020. https://www.filesforprogress.org/memos/national-investment-authority.pdf.

39. Robert C. Hockett and Saule T. Omarova, "Private Wealth and Public Goods: A Case for a National Investment Authority," *Journal of Corporation Law* 43 (2017): 437.

40. James Olson, *Saving Capitalism: The Reconstruction Finance Corporation and the New Deal, 1933–1940* (Princeton University Press, 2017).

41. Daniel Denvir and Tim Barker, "Monetary Politics," December 22, 2022, The Dig Radio, 1:46:49, https://thedigradio.com/podcast/monetary-politics-w-tim-barker/.

42. Brian Tumulty, "Infrastructure Financing Authority Opposed by Municipal Securities Groups," *The Bond Buyer*, June 25, 2021. https://www.bondbuyer.com/news/infrastructure-financing-authority-opposed-by-municipal-securities-groups.

43. "1932–1934 Berwyn School Fight," Tredyffrin/Easttown School District. https://www.tesd.net/Page/16810.

44. "History of the Tredyffrin Easttown School District," Tredyffrin Easttown Historical Society. https://www.tehistory.org/hqda/html/v08/v08n4p080.html.

45. Esther Cyna, "Equalizing Resources vs. Retaining Black Political Power: Paradoxes of an Urban-Suburban School District Merger in Durham, North Carolina, 1958–1996," *History of Education Quarterly* 59, no. 1 (2019): 35–64.

Chapter 8: Solidarity or Markets

1. Frédéric Lordon, "The French Uprising," *New Left Review*, March 30, 2023. https://newleftreview.org/sidecar/posts/the-french-uprising.

2. Michael Roberts, "What's the Problem with Pensions?," *The Next Recession*, March 31, 2023. https://thenextrecession.wordpress.com/2023/03/31/whats-the-problem-with-pensions.

3. Teresa Ghilarducci and Tony James, *Rescuing Retirement: A Plan to Guarantee Retirement Security for All Americans* (Columbia University Press, 2018).

4. "What Role Does State Government Play in Funding Teacher Pensions?," Center for Retirement Research at Boston College, September 24, 2024. https://crr.bc.edu/what-role-does-state-government-play-in-funding-teacher-pensions/.

5. Mark Lieberman, "Many Educators Across America Are on the Verge of a Retirement Benefits Boost," *Education Week*, December 23, 2024. https://www.edweek.org/teaching-learning/many-educators-across-america-are-on-the-verge-of-a-retirement-benefits-boost/2024/12.

6. As Elon Musk ruined Twitter, I found myself using TikTok as a platform and found some success making short videos about the budget crises I researched. Every video I posted got comments from viewers, many of whom asked me to look at a new district. As of this writing, there are more than one hundred requests I haven't gotten to yet, and TikTok is still owned by ByteDance, but a law signed by the Biden administration and delayed multiple times by the second Trump administration will force them to sell it to an American company or face a ban. The link to my account is https://www.tiktok.com/@schooldaves.

7. Hosts of Cut, Fire, Close, and David Backer, "Cut, Fire, Close," August 15, 2022, Apple Podcasts, 42:42, https://podcasts.apple.com/us/podcast/182-cut-fire-close/id1080145136?i=1000665447705.

8. Martin Slagter, "'How Did This Happen?' Ann Arbor Schools Assess Damage of $25M Projected Shortfall," *MLive*, March 20, 2024. https://www.mlive.com/news/ann-arbor/2024/03/how-did-this-happen-ann-arbor-schools-assess-damage-of-25m-projected-shortfall.html.

9. Ann Arbor Public Schools, "General FY 2023-24 Budget Amendment," March 22, 2024, YouTube, 1:30:22, https://www.youtube.com/watch?v=YcCdc5iBqRQ.

10. Municipal Employees' Retirement System of Michigan, "Unfunded Liability," *MERS of Michigan*. https://www.mersofmich.com/employer/trending-topics/unfunded-liability.

11. Michigan Office of Retirement Services, "Employer Contribution Rates: Terms, Definitions, and Descriptions," Michigan.gov. https://www.michigan.gov/psru/administration-and-compliance/contribution-rates/contribution-rates-for-university-employers/definitions/employer-contribution-rates-terms-definitions-and-descriptions.

12. Municipal Securities Rulemaking Board, *Official Statement* Electronic Municipal Market Access (EMMA https://emma.msrb.org/P21707092-P21312872-P21745003.pdf..

13. Michigan Office of Retirement Services, "Employer Contribution Rates: Terms, Definitions, and Descriptions," Michigan.gov. https://www.michigan.gov/psru/administration-and-compliance/contribution-rates/contribution-rates-for-university-employers/definitions/employer-contribution-rates-terms-definitions-and-descriptions. The giving-taking action makes me think of philosopher Jacques Derrida's book *Given Time: I. Counterfeit Money*, which is a reflection on the contradictions of money that begins with a poem about someone giving a homeless person a fake coin. Jacques Derrida, *Given Time: I. Counterfeit Money* (University of Chicago Press, 1992).

14. See the youtube link.

15. Heather Catallo, "Bus Aide Attacked Special Needs Student; Mom Says Ann Arbor School Hid Incident for Weeks," *WXYZ*, July 27, 2023. https://www.wxyz.com/news/local-news/investigations/bus-aide-attacked-special-needs-student-mom-says-ann-arbor-school-hid-incident-for-weeks.

16. Natalie Anderson, "Trustee Townsend Gides Resigns from AAPS Board," *The Michigan Daily*, September 22, 2023. https://www.michigandaily.com/news/news-briefs/trustee-townsend-gides-resigns-from-aaps-board/; https://www.freep.com/story/opinion/contributors/2024/04/23/ann-arbor-school-district-budget-layoffs.

17. Joey Cappelletti, "Israel-Palestinians Conflict Sparks Debate at Ann Arbor School," Associated Press, January 17, 2024. https://apnews.com/article/israel-palestinians-ann-arbor-school-peace-773c1306cde271e00d3c5e9591e48cf6.

18. Michigan Education Association, *Background on State Budget: MPSERS and OPEB*, 2024. https://mea.org/wp-content/uploads/2024/05/Background-on-State-Budget-MPSERS-OPEB.pdf.

19. Ryan Frost, "State Taxpayers' Share of MPSERS Debt Would Increase Under Various Proposals," *Reason*, June 19, 2024. https://reason.org/backgrounder/state-taxpayers-share-of-mpsers-debt-would-increase-under-various-proposals/.

20. Michael A. McCarthy, *Dismantling Solidarity: Capitalist Politics and American Pensions Since the New Deal* (Cornell University Press, 2017).

21. McCarthy, *Dismantling Solidarity*, 10.

22. Aldeman, Chad. "How Much Do School Districts Spend on Teacher Pensions?" *Teacher Pensions*, June 6, 2023. https://www.teacherpensions.org/blog/how-much-do-school-districts-spend-teacher-pensions..

23. Aldeman, "How Much Do School Districts Spend on Teacher Pensions?"

Chapter 9: Is There Really a Teacher Pension Crisis?

1. Andrew G. Biggs, "The Long-Term Solvency of Teacher Pension Plans: How We Got to Now and Prospects for Recovery," *Educational Researcher* 52, no. 2 (2023): 98–115.

2. Public Plans Data. https://publicplansdata.org.

3. I can't get into the politics of pension accounting reform right now, but it's important and I'd like to write about it in the future. See Tom Sgouros, "The Case for New Pension Accounting Standards." Presentation at the NCPERS Annual Conference, May 22, 2019. https://www.ncpers.org/files/Conference%20Docs/Annual%20Conference/2019/PPTs/Tom%20Sgouros_Wednesday%20GS.pdf.

4. PowerSchool, "10 Predictions for K-12 Education Finance." https://www.powerschool.com/whitepaper/10-predictions-for-k12-education-finance/.

5. Equable Institute, "Hidden Education Funding Cuts," February 2023, https://equable.org/wp-content/uploads/2023/02/Equable-Institute_Hidden-Education-Funding-Cuts_Final.pdf. "For a critique of Equable's report, see National Association of State Retirement Administrators (NASRA), "Equable Analysis: The State of Retirement Systems." https://www.nasra.org/Files/NASRA%20Equable%20Analysis.pdf (accessed October 2023).

6. "The Next 10 Years of Education Finance," Jess Gartner et al., Allovue, September 2023, https://www.aasa.org

7. Richard W. Johnson and Erald Kolasi. "How Have Teacher Pensions Changed Since the Great Recession?," Urban Institute, February 10, 2020. https://www.urban.org/research/publication/how-have-teacher-pensions-changed-great-recession.

8. Equable, "Hidden Funding Cuts," https://equable.org/hidden-funding-%20cuts/?utm_source=davidibacker&utm_medium=email&utm_campaign=the-ideology-of-322.

9. National Association of State Retirement Administrators (NASRA), "Equable Analysis: The State of Retirement Systems," p. 1.

10. Robert M. Costrell, "The Three R's of Teacher Pension Funding: Redistribution, Return, and Risk," *Educational Researcher* 52, no. 2 (2023): 91–97.

Chapter 10: Green Fiscal Mutualism

1. Doug Henwood and Liza Featherstone, "The Pension Crisis: How Wall Street Is Destroying Retirement," *In These Times*, January 22, 2018. https://inthesetimes.com/features/pension_crisis_wall_street_social_security.html.

2. C-SPAN, "Doug Henwood on the Pension Crisis," *Washington Journal*. https://www.c-span.org/program/washington-journal/doug-henwood-on-the-pension-crisis/497389.

3. Max B. Sawicky, "No, Pensions Aren't All Collapsing, and We Don't Need To Scrap Them," *In These Times*, January 25, 2018. https://inthesetimes.com/article/no-we-shouldnt-replace-pensions-by-expanding-social-security.

4. Doug Henwood and Liza Featherstone, "Yes, Pensions Are Collapsing, and Progressives Can't Remain in Denial," *In These Times*, January 29, 2018. https://inthesetimes.com/article/yes-pensions-are-collapsing-and-progressives-cant-remain-in-denial.

5. Max B. Sawicky, "Pensions, Wall Street, and Social Security," *Jacobin*, February 13, 2018. https://jacobin.com/2018/02/pensions-wall-street-social-security.

6. Vrinda Mittal. "Desperate Capital Breeds Productivity Loss: Evidence from Public Pension Investments in Private Equity," available at SSRN 4283853 (2024).

7. Liliana Doganova, *Discounting the Future: The Ascendancy of a Political Technology* (Princeton University Press, 2024).

8. Equable, "What Is the Assumed Rate of Return?," https://equable.org/article/what-is-the-assumed-rate-of-return/.

9. Doganova, *Discounting the Future*, 22.

10. Michael R. Glass and Sean H. Vanatta, "The Frail Bonds of Liberalism: Pensions, Schools, and the Unraveling of Fiscal Mutualism in Postwar New York," *Capitalism: A Journal of History and Economics* 2, no. 2 (2021): 427–472. See also Sean H. Vanatta, "The Financialization of US Public Pension Funds, 1945–1974," *Review of Social Economy* 82, no. 2 (2024): 261–293.

11. "Official Statement from Budget Director Annette Guzman," *Politico*, 2024. https://www.politico.com/f/?id=00000191-db95-ddb9-a3d3-fbb7527e0000&.

12. "Experience Review: January 2017 to December 2021." *Municipal Employees Annuity and Benefit Fund of Chicago*, June 2023. https://www.meabf.org/wp-content/uploads/2023/06/E.-MEABF_Experience-Review_March-2023.pdf.

Conclusion: A Plan for Public Education

1. Ashley Koch and Jamie Parfitt, "Newberg School District Faces Budget Debt Amid Pride Controversy." KGW, June 6, 2024. https://www.kgw.com/article/news/local/the-story/newberg-school-district-budget-debt-board-pride/283-17bc272d-52ca-44e4-b278-8ca5d0851a68.

2. Beth Slovic, "Newberg School Board Members Violated Open Meetings Law, Judge Finds," *Oregon Live*, February 4, 2024. https://www.oregonlive.com/education/2024/02/newberg-school-board-members-violated-open-meetings-law-judge-finds.html.

3. Mike Benner, "Newberg School Board Bans Pride and BLM Flags," *KGW*, August 11, 2021. https://www.kgw.com/article/news/local/newberg-school-board-bans-pride-blm/283-a4998b43-caa2-496b-8f03-5aeae285c160.

4. Diane Megaw, "Oregon School Districts: Calls for Superintendent's Dismissal Following Newberg-Dundee Budget Deficit," *Daily Tidings*, June 12, 2024. https://www.dailytidings.com/oregon-school-districts-calls-for-superintendent-dismissal.

5. Carey Martell, "Newberg-Dundee School District Budget Crisis Caused by Illegal Spending on Staffing Agencies; Board Was Aware," *Yamhill Advocate,* July 28, 2024. https://www.yamhilladvocate.com/2024/07/newberg-dundee-school-district-budget-crisis-caused-by-illegal-spending-on-staffing-agencies-board-was-aware/.

6. Karli Olson, "Newberg High School Students Walk Out in Protest After District Announces $3.7M Budget Shortfall," KPTV, May 29, 2024. https://www.kptv.com/2024/05/30/newberg-high-school-students-walk-out-protest-after-district-announces-37m-budget-shortfall/.

7. John Rogers, Rachel White, Robert Shand, and Joseph Kahne, *Costs of Conflict: The Impact of School Closures on Students and Communitie,* UCLA's Institute for Democracy, Education, and Access, Los Angeles, 2024.

8. Andrew Yamakawa Elrod, "What Was Bidenomics?," *Phenomenal World*, September 26, 2024. https://www.phenomenalworld.org/analysis/what-was-bidenomics/.

9. Adam Tooze, "Great Power Politics," *London Review of Books* 46, no. 21 (November 7, 2024). https://www.lrb.co.uk/the-paper/v46/n21/adam-tooze/great-power-politics.

10. The critical macroeconomist Daniela Gabor, whose work critiquing the de-risking state is essential reading, made an interesting comment to me during an event once. It was a book launch for Melinda Cooper's *Counterrevolution* and Liliana Doganova's *Discounting the Future.* Gabor was responding to Cooper, and during the Q&A I asked them both whether the elective pay program in the IRA is a communist potentiality. Cooper said yes, and Gabor, using her formulation that the IRA is too many carrots for capital and not enough sticks, said she thought the tax credit program was a "carrot for progressives." A dialectical object for sure!

11. Undaunted K12, "Elective Pay Database." https://www.undauntedk12.org/elective-pay-database.

Index

Publishing in the Public Interest

Thank you for reading this book published by The New Press; we hope you enjoyed it. New Press books and authors play a crucial role in sparking conversations about the key political and social issues of our day.

We hope that you will stay in touch with us. To keep up to date with our books, events, and the issues we cover, follow us on social media and sign up for our newsletter at thenewpress.org.

Please consider buying New Press books not only for yourself, but also for friends and family and to donate to schools, libraries, community centers, prison libraries, and other organizations involved with the issues our authors write about.

The New Press is a 501(c)(3) nonprofit organization; if you wish to support our work with a tax-deductible gift please visit https://thenewpress.org/donate/ or use the QR code below.

About the Author

David I. Backer is an associate professor of education policy at Seton Hall University whose research, teaching, and organizing focus on ideology and school finance. A former high school teacher, his research has appeared in *Harvard Educational Review*, *Journal of Urban Affairs*, *Journal of Education Policy*, *Journal of Educational Human Resources*, *Journal of Educational Administration and History*, as well as popular venues like *Crain's Business Chicago*, *Phenomenal World*, *African American Policy Forum*, *The American Prospect*, *n+1*, *Dissent*, and *Jacobin*.

www.ingramcontent.com/pod-product-compliance
Lightning Source LLC
Chambersburg PA
CBHW031909020426
42338CB00031B/1697/J

* 9 7 8 1 6 2 0 9 7 8 8 5 6 *